Welcome home,

back hole.

lots of love

cousining boy and
he with re tots

x x x

# FOLKSONGS AND FOLKLORE
# OF SOUTH UIST

# Folksongs and Folklore
# of
# South Uist

by

MARGARET FAY SHAW

THIRD EDITION

ABERDEEN UNIVERSITY PRESS

1986

*Aberdeen University Press*
A member of the Pergamon Group

ISBN 0 08 032471 1

© *Margaret Fay Shaw 1986*

FIRST EDITION 1955
SECOND EDITION 1977
THIRD EDITION 1986

Chuidich an Comann Leabhraichean am foillsichear le cosgaisean an leabhair seo.

*Printed in Great Britain
The University Press
Aberdeen*

To

H.C.S. AND F.P.S.

# CONTENTS

★

# CONTENTS

# CONTENTS

# CONTENTS

# CONTENTS

## DO'N TÉ A CHRUINNICH NA H-ÒRAIN

*Le Fred T. Mac 'ill' Ìosa*

Thàinig mi tarsuinn air uaimh an òir,
Leabhar luachmhor bho'n a' bhean chòir;
'S mór an spéis, an tlachd, 's an ùidh
Thug i do chainnt 's do cheòl Uibhist.
An éibhleag anns an gann bha 'n deò
Shéid ise oirre, 's thug i beò a rithist;
Maireadh a h-ainm air chuimhne
'Nar dùthaich, 's air taobh thall na doimhne:
Sin agaibh Maighread chòir,
Bean uasal Eilean Chanaidh.

xi

# PREFACE

★

This is the third printing of *Folksongs and Folklore of South Uist*. I am pleased to have this memory of life on a South Uist croft, and of my friends who gave me all this book contains, particularly Peigi and Mairi MacRae. I am grateful to them all for giving so generously of their splendid heritage.

I thank the Gaelic Book Council for their generous grant towards the production of this edition.

MARGARET FAY SHAW

*Isle of Canna, 23 June 1986*

# ILLUSTRATIONS

★

# ILLUSTRATIONS

*All the photographs used for illustrations in this book were taken by Margaret Fay Shaw*

xiv

# INTRODUCTION

★

THIS book contains folklore and folksongs taken down in a small community on the south side of Lochboisdale on the Island of South Uist in the Scottish Hebrides, where I lived during the years between 1929 and 1935 and near where I have lived ever since. It is an attempt to give a true record of a splendid people who are crofter-fishermen, of their occupations, interests and pleasures. Their generosity and patience have made this book.

South Uist is an island of sharp physical contrasts. It is twenty-two miles in length from south to north and some five miles in width. The west side is the flat *machair*, which is grassland that covers the mile-wide plain of sand that stretches along the shore of the Atlantic through all the Outer Hebrides. Here is the best crofting land, where most of the population of 2,700 live. It is excellent for grazing cattle and growing oats and bere, a four-rowed barley. In summer the Atlantic, which on fine days is of an extraordinarily deep blue, breaks on the wide beach of white sand. The *machair* is carpeted with wild flowers, the air filled with the song of skylarks, the call of lapwing and corncrake. In winter it is swept by fierce westerly gales and the tremendous seas threaten to break through the dunes and flood the land, some of it well below sea-level.

The east side of the island is wild and boggy moorland that rises to a line of high hills of strange contour that lie the length of the island. Three long sea lochs, Skiport, Eynort and Boisdale, opening into the Minch, cut through these hills. Crofter-fishermen live beside these lochs, as on the western plain, but the poorness of their land is compensated by the safe anchorage for boats and the access to the Minch for fishing.

Innumerable fresh-water lochs are studded over the island, often with small

I

islands on which are ruins of prehistoric forts, and their waters are famed for brown and sea trout and the many varieties of wild duck that feed there in autumn. The only trees are a stunted monkey-puzzle on an island in Loch an Eilein and some small aspens, rowans and willows in some sheltered places. But trees are not missed. There is colour and form of indescribable beauty whenever there is the least clarity, though in the half-dark days of winter it could be desolation such as Noah might have seen when the waters of the flood were still receding.

My first months in South Uist were spent in the village of Lochboisdale, the port of the island. It had charm and friendliness, but there was not the opportunity for a beginner to speak Gaelic nor to hear the old traditional songs and observe crofting life. But not long after my arrival I was invited to dinner at Boisdale House, where my host, Mr. Donald Ferguson, asked two sisters, cousins of his, to sing to his guests. Their voices were clear and true and their songs were golden. I asked one if she would teach me a certain air and she replied that she would be pleased to do so if I would come to her house in Glendale. On a sharp, cold January morning with the land white with frost I crossed Loch Boisdale in a sail-boat and walked the path to the cottage of Peigi and Màiri MacRae, where I was soon to make my home for the rest of my years in South Uist.

Glendale, the township where the MacRaes lived, was some two miles by path from a side road, and the easiest access to it was by sea. We usually journeyed to and from Lochboisdale in a sail-boat, the heavily built seventeen-foot type with a lug sail barked a red brown, which is the custom in the Hebrides. Such a pleasure on a fine day, it could be a terrifying experience on a black stormy night, tacking and threading between submerged rocks with a strong tide against a wind at gale force. But the men in the Hebrides are accustomed to using sail, and during the wars, when many ships were torpedoed or mined, crews were sometimes saved through having Hebrideans amongst them experienced in handling small craft under sail, who were able to take charge of life-boats and bring them to safety, sometimes over great distances.

There were thirteen houses within the radius of a mile beside the sea loch and all had crofts of about five acres of peaty soil. Yet their potatoes produced an excellent crop, and enough oats were grown to feed their cattle through the winter. Each of the crofts had two cows with followers, and six of the crofts owned a few sheep. They were grazed on the hill which was their common land in the summer months and brought back to the shelter of the croft when the harvest was secure. The cattle were Highland or Highland-Shorthorn cross, which can stand the wet and stormy weather. The sheep were a small type of Black-face that is indigenous to the Hebrides, whose mutton is delicious and whose wool is handspun for blankets and tweed, the women not only knitting the socks and sweaters but heavy underwear for the men.

It was necessary for the men to have other work than crofting. Many were part-time fishermen. Lobster fishing was profitable if the lobsters reached London or Birmingham alive. Herring was precarious but could pay well and salt herring was a mainstay of the diet of the people. Others were deep-sea sailors on cargo or passenger ships sailing from British ports to all parts of the world.

The spring work of the croft began in February, when seaweed, used as fertilizer, was cut with a saw-toothed sickle called a *corran* on the tidal islands of the loch at low water of a spring tide. It was bound together in great bundles called *maoisean* and towed ashore at full tide so high that it could be left on the grass verge. The crofters then carried it in creels on their backs to the field, where it was left in a heap for a fortnight before being spread on the ground. There it was left until black and dry, the new grass showing above it, when the ground would be ready to turn. The fields were too small to use a horse-drawn plough, so the ground was dug with a spade or a footplough called a *cas-chrom*. This primitive-looking implement, whose name means crooked-foot, is of a type that has been used in various parts of the world since man first tilled the soil. The foot of the *cas-chrom* is made at an angle of 110 degrees to the long handle and the point is tipped with iron, which is pushed into the earth by the pressure of the man's foot on the wooden pin at the bend of the *cas*. It enters the ground at a slant, is tipped back and rolled to the side, where it deposits the clod. Though it does not reach the same depth as a spade, it cuts more evenly and without the back-breaking effort. The clods were then broken up with a heavy wooden rake of five thick teeth called a *ràcan*, and the field was harrowed by hand before the oats were sown.

The crofters planted their potatoes in 'lazy-beds' or *feannagan*. The plot was divided into long rectangles five feet wide and, with a rope as a measure, each rectangle was cut with a spade the length of the plot to the depth of five inches, this cutting along a rope line being known as *susadh*. A strip of seaweed three feet wide was spread down the centre of each bed. The crofter then turned a foot-wide clod or *ploc* to each side of the cut with a spade and laid it on the seaweed so that the strip was covered by a foot of earth on each side, with a gap or *taomadh* of seaweed being left exposed. The two-foot-wide ditch or *claise* between the beds would be as deep as two feet to drain the ground, which was largely peat and often water-logged. The potatoes were then planted with a dibble or *pleadhag*.

Much of the work was done on a communal system: the lamb marking, the

3

sheep clipping, when the men used to shear and the women fold the fleeces, and the dipping to control sheep scab, which was required in Uist by law four times a year. In June the peat was cut. The men would take each house in rotation for the days, usually not more than two, that each required for the year's fuel. Six men were needed to cut the MacRaes' peat, and it was referred to as 'three irons' or *tréisgeirean*, which meant that three men would cut and three men catch and lift the peat to the bank. On these days the women of the crofts would gather at the house of the one whose peat was being cut and help prepare a dinner for the men, of mutton or salt herring and potatoes. They would carry buckets of a drink called *deoch mhineadh*, which is cool, clear water with oatmeal stirred into it, out to the moor to refresh the workers. After the peat was cut it was left lying by the bank for a month, when three peats were stood on end with another on top. Later these were gathered to make small stacks until, at the end of the summer, when dry enough for burning, they were carried home to make the great stack by the house for the year's use. The peat in Glendale was of particularly good quality, being black and hard and burning long and well until reduced to a fine white ash. These peats have different names according to their size and position. The long, flat rectangle as it was cut was called *fàd*, the small broken pieces found at the bottom of the peat bed *caorain dubha*.

In midsummer the hay and oats were cut with a sickle or a two-handled scythe and made into stooks in the field until the time when it was carried home to the shelter of the byre, where it was built into great stacks or *mulain*, the tops thatched with bracken and secured with ropes against the winter gales. The potatoes were dug in October and stored in the byre.

The women worked extremely hard. Though the men would return from the sea in early spring to cut the seaweed and turn the ground, the women carried the creels, helped with much of the planting, harvesting and carrying home the peats. They never complained of the scarcity of many things that the townsfolk are unable to do without. Nor in those black depression years did they ever voice the worry for their menfolk waiting interminably for a ship in a far-away city.

Most of the people lived in thatched houses which provide the ideal shelter, being warm and secure in the storms of a Hebridean winter and cool in the hot days of summer. It is not only that the thick walls of natural stone and thatched roofs fit into the landscape to the delight of the eye, but it is a design which has evolved through the centuries as being the best type of house for the Hebridean climate. The walls of the house are double, with a packing of earth or small stones between. They measure four feet thick, have rounded ends and are six feet high. The roof of wooden beams holds a layer of sods pinned together shingle fashion with wooden pins. The thatch of rushes or wheat straw is laid on top in such a way as to shed rain, and it is held down by ropes secured with stone weights, which reminded Dr. Samuel Johnson of curling pins. The low door opens into a narrow passage that leads both to the kitchen and to the *seòmbar* or best room, in which are two built-in beds, best furniture, lace curtains at the window, with treasured photographs and ornaments on the mantelpiece. Another small room, the length of the passage, opens off the kitchen and is called the *clòsaid*. The walls are lined and papered, the floor of the room is of wood, the kitchen and passage of hard clay often sprinkled with white sand. The two chimneys at either end with open fires burn peat whose pungent aroma permeates everything in the house.

The MacRae cottage was on the slope of Easival and faced the north. To one who had been brought up in a wooded Pennsylvania valley and had never known a land without trees the contrast of Uist with nothing higher than the heather and the hay was to discover a new earth. The view from Peigi's door was of the life of the island: the small figures going about their crofts, the scholars crossing the hill to school, the solitary figure with a staff herding cows, the boat being dragged ashore, the brown sail on the loch, the smoke of the kelp fires on the sand dunes in the west; overhead the long approach of the flight of wild geese and swans. One watched the shore to see the state of the tide which governed the time of work on the sea. The direction of the wind was always noted, the shape of the clouds—as that strange cloud called *craobh* which stretched like a narrow blanket from north to south above the hills and gave the direction of the wind to-morrow. Winter nights brought an amazing vision of stars. Northern lights, called by the Gaels *Fir-chlisne*, men of the tricks, or the leaping, darting ones, appeared in long shafts of white, green and reddish light to form ribbon-like folds on the centre of the sky.

The sun in the winter months barely rose behind the hill and never shone on the cottage for weeks. But the hill gave protection from the south-westerly gales. The house had originally been a *taigh dubh* or black house, which is the oldest type of dwelling in the Hebrides and now rarely seen. Then the inside walls were not lined and the place for the fire was laid on the floor. The opening in the thatch for the smoke to escape was never directly over the fire in case of rain, but fire and door and chimney-vent were made according to rules that would draw the smoke out. But wind and rain will defy many better chimneys, and at times the smoke would gather in the rafters, and to avoid it one had to sit on a low stool. Peat smoke is not harsh and is said to be a disinfectant. The people have been accustomed to it since fires under cover began. The pleasant thing about such a fire was that there was room to gather round it in the true sense. The light was then the crusie lamp or *crùisgein*. The fuel was fish liver oil, and the wick was made of the pith of rushes or *luachair*, which was dried by the fire and then plaited.

The MacRaes had rebuilt the house to the plan of the other thatched houses in Glendale. The door was barely five feet high, particularly suitable for the little MacRaes, and it was painted bright blue. The kitchen was neat and gay, with a dresser filled with pretty dishes. All the furniture had been made on the island—the meal chest, the table, the long bench below the window, the low armchair and milking stools beside the fire. In the corner was the spinning wheel, with the basket of *rolagan* waiting to be spun. There were always a cat and kittens and a clever collie dog in the house. Every creature they possessed was a personality to the sisters. The sheep were given names and the roman-nosed ram with his great curling horns would call in the kitchen for his titbit. The cow was not only valuable property but one deserving constant care with true affection.

In the summer Peigi would have washed and dyed the fleeces. Then she would card the wool, combing, cleaning and making it into *rolagan* for spinning in winter. Peigi was continually singing as she spun. The rhythm of her foot on the treadle brought forth the songs as naturally as her fingers turned the wool to yarn. When there was sufficient for a length of tweed we took it in a sack across the hill to Peigi Iain Bharraich, the weaver, who lived with her sister in a house just big enough to hold themselves and the loom. When word came that it was ready it was collected and preparations were made for the great event of a *luadhadh*, or waulking, which is when the cloth is shrunk and made ready for the tailor, as I have described it in the preface to the songs. My first *luadhadh* was held in Peigi's byre. The planks that served as a bridge across the burn were made to serve as the table. A lantern hung from the rafters and shone down on the singers in their rough aprons, their heads tied in kerchiefs, their sleeves rolled high. The air was potent with the smell of hot urine, but no substitute will give the softness of texture nor set the colour, especially of indigo. When finished the tweed was thoroughly washed in a running stream and dried on the heather, exposed to the sun and wind for several days until perfectly clean.

The women kneaded and pushed the cloth round and round the table with song after song. The one who sang the verse line would give turns and grace notes to take in all the syllables, always in absolute time and with a rhythm that was marvellous to me. When it was thought to be sufficiently shrunk and the feel of the texture right, one would measure the length with her third finger. If not yet shrunk enough they would give it another song, always keeping it moist. When ready at last it was rolled up tightly and two women

6

would face across it and, clapping the roll, would sing the *òran basaidh*, or clapping song, called in Glendale the *coileach*, in quick 2/4 time, which was for the purpose of finishing the *luadhadh*. The company would shout 'Give them the *coileach*!' for the words of these last songs are to a great extent extemporized and consist of witty and ribald remarks about the people present with reference to their actual or possible love affairs.

The singers then washed and changed, to gather with the other members of the party in the kitchen, where a dram was passed and tea with scones and cake. Then began the singing and dancing, with great hilarity. Those were days when a wearer could regard his homespun from the Hebrides with the thought of the songs and gaiety that went into the making of it.

It was in the MacRaes' house on winter nights that most of the contents of this book were taken down. From spring until autumn everyone was too occupied with work on the croft to spend time at the fireside. The long day-light of spring and summer (at midsummer it is twilight all night) make it possible to work outside until bed-time. But when the nights drew in and the harvest work was done, then began the *céilidh*, a word that means the gathering of friends to talk and sing and entertain each other. There were no radios and few newspapers but no lack of good company. There were many tales told of olden times. The ship that was wrecked behind Eoligarry full of gold when Ranald's grandfather was a lad. The diver came and they recovered the gold and it was ferried across to Pollachar. It was in bags, and the one in charge would give them a little if they would bring needle and thread and sew up the bags! Of the time when their old landlords, the MacDonalds of Boisdale, lived at Kilbride House, which stood by the shore on the Sound of Eriskay. All that remains to-day is the great garden wall. There were witches in those days who would come from Skye to steal the cream or *toradh* off the chief's milk. I was told of a boat coming home to Eriskay and how it passed an egg-shell floating in the channel. One of the men was about to sink it with his oar when another warned him against it. Later, when the boat was in Skye, that man was befriended by an old *cailleach* 'for the reason you did not sink me when I was in the egg-shell that day'. Witches were said to have the power of raising storms by knots that were tied in a piece of wool. Each knot meant a different strength of wind, and as each knot was loosened the wind increased. This piece of wool is called a *snàithlin*, and it had another use which is known to-day when it is made by one who has the power to remove the curse of the evil eye on cattle. A woman, whose mother's cow was so afflicted, told how her mother, finding nothing to cure the beast, walked a long way to the house of a man with this power. He named the one who had put the illness on the cow and he made a *snàithlin* for her with a certain prayer or incantation for the cure,

7

but not in her sight. She was told to conceal it on the cow and that it would recover, which it did. I was always told that these incantations were made in the name of the Good One.

My hosts had their own experiences of this sort. When Peigi and Màiri were children they lived for a time in South Glendale by the side of the narrow sound between South Uist and Eriskay. Their only neighbour was a very old woman called Catriona nighean Eachainn who lived alone in a little house close by. She had the name of being a witch and of having communications with the spirit world. It was sometimes possible to find a young girl to stay with Catriona, but the older women were much too frightened to share a bed with her for even one night. It was Mrs. MacRae, Peigi's mother, who cared for her. Her husband, Andrew MacRae, was a shepherd and his sheep were on wild and lonely hill pasture difficult to guard. Once he lost a ram and searched for it for three weeks without success. He was told to ask Catriona, who had the gift of 'seeing' the lost, but he had no faith in her 'sight'. However, he was persuaded to call on her one evening and ask her help. She told him that she could do nothing at that time of the night but he must come the next morning. When he returned the next day she asked him what way he would take. He replied that he did not know. She then said to go such a distance and there follow the *gàradh-crìche*, a grass dyke that was made in the old days as a boundary, and that he would meet the ram facing him. He followed her directions and he met the ram as she described. This type of divination is what is known as making a *frìth* for what was lost. As Màiri described it: 'She would rise early in the morning and make the prayer for it. She would go out without taking food or drink, and the very first creatures she would put her eyes on, the hens, the cock, the ducks, the cow, how they would be standing, lying or what way they would be facing, from them she would make her *frìth* and know where the ram would be found.'

When Peigi and Màiri went to her cottage to sit at the fire with the little lass who stayed with her, she told them to move to make room for friends coming in the door. Without delay they gave her guests the entire fireside. Her callers came at night, and she would have long conversations at the door. One night the little lass was awakened by rapping and told Catriona there was someone at the door. She was told to be quiet. The rapping continued, and at long last the old woman rose and dressed, took up the tongs and left the house. She was gone all night, and the day was breaking when she returned and got back into bed. When the child arose she saw that the old woman's face and wrists were scratched. She started to make up the fire, but she could not find the tongs. She asked Catriona where they were and was told to go to the shore below the house and she would find them by a certain big stone. They were where she said, and with blood on them. This occurred in 1898. In Gaelic folklore anything made of iron is considered a defence against evil spirits. I was told of the head of the tongs being put in the fire during thunderstorms with an incantation being said by the person that put them there.

Second sight, which is the ability to foresee what is to happen, is well known, and the possessor is never envied. There is no doubt that it exists and that it is inherited. In most instances the seer foresaw tragedy, as in the case of the girl who saw seaweed about the necks of two young men at a dance at Garrynamonie, and they were drowned together soon after. They said it was possible for one without the gift to see the apparition if he would clasp the hand or put his foot on that of the one who was seeing it. There were well-attested stories of this foresight and the disasters that followed which I personally fully believe. There are two types of phenomena of foretelling or foreseeing the future which they described, and which may not be connected with a death. One is known as *manadh*, or a supernatural warning from inanimate objects. You hear a knock at the door and find no one there. But later the same knock comes and there *is* someone there. Or dishes would move about, the chest lid flies open, and soon after a death comes—and these same dishes and the supplies from the chest would be needed. The second is the *taibhse*, which is an apparition, and they described it as someone 'seeing yourself standing at the house six years before you came'. An instance of both these signs was given by a neighbour. Her father as a young lad was returning home from the shop with his parcels at dusk. It was a lonely walk and as he came down the brae by a certain big stone he saw a young girl lying on the grass with brilliant red hair spread about her. She wore a dark dress and white stockings. He dropped his parcels and fled home to say that he had seen a ghost. Some months later he was in the kitchen at Boisdale House when the new servant from North Uist came in. It was the same girl, with her red hair and white stockings. She later married a MacDonald, and they built a house near the stone where he had seen her wraith. I myself knew Mrs. MacDonald, who was known as Kirsty Ruadh. Though more than ninety years, her hair still showed the red. Her youngest son was lost on the fishing boat *Cheerful*. A storm came up suddenly when they were lifting the herring nets. The ropes were not cut quickly enough to free her and the weight of the fish dragged her under. Kirsty never again touched herring from that day, though it was the main diet of the isles.

The instance of the *manadh* was when the neighbour's father was waiting one evening for his wife to return. He was sitting at the fire, which was in the centre of the floor, and had his two children about him. He heard a heavy breathing at the door and went to see, but there was no one there. He heard it again. He listened—it was the breathing sound his asthmatic brother made, and he was deep-sea sailing and had not been home for years. The 'breathing' entered the room. In terrible fright he gathered up the children, jumped into bed and hid beneath the clothes. The 'breathing' crossed the room, seemed to move furniture about and then ceased. When his wife returned he told her what had happened, and they were sure that some misfortune had come to the brother. He must be dead. Late that same night a knock came at the door and in came the brother. On unexpected leave, he had arrived without word.

The only experience I ever had of this kind was in a dream. I had had to return to America for some months, and while there my thoughts were most of the time of Glendale and when I would return again. Màiri had a dog, a small black-and-white collie, of which I was very fond. This night I had a most vivid dream. I had just arrived at the MacRaes', Màiri was baking, covered with flour, and I was so happy to be there, embracing her, cuddling the cat and then turning to the dog, who ran out of the door. I called him and then asked Màiri to call him back that I might greet him too. But she replied, 'He can't come back.' 'But he has just run out,' I said. She shook her head, 'He will never come back.' I was greatly distressed and woke up. That day I wrote to Màiri and told her that I had had an unhappy dream about the dog and hoped nothing had happened to him. Her letter told me that she had had to have him put down at the time of my dream and she had not wanted to tell me.

Less credible tales of the supernatural exist in the folklore of Uist. Peigi's neighbour Seonaidh Caimbeul, the bard, told me how a shepherd lived in his father's cottage on the wild, high slope of Beinn Mhór. He had a young wife and one child, a little girl, and she was deaf and dumb. The shepherd's father was an old man of evil temper, and this night he grew ill and died. The shepherd and his wife placed him in a bier, and in the early morning the shepherd left for the village far off to bring help. Evening came, it grew dark and stormy, and the shepherd was not returning. The mother with her little child sat by the fire in silence. She heard the corpse move. The child looked up and spoke her first words, 'Grandfather is rising. He will eat you, but he won't touch me.' The mother caught up the child and fled to the one other room. She barred the door and put everything she could move against it. The old man rose up and came to the door, and he began to dig away the earth under the lintel with his hands until his head appeared, his shoulders—but at that moment the cock crew and he lay still. He was there until the shepherd with his friends arrived and they lifted him back on the bier. They took him away next day and buried him in a graveyard on the north side of Loch Eynort at a place called An t-Uchd Buidhe on the beach. There is a hole where he is buried, and that hole can be seen to this day. People say it can never be filled.

Tales were also told about supernatural animals such as sea cattle and water horses. I heard of the sea cattle from Angus John Campbell, who told of an old man on the small island of Mingulay finding a strange cow among his own herd one morning. She was a good milker, better than the others, so he kept every calf that came from her and did away with all his own. The cattle at that time were kept under the same roof along with the folk, and this night the old man was talking to his wife about the stray cow getting rather old, and they decided to kill it next day. In the morning when he let them loose the old cow made for the shore and all the rest followed her, to disappear into the sea. That night the old man was without a cow to his name. Though I heard no account of the actual appearance of the water horse, he is known in Glendale, as he is in every part of the Hebrides. The *each-uisge*, as he is called, becomes a handsome young man at night and he comes about the house to court pretty girls. At daylight he changes into a savage horse that drags his victim into the loch. He has a weakness which results in his being recognized. He likes to have his head rubbed, and while his sweetheart puts her fingers through his hair she feels the sand and the bits of water-weed and so knows who her lover is. Peigi MacRae gave me a song which is incomplete, but the words were collected in Dalibrog sixty years ago by Dr. George Henderson. It is the pleading of a girl to her supernatural captor to free her and let her go home as he found her. It is included in this book. In Glendale an *each-uisge* was said to live in Loch Kearsinish.

The reminiscences of the older men, of what happened in their lives and the lives of their fathers and grandfathers, were vivid and extensive. It was less than a hundred years since the evictions were made by the chiefs and landlords of the Highlands and the Hebrides. They cleared the people from the best land to make sheep farms, which then was the great profit-making scheme. They were made to live near the shore and gather seaweed to burn for kelp that was transported south for the manufacture of soda. But when it was found possible to make soda by cheaper means this work was abandoned. Then followed poverty made worse by the potato blight, as in the case of Ireland. It happened in South Uist, as in many another part of the west, that factors, estate officers, and police were sent to force hundreds aboard ships for Canada. Those that refused had their houses burned and possessions confiscated to prevent their having any shelter or means. The ships lay in Loch Boisdale while the families were rounded up and put on board, some tied with ropes to prevent their escape. Those who did escape managed to hide in the hills until it was possible to make their way to the Lowlands. When the conditions of starvation and

INTRODUCTION

want were made known in the south, funds were gathered, and it was said that
the agents for the landowners would distribute the money to the immigrants on
their arrival in Canada. It never reached there, and the wretched people
landed with barely enough clothing, no money, no work and no language but
Gaelic, to wander about the country, many of them dying of cold and disease.
There are many sad songs still sung in Uist composed at the time either by
those that left their island or who watched them depart. The years that
followed were hard in South Uist. They lived in poverty, boiling the roots of the
silver-weed and the leaves of nettles, and always in fear of eviction. But in
1883, through the agitation of the Highland Land League, a Royal Commission was set up to investigate their grievances, and it travelled through the
Highlands and Islands, having meetings where representatives of the crofters
and landowners were able to give their evidence and could be cross-
examined.[1]

As a consequence of the Report made by this Commission, the Crofters Act
was passed in 1886, granting security of tenure at fair rents to smallholders in
the Highlands and Islands. It became impossible for any landlord to evict a
crofter so long as he tilled the ground according to the laws of good husbandry
and paid his fair rent. Some of the great sheep farms were broken up and given
back to the people and the crofts became theirs.

There was another tragedy when in 1897 the island had a contagious and
deadly fever. They told how it came to Glendale and that nine coffins were
carried out of a house below Seonaidh's where only the walls are standing.
They never wanted to turn the ground about that house, for they felt the
fever might still be in it. People were too afraid to go to the sick and would put
milk in a pail on a long pole and pass it through the window to the bedside.
The parish priest of Dalibrog, Fr. George Rigg, a young man, met a martyr's
death in this epidemic attending a fever-stricken woman in Glendale whom no
one else would go near. Several Gaelic elegies on him are still known in Uist.
A neighbour, Màiri Mór an t-Saighdeir, was a young wife at the time and her
husband became ill. Neighbours took her two little children while she stayed
alone with him. He died by the fire in his clothes, his big sea jacket and boots.
A man was given a dram and he took the coffin into the house, and when all
was ready they pulled it out with ropes. After it was away Màiri climbed to the
roof and set fire to the thatch, and the house burned to the ground.

\*　　\*　　\*　　\*　　\*

[1] The testimony given by the South Uist witnesses to this Commission is printed in their
first volume of Minutes of Evidence, and should be read by anyone interested in the history of
the Island, as should the letters of Bishop Angus MacDonald, printed in the Appendix to the
Commission's Report.

# INTRODUCTION

I have given the collection I made of sayings and proverbs that I heard among my friends. They are certain to know many more, and many more again must have been forgotten by now. As for customs and beliefs, I was told not to begin a new work on the third of May or I would be a life-time finishing it, and not to cut hair or nails on a Friday or a Sunday. I was told it was dangerous to bring a third light into a room. This was considered a sign of death; another sign of death was to hear a cock crowing before midnight. I remember one whose neck was drawn at once because he made the mistake of crowing at that time. I asked if it were a sign of bad news, and the reply was: 'Whatever it is, I don't like to hear it.' The origin of such beliefs was lost or else rationalized, as when the little plate of salt and nails placed on the corpse was said to be to keep it from swelling. The time was remembered when new babies used to be passed over the fire, but the reason was forgotten. No sailor should wear clothes dyed with the lichen *crotal*, for 'what came from the rocks will return to the rocks'. A boat on the water, a funeral party, a wedding party or the lads on Hogmanay Eve should all turn sunwise (from left to right) when entering or leaving the house or the graveyard. There were probably good reasons originally for some of these things, but as it was tactless of me to ask I did not hear them.

There was a large glossy Molucca bean called *Cnò Mhoire* (*Entada gigas* = *E. scandeus*), or Mary's Nut, found in the seaweed on the Atlantic shore, where it was brought by the Gulf Stream from the West Indies. This bean brought luck to the finder, who carried it with him, and I have seen one made into a neat snuff-box for an old lady. Another smaller bean (*Mucuna urens* or *Dioclea reflexa*) found in the seaweed which comes from the same source sometimes has a mark like a cross and is called *Àirne Mhoire* or Mary's Kidney. Young women used to use it as a charm to guard virtue, and it was also held in the hand during childbirth.

The *first* bumble bee of spring brings good luck. Put her in the wool bag for good fleeces, in the purse for money, and in the house for contentment.

Of the celebrations of feast days in Glendale, the ritual performed on New Year's Eve by the lads of the township was of great antiquity and possibly pre-Christian. Known as Hogmanay to the Scots and *A' Challuinn* to the Gaels, it began as soon as darkness fell. The sound of boys' voices calling '*A' Challaig seo! A' Challaig seo! Chall O! Chall O!*' was heard in the distance, and when they reached the house they walked round it sunwise, chanting Hogmanay ballads or *duain*, two of which I have given in this book. While they chanted we sat in silence, and then the door was opened for them to enter. The torch-bearer passed his brand of smouldering sheepskin three times round the head of the wife (a very bad omen if it should go out during this ceremony), and then she produced the three round bannocks which the leader of the boys carefully put in his bag and then gave another one to her in return. Other good things were put in the bag for the feast at the end of their journey. When they left and the door was closed they called out the blessing of God on the house for its hospitality. After midnight came the 'first footing', men either singly or in pairs to be the first to bring good wishes for the new year. They carried a bottle of whisky to give all in the house a dram. Using the one glass, the guest would fill it and then pass to everyone present. It was not necessary to finish the contents but only to put the lips to the glass and give the salutation to each person by name. Then the owner of the house would give a glass from his own bottle. It was wise to take little, as the 'first footing' might continue until daybreak and all who called during that day might bring, and certainly be given, refreshment. It was said to be good luck to the unmarried members of the house if the first man to enter was fair while the daughter or the mistress was dark, or the other way about.

The first of February is St. Bride's Day. In Gaelic tradition she was the foster-mother of Christ, and her name is in many ancient prayers. The oyster-catcher, the black-and-white shore bird with scarlet legs and beak, is said to be her servant and is called in Gaelic *Gille Brìghde* or servant of Bride. The story is told that he once concealed Christ from his enemies by covering Him with seaweed and for that service he wears a cross on his back. The sea water is said to become warm on her day.

I was told no traditions of Easter, save that of an old man who said if I were to rise at dawn on Easter morning and go to the rim of the eastern sea I would see the sun dance. The *Duan na Càisg* given by Seonaidh Caimbeul, the bard, must have been recited on Good Friday, but there was no remembrance of it being done.

St. Michael's Day, or Michaelmas, on the twenty-ninth day of September, was the day for baking the special cake, *strùthan*, whose recipe I have given. Hallowe'en was a night of much jollity, when the house was invaded by visitors in the ugliest disguises they could contrive of sheepskin and unravelled rope. One little boy spent the day carefully removing the entire skin off the head of a sheep so he could slip it over his own head like a bag, with ears intact. Màiri made a bowl of *fuarag*, thick cream and oatmeal in which was put the silver sixpence, the thimble and button, and we all had a spoon to feast from the same dish. There was the foretelling the future of sweethearts by putting two nuts in the fire, and if they exploded together 'they were away together'. Or dropping the white of egg into a glass of water to see if it would rise 'in wee trees', which was a happy omen, but not if it stayed on the bottom. They would stand two straws near together in the ashes and watch how they would move, whether they fell away from or towards each other.

# INTRODUCTION

Christmas Eve I walked with my Catholic friends to midnight mass at Dalibrog. It was a long five miles in the dark, and as we made our way west with a storm lantern around the slope of Carrisaval we could see far away many tiny lights scattered over the black *machair* moving north towards the church. Others joined us out of the darkness, and we made a long and cheerful procession. The Christmas story was read in Gaelic and they sang the Gaelic Christmas hymn, *Tàladh Chrìosta* or the Christ Child's Lullaby. It has recently been found that Father Ranald Rankin composed the words of this beautiful hymn in 1855, and it was first taught to the people of South Uist and Eriskay by Father Allan McDonald, who had it printed with other Gaelic hymns for private circulation. The tune was originally a waulking song, and I have given the version that is sung in South Uist. After church, shaking hands with each other and giving the wish of *Nollaig shunndach*, we walked the long road home in the early hours of the morning. There waiting was the feast of mutton, cooked the evening before, for it is the custom to kill a sheep for the first food on Christmas morning.

One old custom still kept up was the *réiteach* or formal betrothal. The young man took an older friend with him to call on the parents of the young woman. After conversation about many things, the friend would begin to extol the young man's character and his qualities for making a good husband for their daughter, while she would make her feelings known by staying in their presence with obvious pleasure or by leaving the room. Whatever the opinion of the parents, unless there was some serious reason for their refusal, the daughter made her own decision. If she stayed, she would seat herself at the table opposite the young man. Her father would say '*Ma tha ise deònach, tha mise ro-dheònach, agus mura bi sin mar sin, cha bhi so mar so*' (If she is willing, I am very willing, and if that weren't so, this wouldn't be so). The young man would catch the girl's hand, and they would divide a dram between them, drinking from the same glass. The banns were called three Sundays in succession, and on the Tuesday morning after the last calling the wedding took place.

The greatest chore for a wedding was the plucking and cooking of innumerable hens presented for the party by friends of the bride and bridegroom all over the island. A delegation was formed just to deal with this part of the feast, which consisted of cold chicken, roast mutton, scones and bannocks, fresh and salt butter, new cheese and many another special delicacy of the island, with the ever-present tea, and whisky and port wine for the toasts. Chickens were considered such an essential part of these feasts that when an epidemic killed a lot of hens in the island, Seonaidh Caimbeul, the local bard, made a song about it in which he refers to the grief of prospective brides at the impossibility of making proper wedding feasts without them.

15

# INTRODUCTION

After the religious service the wedding party was met at the church door with the firing of guns and the skirl of bagpipes, which, playing the fine tune *Highland Wedding*, led the procession home to the wedding breakfast. The celebration continued through the day and night. The guests sat down to the banquet in relays while songs and toasts were given, the songs often starting with a new song composed by the local bard specially for the occasion. Dancing began with a Scots foursome reel for the bride and groom and best man and first bridesmaid. Then the guests joined them on the floor and danced until morning. South Uist is famous for its pipers and a great delight of such a day was to listen to their perfect playing and their timing and pointing of the lovely tunes.

Dancing the Highland dances was one of the joys of life in the Hebrides. In Glendale we danced in the kitchen to the pipes of Angus John or James Campbell, or to Donald MacRae playing the accordion, locally known as the 'box'. For more important parties we used to go to the school-house, where there was room for many to gather and dance the favourite country dances, the Petronella, Quadrille and Eightsome Reel, and to shake the house with the lively Scottische and the old dances native to South Uist. Sometimes it was necessary to walk more than five miles to these dances, and ever-memorable was the boundless energy of Màiri Anndra, who would dance all night and walk the long road home to put on the kettle and begin her daily tasks while her companions lay stretched on their beds too tired to remove their shoes.

Màiri Anndra was the best of companions, and a tremendous help to me in taking down songs. She and her sister Peigi had a remarkable memory for songs, a keen ear and excellent Gaelic, though she had never been taught to read or write her native language. From the beginning she understood what I was trying to do, and the difficulties with which I had to contend. She would take, and make others take, hours of effort to have me put down a song correctly. She made certain that I had the sound of the words down right, no matter in what spelling, for they were of the utmost importance in noting down the tune. Whoever was singing the song had to suffer by being made to repeat it over and over again. (Since those days the invention of wire and tape recorders has relieved folksong collectors and singers from this burden.) With a tuning fork to find the key, I would struggle to write down what I heard. Then I was made to sing it, and while the guest might from kindness smile approval—not Màiri Anndra. Her pride was in my getting it down as she knew I wanted—exactly as it was sung. Sometimes we had what she called a 'scholar' with us, such as Angus John Campbell, who could write down the words and who knew himself a large number of songs. But often correction of the text had to come afterwards, when the singer would repeat the words to me slowly.

16

# INTRODUCTION

Time meant nothing to us, as we worked at what we all enjoyed. When one song was declared to have been correctly taken down, someone would suggest another. The singer would be reluctant to sing it if she knew only the chorus and one or two verses, as she felt that doing so was not doing justice to the song. But often other people present would remember other verses, and I have known a song to begin with one verse and end with eleven.

Besides helping me with the songs, Màiri Anndra helped me to search the glen for recipes for dyes, medicinal cures and proverbs, and saw to it that I understood what I was writing down. All my friends were most generous in giving me information and help. My sorrow is that some of them have not lived to see the book in print, for it is rightly to be regarded as belonging to them all.

It is now nearly twenty years since I left Glendale to live, fortunately, not far away, and since those days many changes have come over the glen. The children I knew have grown up, gone away or married; some of them fought in the last war or served in the Merchant Navy, two giving their lives for their country. A road has been built out to the glen, and is already falling into disrepair. Seonaidh Caimbeul celebrated its construction with a poem; this and songs on the wartime shortage of tea and tobacco were among the last of his compositions. He and his wife Peigi are now both dead, as is his brother Iain, men noble in character and sharp in wit, and there is no bard now living in the glen to preserve the memory of events and personalities there in Gaelic verse.

The school in the glen has been closed, for there are now no children to attend it, though recently three babies have been born, and the school may open again. Peigi Nill now sings lullabies to her grandchildren.

The thatched houses, so warm and safe in the winter storms, have been condemned to extinction by an unimaginative authority which prefers two-storey wooden Swedish prefabricated houses, planned for a totally different climate, the height of which exposes them to every gale that blows in Uist. No thatched house may now be built, but Peigi and Màiri Anndra still inhabit theirs and keep it up, and are themselves as lively and tuneful as they ever were. Peigi in spite of her years is a frequent visitor to my house on the Isle of Canna, and has now recorded on wire more than 200 songs and several anecdotes, after telling us that forty or fifty songs exhausted her memory. Her voice is now preserved for posterity.

In spite of all the pressure exerted by English-language schools and broadcasting, and the influx of strangers during the war years, South Uist still retains in greater measure than any other part of the Highlands and Islands the great traditions of its Gaelic past. That this book may help to preserve something of this great tradition and obtain for it a wider respect and recognition, is my humble hope.

In conclusion I acknowledge with gratitude my indebtedness to the friends who helped me make this collection of songs and folklore: Angus John Campbell, son of Iain Campbell and nephew of Seonaidh Campbell, South Lochboisdale; Fred T. Gillies, Esq., Lochboisdale; the Rev. Murdo MacLeod, formerly Church of Scotland minister at Dalibrog, now at Valparaiso; Alasdair Fraser, schoolmaster, Dalibrog; the Rev. Murdo MacDonald, Taynuilt; Neil MacLennan, postmaster, Lochboisdale, and to all my friends in South Lochboisdale and elsewhere in Uist, to whom I have already referred. For help in correcting this work in manuscript and in proof I am indebted to the Rev. John MacCormick, now parish priest of Benbecula, and Angus Matheson, M.A., Lecturer in Celtic at Glasgow, natives of Uist; to the Rev. John MacLean, Bornish, and John MacLean, M.A., headmaster of St. Kieran's School, Campbeltown, natives of Barra; to Calum MacLean, Raasay; and to my husband, John Lorne Campbell, for his help in correcting and translating, and in seeing the book through the press. I am also greatly indebted to Miss Sheila Lockett who has drawn the tunes and map with such care and skill for photographic reproduction.

I acknowledge with gratitude the permission given by the American National Geographic Society to me to reproduce seven of my photographs which were first used to illustrate my article 'Hunting Folksongs in the Hebrides' that was published in their magazine in February 1947; the permission given by the Journal of the English Folk Dance and Song Society to reprint thirteen Gaelic folksongs from Uist which I first printed in their fifth volume; and that given by Glasgow University Library to reprint the words of the song A Ghaoil lig dhachaigh dha m' mhàthair mi discovered by my husband in the papers of the late Dr. George Henderson.

I am indebted to the MacCaig Trust and the Scottish Country Dance Society for generous grants towards the cost of producing this book, and also for very generous gifts towards the same end from my friends Betty Gordon, Jean Milligan, Elizabeth and Francis M. Collinson, and one who wishes to remain anonymous.

Isle of Canna
January 1955

# ÙRNAIGHEAN AGUS
# LÀITHEAN FÉILLE

## PRAYERS AND SAINTS' DAYS

★

### ÙRNAIGH

Gum b'ann 'nad ainm, m'eudail,
A laigheas 's a dh'éireas (mi),
A thogas mo làmh, a shìneas mo chas,
Buileachas is mathas Mhic Dé
As gach nì bhuineas dhòmhsa.

### PRAYER

In thy name, my love,
May I lie down and rise,
Raise my hand and stretch my foot,
And may the bounty and the goodness
Of the Son of God be in everything
That I possess.

★

### SMÀLADH AN TEINE

Smàlaidh mise nochd an teine,
Mar a smàladh Muire 'n t-aingeal.
Có bhios air an fhaire nochd?
Muire gheal 's a Mac,
'S aingeal geal an dorus an taighe
Gus an dig a' là màireach.

### SMOORING THE FIRE

I shall smoor the fire to-night,
As Mary would smoor the fire.
Who shall be on watch to-night?
Bright Mary and her Son,
And a white angel at the door of the house
Until to-morrow comes.

*Note:* The prayer for 'smooring' or smothering the fire is said when covering the burning peats with ashes to keep them alight until morning. The first thought of the housewife is the fire, for, kindling being very scarce, it must not be allowed to go out. At night the live peats were well covered and in the morning they were 'lifted' from the ashes and the new peats added, which soon were ablaze.

19

## ÙRNAIGH

Ìosa an t-ainm os cionn gach ainm,
 Beatha an anma gu léir:
Ged as tric a thoill mi t'fhearg
 Bidh mi leanmhainn as Do dhéidh.

## PRAYER

Jesu, the Name above every name,
The entire life of the soul:
Though often I deserved Thy anger,
I will follow after Thee.

★

## FÀILT' AN AINGEIL

Aingeil Dhé fhuair mar chùram
O Athair na tròcaire
Buachailleachd naomh a dhèanamh ormsa,
An diu 's a nochd;
Dìobair bhuam gach uile chunnart,
Stiùir mo thriall gu slighe na còrach:
Guidhim ort, a Dhia, solus ùr romham,
'S bi fhéin 'nad chairt-iùil os mo chionn
Nochd 's gu sìorruidh, Amen.

## PRAYER TO THE GUARDIAN ANGEL

Angel of God, whom the Father of Mercy
Has entrusted with my spiritual protection,
To-day and to-night banish from me every danger.
Direct my path in the way of righteousness,
I pray Thee make a new light before me,
Be Thou from above my compass to-night and for ever, Amen.

# PRAYERS AND SAINTS' DAYS

## LATHA MUIRE

Cuiridh Brìd' a cas ann,
Cuiridh Muir' a bas ann,
Cuiridh Pàdraig a spòg mhór ann,
Bidh e blàth gu leòr an uair sin.

## LADY DAY

(St. Bride's Day, 1st February[1])

(St.) Bride will place her foot in it (*i.e.* the sea),
Mary will put her palm in it,
(St.) Patrick will put his big hand in it,
It will be warm enough then.

The sea water is said to become warm on St. Bride's feast day. In the Old Style this was eleven days later than at present. Actually the sea is coldest in the spring and warmest in the autumn. In Fr. Allan McDonald's papers, there is a version of this saying in which the last line is

'S thug Pàdraig a' chlach fhuar as.
St Patrick has taken the cold stone out of it.

which makes better sense.

★

Reothart mór na h-Éill Moire,
'S bòlaich na h-Éill Pàdraig.

The big spring-tide of Mary's Day,
And the swell of the sea on St. Patrick's Day.

★

## LATHA CHALUM CHILLE[2]

Diar-daoin Là Chalum Chille chaoimh,
Là chur chaorach air seilbh,
A dhol dheilbh beairt, 's a chur bà air laoigh.

## ST. COLUMBA'S DAY
(9th June)

Thursday the day of kindly Columba,
The day to gather the sheep in the fold,
To set the loom, and put cows with the calves.

[1] See *Carmina Gadelica*, Vol. I, pp. 167, 172.  [2] *Cf. Carmina Gadelica*, Vol. I, p. 162.

# PRAYERS AND SAINTS' DAYS

## BEANNACHADH CRUIDH

Buachaille Chalum Chille
A bhith mu'r casan, 's guma slàn
A thig sibh dhachaigh.

## BLESSING THE CATTLE

May the shepherd of St. Columba
Be about your feet, and may you come home safely.

(St. Columba is the patron saint of cattle in the islands.)

★

## LATHA PHEADAIR

Là Fhéill Peadair, Latha Muire,
Latha mór air son gruth is uachdair
Nuair bhiomaid air an àirigh.

## ST. PETER'S DAY

(29th June)

The feast day of Peter, Lady Day,
The great day for the curds[1] and cream
When we would be at the sheiling.

★

## LÀ FHÉILL MÌCHEIL

Là Fhéill Mìcheil nì sinn strùthan,
Gabhaidh sinn dheth gu cridheil càirdeil,
Mar bu chòir a bhith.

## ST. MICHAEL'S DAY

(29th September)

On St. Michael's Day we will make a cake[2],
We will partake of it in a joyful friendly manner,
As is proper.

[1] 'Gruth'—crowdie in the Highlands.        [2] See p. 58 for recipe for 'strùthan' cake.

# DUAIN

## BALLADS

★

### HOGMANAY

On Hogmanay, New Year's Eve, the boys of the South Side would gather at the house of Alasdair MacDhubhghaill and try to lift a weight. Those with strength enough were regarded as fit to join the older lads in their journey from house to house. One carried a sack and another a stick on which was tied a sheepskin and rags dipped in tallow and set alight. At the door of each house they recited the Duan. With the saying 'Fosgail an dorus is lig astigh mi', the wife opened the door and the boys trooped in. The one with the torch swung it round her head three times. It was the prophecy of death if it should go out during this action. The wife took from the meal chest three bannocks and presented them to the boy with the sack. After putting them in the sack he then returned one. Any presents of food were then welcomed and put away in the bag. They then left and any lad in the house was welcome to accompany them. Out again in the dark, they shouted their blessing on the house of hospitality. 'Beannachdan Dhia 's na Callaig libh'—'the blessing of God and of Hogmanay be with you.' They would visit all the houses from Alasdair's to Raghnall Beag's, then return to Màiri Mór an t-Saighdeir's, where they divided the contents of their sack.

Many ballads were kept alive through this custom.

# 1. DUAN CALLAIG

Tha mise nochd a' tighinn dh'ur n-ionnsaigh
   A dh'ùrachadh dhuibh na Callaig;
Cha ruig mi leas a bhith 'ga innse,
   Bha i ann ri linn mo sheanar.
Mo chaisean Callaig ann am phòcaid,
   'S math an ceò thig as an fhear ud:
Théid e deiseal air na pàisdean,
   Gu h-àraid air bean an taighe.
Bean an taighe is i as fhiach e,
   Làmh a riarachadh na Callaig.
Rud beag do shochair an t-samhraidh
   A' cumail geall air aig an aran.
     Fosgail an dorus is lig a staigh mi!


## HOGMANAY BALLAD

I am coming to-night to you
To renew for you Hogmanay.
I have no need to tell you of it,
It existed in the time of my grandfather;
My Hogmanay skin-strip[1] is in my pocket
And good is the smoke that comes from it.
It will go sun-wise round the children
And especially round the housewife.
'Tis the housewife who deserves it,
Hers is the hand for the 'Hogmanay'.
A small thing of the good things of summer [2]
To keep a promise got with the bread.
     Open the door and let me in!

---

[1] The 'caisean', or 'caisean-uchd', is a strip of skin from the breast of a sheep killed at Christmas or New Year. It is tied to a stick and set alight. See *Carmina Gadelica*, Vol. I, p. 150, and Vol. II, p. 243.

[2] *E.g.* butter.

## 2. DUAN CALLUINN

A' challaig seo, a' challaig seo,
Chall O, chall O!

Mise nochd a' tighinn air Challaig,
   Gille beag nan casan rùis'te;
Cha n-eil orm ach smachd na h-òige
   'S ma bhios mi beò nì mi diùmlach.
Coisnidh mi biadh agus aodach,
   Ma gheibh mi saoghal is ùine;
Ge bè bheir dhomh a' Challaig a nochd
   Guma math théid a' bhliadhn' ùr leis!
     Fosgail an dorus is lig a staigh mi!


### HOGMANAY BALLAD

Hogmanay, Hogmanay, Chall O, Chall O!
I am coming to-night on Hogmanay
A little lad with bare feet;
I am still under the discipline of youth
And if I live I shall make a warrior.
I shall earn food and clothing
If I shall get long life and time;
Whoever will give me my 'Hogmanay' tonight,
May the New Year bring him prosperity.
     Open the door and let me in!

From Angus John Campbell and Donald Currie, South Lochboisdale.

## 3. DUAN NA CÀISG

Triùir a nochd mar oidhche Chàisg, Mar mhì-mhùch-ainn mhàch-ainn, sgiath;

A nochd oidhch' a' chroch-aidh chruaidh, Crann cruaidh air na chroch-adh Crìosd.

A nochd oidhch' a' chroch-aidh chruaidh, Crann cruaidh air na chroch-adh Crìosd'.

Crìosd—a cléir-each os ar cionn Dh'òrd-aich Dia nan Dùl a bh'ann.

1. Triùir a nochd mar oidhche Chàisg,
   Mar mhì-mhùchainn, mhàchainn sgiath;
   A nochd oidhch' a' chrochaidh chruaidh,
   Crann cruaidh air na (ris an do) chrochadh Crìosd'.

2. Crìosda cléireach os ar cionn
   Dh'òrdaich Dia nan Dùl a bh'ann;
   Dia na gile (gealaich), Dia na gréine,
   Dh'òrdaich gach nì is bàrr féileadh.

3. Is uasal bannag, is uasal bochd,
   Is uasal Fear na h-oidhche 'nochd;
   Brìde a shuidh (chaidh) air a glùin
   Is Rìgh nan dùl a chaidh (bha) 'na h-uchd.

4. Is mise an cléireach stucanach
   A' dol timchioll nan clach stacanach,
   Is mise an cléireach, 's math mo bhriotal,
   Dol timchioll nan clach a bha sliochdmhor.

26

5. Is léir dhomh tulaich, is léir dhomh tràigh,
Is léir dhomh na fir air an t-snàmh,
Is léir dhomh caladh (calpa) caol cruaidh
A' tighinn air tìr gun chàirdeas ann.

6. Is iomadh gille, is iomadh cù,
Is iomadh taigh mór air an tulaich
Gun arm gille, gun arm bréige,
Gun arm dhiubh tachairt r'a chéile.

Mise teachdaire Mhic Dé 'san dorus
'S lig a staigh mi.

## THE LAY OF EASTER

1. Three to-night as (on the) night of Easter,
Like [                                    ] of shields;
To-night is the night of the cruel Crucifixion,
Of the hard cross whereon Christ was hung.

2. Christ is the cleric over us
Ordained by God of the Elements[1];
God of the moon, God of the sun,
Who ordained every thing and supreme generosity.

3. [2]Noble the gift, noble the poor,
[2]Noble the Man of this night;
St. Bride went on her knee
With the King of Elements in her lap.

4. [2]I am the cleric established
[2]Going round the founded stones,
I am the cleric, good is my talk,
Going round the stones that were fertile.

5. I see hills, I see shores,
I see men swimming,
I see a slender hard column [?]
Coming ashore without[3] friendship there.

[1] Also 'Dia an tùir'—God of Intelligence (same reciter).
[2] Carmichael's translations of these lines. See *Scottish Gaelic Studies*, Vol. IV, p. 150, for full collation.
[3] All the other versions have the opposite—'with friendship'—which makes better sense.

6. Many a servant, many a dog,
   Many a great house is on the hill
   Without a servant's weapon,[1] without a weapon of falsehood,
   Without a weapon of these meeting together.

   I am the messenger of the Son of God at the door,
   Let me in.


The text of this poem was taken down from the recitation of Seonaidh Campbell, North Glendale, South Uist, on 28th November 1933. Mr. Campbell, who was over seventy years of age, was a native of Loch Carnan, South Uist, and learnt it there when he was a child, but from whom he could not remember. The text is very obscure; the reciter himself varied it and did not profess to be able to explain all the expressions in it. It is interesting to note that there are similarities between this 'Duan' and five poems printed in *Carmina Gadelica*, of which three were collected in the same district. I published this 'Duan' in *Scottish Gaelic Studies*, Vol. IV, 1935, Oxford University Press. In the preface of *Carmina Gadelica*, written on St. Michael's Day, 1899, Alexander Carmichael said that reciters from whom he had taken down this kind of material were nearly all dead by then, leaving no successors. This was an exaggeration. The tune was recorded by Rev. John MacCormick and my husband from Peigi Nill Currie on 17th May 1954; a version from Eriskay was published by Mrs. Kennedy Fraser, Vol I, p. 159, entitled 'Christmas Duanag'. Note also the resemblance to the tune of 'Gura mise tha fo éislein', p. 216.

Mode: Irregular, no 5th or 6th.


[1] *Carmina Gadelica*, Vol.I, p. 160. The equivalent passage there has 'farmad' (= envy) for 'arm', which makes better sense.

# 4. DUAN NA CEÀRDAICH

1. Latha dha'n Fhinn air luachair leobhair—
    A cheathrar chrodha dha'n bhuidhinn—
   Mi fhìn is Osgar is Daorghlas,
    Bha Fionn fhéin ann, 's b'e Mac Cumhail.

2. Chunnacas a' tighinn o'n mhunadh
    Fear fada dubh 's e air aona-chois,
   Le bharran dubh ciardhubh chraicinn,
    Le aparan dha'n éideadh chianda.

3. Labhair Fionn a bha 'sa chuideachd
    Ris an urra a bha dol seachad—
   'Co i' n tìr dha'm bheil do chuideachd?
    Bu tu urra nan cochall craicinn.'

4. 'Mac a' Lìobhainn m'ainm baistidh,
    Nam biodh agaibh orm beachd sgeula,
   Bha mi uair ag uallach ghobhar
    Aig Rìgh Lochlainn as a' Ghealbhain.'

5. Bha mo chàirdean 'sa Bheinn Dòbhrain
    Far an d'fhuair mi m'àrach òg
   Aig nighinn duibh Mhic Asgaill,
    'S bu mhath i an ceann na cloinne.

6. 'Ach tha mi 'gur cur fo gheasaibh
    O's sibh luchd freasdail na ceàrdaich
   Ann an gleannan dubh siar an domhain
    'S cian o dhorus mo cheàrdaich.'

7. 'Có an rudha am bheil do cheàrdach
    No 'm b'fheàirrde sinne 'ga faicinn?'
   'Ma dh'fhaodas mise cha n-fheàirrde,
    No dé mas fheàirrde sibh a faicinn?'

8. Thug iad an sin air an t-siubhal
    'Na chóigeamh luimeanach,
   An gleannan dubh siar an domhain
    Chaidh iad 'nan ceithir buidhnean.

9. Bu bhuidheann dhiu sin an gobha,
    Bu bhuidheann eile dhiu Daorghlas,
   Bu bhuidheann dhiu Dearg mac Dreighinn,
    'S bha Fionn air deireadh 's e 'na aonar.

29

10. Cha ghearradh an gobha ach aona-cheum
   Air gach gleannan siar fàsaich;
   Cha n-fhaiceamaid ach air éiginn
   Sgòd dha éideadh air a mhàsan.

11. 'Fosgail, fosgail' ars an gobha—
   'Put romhad e' arsa Daorghlas;
   'Cha n-fhàgainn dorus mo cheàrdaich
   An àit' gàbhaidh 's mi 'nam aonar.'

12. Fhuair iad an sin builg ri'n séideadh,
   Fhuair iad an sin éideadh ceàrdaich,
   Fhuair iad an sin ceathrar ghoibhnean
   Do dhaoine déisneach, mi-dhealbhach.

13. Ceithir làmhan air gach gobha,
   Lomhainn is teanchair iarainn;
   Thuirt an tì a bha 'gam freagairt
   'S cha bu mhiosa fhreagradh Daorghlas.

14. Daorghlas fear aire na ceàrdaich,
   Leis 'm bu ghnàth a bhith 'na sheasamh,
   'S e cho dearg ri gual' an daraich
   'S a shnuadh air thoradh na h-oibreach.

15. Labhair fear do na goibhnean
   Gu gìomach agus gu guamach:—
   'Có e 'm fear caol gun tioma
   A mhill orm m'innein cruadhach?'

16. Caoilte ag ràdh ri Daorghlas
   'Fàgaibh an t-ainm sgaoilte bhuaibh.'

17. Fhuair iad an sin 'nan sìneadh
   Na lannan dìreacha daithte,
   'S an claidheamh luinneach air a dhianamh
   Le Clanna Sìomain na faiche.

18. 'Fead' agus 'Faoidh' agus 'Éigheach'
   An còmhlan mhic na ceàrdaich;
   Dà làimh dhiag a bha aig Diarmaid,
   'S iomadh duine riamh a mharbh iad.

19. Claidheamh luinneach an làimh Mhic Cumhail, (?Ghuill)
   Nach do dh'fhàg fuil (fuidheall) feòla caoineadh;
   Mise a nochd sgìth mar thà mi
   An déidh bhith 'g àireamh na buidhne.
   Fosgail seo 's lig a staigh mi.

30

# DUAIN—BALLADS

## THE LAY OF THE SMITHY

1. One day the Fiann were on the plain of rushes, four valiant (members) of the band, myself and Oscar and Daorghlas, and Fionn himself, the son of Cumhal.

2. We saw coming from the hillside, a tall dark one-legged man, with his black, dark hood of skin, and his apron of the same material.

3. Fionn, who was in the company, spoke to the person who was going past: 'To what land does your people belong, you, the person of skinny coverings?'

4. 'Son of Liobhann is my name, if you want to know my story; once I used to herd goats for the King of Norway in Gealbhain.'

5. 'My relations were in Ben Dorain, where I was reared in my youth by the black-haired daughter of the son of Asgall; she was good at looking after children.'

6. 'But I am putting you under spells, since you are people used to smithy work, (to follow me to) a dark glen at the west of the world—it is far from the door of my smithy.'

7. 'On what promontory (said Fionn) is your smithy, or would we be the better for seeing it?'
   'If it is in my power, you will not be the better—or what if you are the better for seeing it?'

8. They then set out, into the bleak province, into the dark glen at the west of the world, they went in four bands.

9. One band was the smith('s), one band was (with) Daorghlas, another band was with Dearg mac Dreighinn, Fionn was the last, alone.

10. The smith only took one step westwards over each desolate glen; we hardly saw a corner of his dress on his backside (*i.e.* he went so fast ahead).

11. 'Open, open,' said the smith; 'push it in before you,' said Daorghlas. 'I would not leave the door of my smithy, in a place of danger, while I was alone.'

12. Then they got bellows for blowing, and smithy-clothes, and four smiths, horrible misshapen fellows.

13. Each smith had four hands, a leash and pincers of iron. The one who was answering them spoke, and Daorghlas answered no worse.

14. Daorghlas, watcher of the smithy, who was used to standing; he was as red as oak embers, and his face looked like the fruit of his work.

15. One of the smiths spoke, in careful tones, 'Who is the lean fearless fellow who has spoilt my steel anvil?'

16. Daorghlas was (thenceforth) called 'Caoilte'—'Leave it a widespread nickname'.

31

17. Then they got the straight, shining swords stretched out, and the keen sword made by the children of Siomain of the green.

18. 'Fead' (Whistle) and 'Faoidh' (Cry) and 'Éigheach' (Shouting), in the band of the son of the smithy; Diarmaid had twelve hands, many a man they have slain.

19. A swift sword in the hand of Mac Cumhail which never left a remnant of flesh lamenting (*i.e.* which always cut right through what was before it); tired am I to-night in my condition, after numbering (recounting) the companies; open the door and let me in.

Taken down from John MacDonald, South Lochboisdale, 30th September 1934. See also J. F. Campbell *Leabhar na Féinne*, p. 65, and Reidar Christiansen *The Vikings in Gaelic Tradition*, pp. 197, 345. The story behind the ballad can be read in the latter.

This was always one of the most popular of the Ossianic ballads amongst the people, and many versions have been preserved; it was frequently recited on Hogmanay (the last verse here makes this clear). The version printed here is worn; Campbell prints one of 46 verses and Christiansen one of 41 verses. Verses 13 and 18 are almost certainly corrupt; 13*c* should probably be:

> 'S na seachd uird a bha 'gan spreigheadh
> Seven hammers worked powerfully   (Christiansen)

Verse 18 should probably read:

> 'Fead' agus 'Faoidh' agus 'Éigheach'
> 'S an 'Comhlann', nic na ceàrdaich;
> Dà lann diag a bha aig Diarmaid,
> 'S iomadh duine riamh a mharbh iad.

'Fead' and 'Faoidh' and 'Éigheach', and 'Comhlann' (*i.e.* names of the swords) 'daughter of the smithy'; Diarmaid had twelve swords, many a man they have slain.

The real point of the story, not touched on in this version, is that the smith declared that the sword must be tempered in human blood; lots were cast, and it fell on Fionn to find a victim; he called at a neighbouring house and found an old woman, who turned out to be the smith's own mother. He told her to go to the smithy, where the smith was waiting behind the door; when the door was opened the smith thrust the sword through her as she entered. He was expecting someone else. Afterwards Fionn fought the smith and killed him (see Christiansen).

A number of versions of this ballad have by now been recorded on wire or tape by J. L. Campbell and others. A tune to which it is sung is printed by Amy Murray in *Father Allan's Island*, p. 100.

# SEANFHACLAN AGUS RÀITINNEAN

## PROVERBS AND SAYINGS

★

## TRIADS

Math air an-duine,
'S math air seann-duine,
'S math air leanabh beag,
Trì mathan a théid a mudha.

A kindness to an indifferent man,
A kindness to an aged man,
A kindness to a little babe,
Three kindnesses that will be forgotten.

★

Giomach, runnach, is ròn, trì seòid a' chuain.

A lobster, a mackerel and a seal, the three heroes of the sea (*i.e.* they can move faster than any other sea animal).

★

Na trì rudan as briagha air an t-saoghal: long fo h-uidheam, boireannach leatromach, agus gealach làn.

The three most beautiful things in the world: a full-rigged ship, a woman with child, and a full moon.

33

# PROVERBS AND SAYINGS

Gille pilleagach, loth pheallagach, agus nighean bhreac-luirgneach, triùir nach ruigear a leas tàir orra.

A ragged young man, a shaggy filly and a freckled-legged girl: three things that should not be despised.

★

Taigh gun chù, gun chat, gun leanabh beag, taigh gun ghean, gun ghàire.

A house without a dog, without a cat, without a baby: a house without cheer, without laughter.

★

Trì nithean a thig gun iarraidh : an t-eagal, an t-iadach, 's an gaol.

Three things that come without asking: fear, jealousy, love.

★

Na ceithir gaoithean as fuaire :
   Gaoth ro' uisge,
   Gaoth ro' shneachda,
   Gaoth ro' tholl,
   'S gaoth nan tonn a' tighinn fo sheòl.

The four coldest winds:
   Wind through rain,
   Wind through snow,
   Wind through a (knot) hole,
   And wind of the waves coming under a sail.

★

# LÀITHEAN SEALBHACH—LUCKY DAYS

Imprig Shathurna mu thuath,
Imprig Di-Luain mu dheas;
Ged nach biodh agam ach an t-uan,
'S ann Di-Luain dh'fhalbhainn leis.

Saturday's flitting to the north,
Monday's flitting to the south,
Though I only had the lamb,
I would go with it on a Monday.

34

# PROVERBS AND SAYINGS

## A' GHAOTH—THE WIND

Nuair bhios a' ghaoth air chall, iarr bho'n deas i.

When the wind is lost (dropped) seek it in the south.

★

Chuala mi ghaoth 's cha n-fhaca mi i.

I heard the wind, but I did not see it.

★

'Thugainn,' ars' an Rìgh; 'Fuirich,' ars' a' ghaoth.

'Come,' said the king; 'Stay,' said the wind.

★

Cha dànaig gaoth riamh nach robh an seòl feareigin.

A wind never blew that did not fill somebody's sail.


★


## AM MUIR—THE SEA

Cha n-fhan muir ri uallach, 's cha dean bean luath maorach.

The sea does not wait for a burden, and a hasty woman will not get shell fish.

★

Cha d'fhuair droch-ràmhaiche ràmh math riamh.

A bad oarsman never got a good oar.

★

'S geur fiacail o'n fhraoch, is maol fiacail o'n tràigh.

Sharp the tooth from the hill, blunt the tooth from the shore; *or*

Is geur fiacail o'n fhraoch, is seachd faobhair o'n fheamain.

Sharp the tooth from the moor, seven times sharper the tooth from (gathering) the
   seaweed.

★

Cha n-eil air an loch nach gabh ligeadh ach a fhàgail far am bi e.

The loch you cannot drain you must leave as it is.

35

# PROVERBS AND SAYINGS

## AN T-IASGACH—FISHING

Anmoch gu loch 's moch gu abhainn.

Late to the loch and early to the river. (Loch fishing is best in the early evening, and river fishing best in the early morning.)

★

Is corrach gob an dubhain.

The fishing hook's point is spiky (*i.e.* the fisherman's livelihood is uncertain).

★

An ceann na bliadhna a dh'innseas an t-iasgair iasgach.

It is at the end of the year that the fisherman tells of his fishing.

★

## AN CAT—THE CAT

Am fear a shuath urball a' chait air a mhìs, thuirt e, ' 'S mór bho'n eireachdas.'
The man who wiped his dish with the cat's tail said: 'This is a long way from elegance.'

★

Draghadh cait an aghaidh urbuill.
Pulling a cat against its tail.

★

Cha do loisg seann-chat e fhéin riamh.
An old cat never burnt itself.

★

Tha miann a' chait 'san tràigh, 's cha doir e fhéin as e.
What the cat wants is on the shore, but he won't take it out himself.

★

An diar 'ga iarraidh air a' chat, 's an cat fhéin a' mialaich.
Asking the cat for a drink when the cat is miaouwing herself.

36

# AN CÙ—THE DOG

Modh a' choin, gabhail ealla ris.

A dog's good manners: having nothing to do with it.

★

Cha truagh liom cù is marag m'a amhaich.

I have no pity for a dog with a mealy pudding (tied) round its neck.

★

Cha dèanar cron air a' ghealaich na coin a bhith comhartaich rithe.

The moon is not hurt by the dogs' barking at her.

★

Cha mhór as diach an cù nach eil eadraiginn a chinn fhéin do dhranndan aige.

A dog is worth little that hasn't a headful of growls.

★

# AN T-EACH—THE HORSE

Is olc an t-each nach giùlain a dhiallaid.

'Tis a bad horse that cannot carry his own saddle.

★

Is luath each iasaid.

Fast goes the borrowed horse.

★

# A' MHUC—THE PIG

Ged a chuirte muc dha'n taigh mhór, dh'iarradh i dha'n chitsinn.

Though a pig were invited to the big house, it would want into the kitchen.

★

Muc shàmhach as mutha dh'icheas.

The quiet pig eats most.

# PROVERBS AND SAYINGS

## NA H-EÒIN—BIRDS

Ugh aig eireig 's bean aig sgalaig.

A pullet's egg and a farm servant's wife—(Two unsuitable things, both too early).

★

'S minig [1] a chreiceadh a chearc 'san là fhliuch.

Pity the one who would sell his hen on a wet day (it would look much smaller).

★

Ge b'r'ith dé gheibh cearc a' sgrìobain, cha n-fhaigh cearc a' ghràgain dad.

Whatever the scratching hen may get, the cackling hen gets nothing.

★

Ugh air an Inid,
Ian air a' Chàisg,
Mura bi sin aig an fhitheach,
Bidh am bàs.

Egg at Shrovetide,
Chick at Easter,
If the raven does not have that, it will die.

★

Gach ian dh'a niod 's a shràbh 'na ghob.

Every bird to its nest and its straw in its mouth.

★

'S toil leis an fheannaig a h-isean carrach gorm fhéin.

The crow likes its own scabby blue fledgling.

★

'S minig [1] a thaobhadh a' chreag 'nuair bhiodh a h-eòin fhéin 'ga fàgail.

Pity the one who would take to the rock when its own birds were leaving it. (Said of someone taking a farm in which his predecessor had failed.)

★

'Cha doir do cheòl do'n chuideachd thu', mar thuirt a' chorra-ghritheach ris an fheann-aig.

'Your music will not take you into company,' as the heron said to the crow.

[1] 'minig' and 'mairg' are confused in this dialect.

Cha dig ugh mór a tòn an dreathain.

A big egg will never come from the wren's backside.

★

Cha chuir is cha bhuain bigean beag,[1]
Gheibh e na dh'fhòghnas dha.

The little bird[2] does not sow nor does he harvest—
He will get what suffices him.

★

# AN TEINE—THE FIRE

Far am bi toit, bidh teine.

Where there is smoke there is fire.

★

Tha a smùid fhéin an ceann gach fòid,
'S a dhòrainn ceangailte ri gach neach.

Every peat has its own smoke,
And every person has his own sorrow.

★

Is minig a bha gabhail mhór a teine beag, agus teine mór a chaidh as.

There has often been a big blaze from a little fire and often a big fire that has gone out.

★

# COMHAIRLE—COUNSEL

'S minig gun dòigh na daoine.

Men are often feckless.

★

Na tog mi gu'n tuit mi.

Don't lift me until I fall.

---

[1] This proverb was said in reply to Peigi MacRae's mother's remark to a certain neighbour
—that he was a very idle fellow.
[2] The meadow or rock pipit. I was told it is ' the little bird that follows the cuckoo'.

# PROVERBS AND SAYINGS

Is math am modh a bhith sàmhach.
It is good manners to keep quiet.

★

Ged as mór na guthan, cha n-fhìor na leathan.
Though the words are big, they are not half of them true.

★

Is mór am facal nach toill 'sa bheul.
It is a big word that the mouth won't hold.

★

Is lugha na frìde màthair an uilc.
Smaller than a mite is the origin of evil.

★

An rud nach binn liom cha chluinn mi.
What I do not like, I do not hear.

★

Na cuir spàin an càl nach ich thu.
Don't put a spoon in kail you won't eat.

★

Ge bè nach gabh comhairle gabhaidh e cama-lorg.
He who won't take advice will take the crooked track.

★

Is fheàrr aon chomhairle bho Dhia na dhà dhiag bho dhaoine.
Better one counsel from God than twelve from men.

★

'S fhada a bhios duine muigh mun doir e dhachaigh droch-theisteanas air fhéin.
A man will be a long time abroad before he brings home a bad report of himself.

★

An rud a nì thu 'sa chùil thig e dh'ionnsaigh an doruis.
What is done in the back corner will eventually come to the front door.

★

Cluasan móra aig saithichean beaga.
Little pitchers have big ears.

40

# PROVERBS AND SAYINGS

Ge bè nach coimhead roimhe, coimheadaidh e fada 'na dhéidh.

He who will not look before him will look far behind him.

★

Ge bè nach doir gnothach dha'n bhaile mhór, bheir e gnothach air ais.

He who does not take a business to the big town will bring a business back with him.
(Said of a man who returned from a jaunt to Glasgow with a black eye.)

★

Is miosa an t-eagal na 'n cogadh.

Fear is worse than war.

★

Tha eachdraidh na bliadhna gu léir aig fear falbh na h-aon oidhche.

The man who goes away for one night has the history of the whole year.

★

Am fear a bhios fada gun éirigh bidh e 'na leum fad a' latha.

He who is late rising will be in a hurry all day.

★

'S minig a bha comas urchair aig fear gun ghunna, is ligeadh fada aig fear gun chù.

Many a time a man without a gun got the chance of a shot, and a man without a dog got a chance of unleashing one.

★

'S fheàrr an còta a bhith fàs fada na bhith fàs goirid.

Better for the coat to grow long than to grow short.

★

Tarraing do chasan a taigh do choimhearsnaich, mus fàs e sgìth dhiot.

Take your feet out of your neighbour's house before he grows tired of you.

(Cf. Proverbs xxv, 17.)

★

# AN OIGHREACHD—THE ESTATE

'S fheàrr caraid 'sa chùirt na crùn 'san sporan.

Better a friend at court than a crown in the purse.

41

Nuair thig bàillidh ùr bidh lagh ùr 'na chois.

When a new factor comes he brings a new law with him.

★

Bithibh a staigh air a' mhaor 's bidh sibh a staigh air a' bhàillidh.

Be in with the estate officer and you will be in with the factor.

★

Is sleamhain a' chlach a tha 'n ursann an taigh mhóir.

Slippery is the threshold of the big house (*i.e.*, the favour of the great is not to be depended on).

★

Uaisle gun chuid, is maragan gun gheir.

Gentry without wealth, sausages without fat.

★

# BEAIRTEAS AN T-SAOGHAIL—WORLDLY WEALTH

Sùil a ghleidheas sealbh.

A (keen) eye keeps cattle.

★

Cha n-fhidir an sàthach an seang.

The replete does not consider the lean.

★

Biodh rud agad 's thig rud ugad.

He that has gets.

★

Is minig a chinn fuidheall fanaid 's a mhith fuidheall farmaid.

An object of ridicule has often succeeded, while an object of envy has often come to nothing.

★

Far am faighear an iomairt gabhaidh na damaich innte.

Where gambling goes on the rogues will get into it.

★

'S fheàrr làn an dùirn do chiùird na làn an dùirn do dh'òr.

Better a handful of craft than a handful of gold.

42

# PROVERBS AND SAYINGS

Ge bè nach cuir 'san là fhuar cha bhuain 'san là theth.

He who does not sow on the cold day will not reap on the warm day.

★

'S minig a bha rath air leiristeach is math-an-airigh gun nì.

Many a time a ne'er-do-well prospered and a well-deserving one failed.

★

Feumaidh fear nan cuaran éirigh uair ro' fhear nam bròg.

The man of cowhide slippers must get up an hour before the man who has shoes.

★

Nuair a throideas an dà mheàirleach, théid an t-ionracan 'na chuid.

When two thieves quarrel the honest man comes into his own.

★

# FEARAS-TAIGHE—THE HOUSEHOLD

Cha chumar taigh le bial dùinte.

A house cannot be kept with a shut mouth.

★

Am fear a nì am prìne cha n-e chuireas am pluc air.

The man who makes the pin is not the one who puts the head on it.   (Said of a person who doesn't finish the work he begins.)

★

Cha dig as a' phoit ach an toit a bhios innte.

Nothing will come out of the pot but the steam that's in it.

★

'S fheàirrde brà a breacadh gun a bristeadh.

A quern[1] is the better for being roughened without being broken.

★

Dh'aithnichinn air a' mhiùg có bheireadh am bainne dhomh.

I'd know by the whey who'd give me the milk.

★

Is furasda fuine dheanamh taca ri min.

It is easy to bake when meal is at hand.

[1] A stone hand-mill.

Cha dean corrag-mhilis ìm, 's cha dean glutaire càise.

Sweet finger does not make butter, and a glutton does not make cheese.

★

Taban gòraig air cuigeal crìonaig.

The foolish one's wool on the cute one's distaff.

★

Gabhaidh dath dubh, 's cha ghabh dubh dath.

Any colour can be dyed black, but black can't be dyed any colour.

★

Meàirleach lìn 's meàirleach sìl, ge bè có meàirleach a gheibh fois, cha n-fhaigh meàirleach an lìn ghlais.

Thief of flax and thief of grain, whichever thief will get (? eternal) rest it will not be the thief of the green flax.

★

# AM PÒSADH—MARRIAGE

Diùghaidh sìde, fliodh shneachda,
Diùghaidh connaidh, fearna fhliuch,
Diùghaidh digheadh, beòir air dhol aog,
Agus diùghaidh an t-saoghail, droch-bhean.

The worst of weather—sleet,
The worst of fuel—wet alder,
The worst of drink—stale beer,
The worst thing in the world—a bad wife.

★

Fàinne òir air stròin muice,
Eireachdas air bean gun bhanalachd.

Finery on an immodest woman (is like) a gold ring in a pig's nose.

★

Sùilean gobhair an ceann nam fear dol a thaghadh nam ban.

Goats' eyes in the heads of men going to choose wives.

★

A' chiad bhliadhna, bliadhna nam pòg,
An darna bliadhna, bliadhna nan dòrn.

The first year, year of the kisses,
The second year, year of the fists.

44

# PROVERBS AND SAYINGS

'S luath ceum fear na droch-mhnatha air a' mhachair Uibhisteach.

Fast the pace of the husband of a thriftless wife on the Uist machair.[1]

★

'S toil liom airgiod [2] a' bhodaich, ach cha toil liom anail a' bhodaich.

I like the old man's money,[3] but I don't like his breath. (Said of a girl who would take an old-age-pensioner as a husband.)

★

Tha mac 'na mhac gu faigh e bean, tha nighean 'na nighinn fad a beatha.

A son is a son until he gets a wife,
A daughter is a daughter the whole of her life.

★

'S fheàrr am pòsadh na 'n losgadh.

It is better to marry than to burn.   (*Cf.* I Corinthians vii, 9.)

★

Bean bheag dha'n fhear mhór 's bean mhór dha'n fhear bheag.

A little wife for the big man, a big wife for the little man.

★

Cha ghabh mi fear gun each, 's cha dig fear eich 'gam iarraidh.

I will not take a man without a horse, and no horseman comes to ask for me.

★

# TOIMHSEACHAIN—RIDDLES

Bodach 'sa chùil 's dà shùil dhiag air.                                    Criathar.

An old man in the corner with twelve eyes.                          A sieve.

★

Ceathrar air chrith,
Ceathrar 'nan ruith,
'S dithis a' deanamh an rathaid,
Aon duine ag éigheach.                                                          Mart.

Four shaking, four running,
Two making (out) the road, and one crying.                    A cow.

---

[1] The flat sandy plain that borders the Atlantic, windswept, cold and without shelter.
[2] 'aran' air uaireannan.
[3] 'bread' sometimes.

## PROVERBS AND SAYINGS

Théid an làir ghlas a Shasunn gun a cas a fhliuchadh.          Litir.

The grey mare will go to England without wetting a foot.      A letter.

(A letter in olden times was grey in colour and known as *làir ghlas*.)

★

Chaidh mi dha'n bheinn, 's fhuair mi e,
Shuidh mi air cnoc, 's dh'iarr mi e,
'S na faighinn e, dh'fhàgainn e,
O nach d'fhuair mi e, thug mi liom e.          Bior 'nam chois.

I went to the hill and I got it.
I sat on a knoll and I sought it.
And if I would get it I would leave it.
Since I did not get it, I took it with me.      A thorn in my foot.


## NA FIANTAICHEAN—THE FINGALIANS

Ruthadh athair an am cadail,
Dh'éireadh Fionn moch 'sa mhaduinn;
Ruthadh athair anns a' mhoch-mhaduinn,
Dheanadh Fionn an ath-chadal.

With a red sky at bed-time,
Fionn would rise early in the morning;
With a red sky early in the morning,
Fionn would go to sleep again.

# SEANN-LEIGHEISEAN

## OLD CURES

★

COLD BLISTER: Rub a Slug (Seilcheag) on it. For a sore lip one chews Tormentil (Cairt Shleamhna). (R. M.)

SORE THROAT: Eat dry sugar. A cup of hot water with a spoonful of treacle on going to bed. (N. M., A. McD.)

EARACHE: Put a limpet on the fire and remove when the juice bubbles. When able to be borne, pour the juice in the ear and stop the ear with a bit of wool that still contains the natural oil. (A. G. C.)

HEADACHE: Boil the leaves of the Buckbean (*Menyanthes trifoliata* or Lus nan Laogh), and drink the water the first thing in the morning. Gather the entire plant, dry it, boil and drink the juice for a severe headache. (P. C.)

ASTHMA: Take a dose of castor oil and vinegar, half and half. (N. M.)

STIFF NECK: Put the tongs about the neck and massage back and forth. (S. C.)

SPRAINS AND STRAINS: Skin an eel in long strips and wrap it round as a bandage with the fat side in. The eel fat soothes and the skin, being elastic, will not bind too tightly. Put sprain in a running stream. (I. C.)

SPLINTERS: To remove a splinter take boiling lard or fat—it must be very hot—and either put it on the place with a limpet shell or dip the finger in. Fat or lard are preferable to butter, as they hold greater heat. (A. J. C., C. E. M.)

47

# OLD CURES

BURNS AND SCALDS: Docken (Copan)—boil the root with a little fresh butter and apply as a dressing on a bandage. Fish oil is used; mushrooms, applied sliced; peat soot from the chimney applied at once (a very sore cure). Eel fat (Sul-easgainn) is very good. (A. G. C., M. M., P. N. C.)

BEALING: Great Plantain (Cuach Phàdraig) and Ribwort (Slànlus)—dip in hot water and apply them as a plaster. They have great healing properties and leave no scar. Tormentil (Cairt Shleamhna) to be made into a paste and applied to any suppurating sore. A turnip poultice or sugar and soap will draw boils. Archangel tar is applied to deep cuts. (Johnny Campbell used it to cure a bad wound in the palm of his hand made by a crab shell and it healed easily without a scar.) (M. M., P. M., P. N. C., A. J. C., S. C.)

INDIGESTION: Take fresh Dulse (Duileasg) from the shore and eat it raw. Carrageen boiled in either water or milk is very soothing to a sore stomach. Boil the entire plant of Tormentil (Cairt Shleamhna) and drink the juice. Also boil nettle tops and drink the juice. This will cure stomach trouble. (S. C., M. M., P. C., A. G. C.)

STOMACH ACHE: When a patient is in desperation, put a rope around his feet and hang him by the heels from the rafters. Repeat at reasonable intervals: 'This will undo the knot in the guts.' (S. C.)

HEARTBURN: Drink hot sea water. For 'Groim-Maothain', a pain that spinners have from swallowing bits of wool while putting it between their teeth when spinning, boil cuddies (cudaigean—tiny codlings) and eat bones and all. (A. G. C.)

CONSTIPATION: For 'stopadh' (tight bowels) take fresh sea tangle, cut in pieces, chew and swallow. Take the root of Buckbean (*Menyanthes trifoliata* or Lus nan Laogh). Clean and boil it in water all day until the juice is dark and thick. Strain and give the patient a teaspoonful, as it is very strong. (S. C.)

CORNS: A poultice of ivy leaves and vinegar. Also Tormentil (Cairt Shleamhna) chewed and applied on a bandage. (S. C., A. G. C.)

CHILBLAINS: When you go to bed at night put your hands or feet in very hot water, then dry thoroughly with an old linen cloth, patting so that the linen takes back all the moisture from the pores. Put them right up to the fire for a good while. Then make an oatmeal poultice, just like porridge without salt, leaving it on until the morning. Then make another poultice and put it on without washing the feet. But at night begin with the very hot water as you did before, and continue for a week and it will cure them. (P. C.)

WARTS: Put nine nines of the joints of the corn (oats) in a secret place, such as under a stone. Do not go near them again, and as they wear away the warts will also disappear. (A. J. C.)

# OLD CURES

SORE FEET: For soreness under the toes from walking barefoot, apply as dressing the little shreds of wool found on the hill and still full of natural grease. Archangel tar is also used. For a sore place—as a cut from a shoe where a shoe rubs—apply Ribwort (*Plantago lanceolata*) or Slànlus (pronounced snà-lus).

SKIN: The fat around the gizzard of a chicken (blonaig circe) melted and applied to the skin for any kind of irritation is excellent. It can be bottled. It is also good for preserving boots.

STYE: Counting (Cunntais an t-Sleamhnain) is an incantation said while pointing a sharp steel instrument at the stye.[1] Boil Bird's Foot Trefoil in water and use as eyewash. Eye-bright (Lus nan Leac) infused in either water or milk to bathe the eyes; rub with pure gold; wash with new tea. The two small white bones found in the head of the haddock, one behind each eye, if pounded into dust and applied to a stye will cure it.                                    (M. M., P. N. C., I. F.)

TOOTHACHE: Mix gunpowder and tallow and put it into the cavity, chewing it in; fill the cavity with Archangel tar. Make a poultice of Archangel tar in a piece of linen and plaster the cheek with it.                              (S. C.)

NOSE BLEED: Put the cold tongs down the back.                        (M. M.)

RHEUMATISM: Boil sea water and put in the sore joints, as hot as can be borne. Put sulphur in the soles of the stockings.                      (C. E. M., A. G. C.)

LUMBAGO: For Sprung Back (Leum Droma) have someone who was born feet first to stand on the back.[2]

SCROFULA: King's Evil (Tinneas an Rìgh). The seventh child of a line of either boys or girls is said to inherit this power, and the charm is handed down from one possessor of the gift to the next, and it is under the greatest secrecy. If divulged, the possessor would lose the power of curing. After seeing the patient, the 'possessor' fills a bottle of water, washes the patient and at the same time recites the charm or incantation, giving the patient a silver coin to be worn on a string about the neck. This is still in practice. A young girl from South Lochboisdale, and a Glasgow boy living with his grandmother in Smerclett, went to Barra for this cure during 1932.

Màiri MacRae knew a man of Harris, when she was there in 19—, who attended a girl with this power (Johann nighean Iain bho Phabaidh). All three patients here mentioned recovered.                                            (M. M.)

[1] See Dr. Alexander Carmichael's *Carmina Gadelica*, Vol. I, p. 73, for the charm.
[2] See *idem*, Vol. IV, p. 207.

JAUNDICE: Yellow Disease (Tinneas Buidhe) is got by fright and must be cured by a fright. Bean Anndra (màthair Màiri Anndra) got jaundice when a young woman from seeing an adder crawl out of a creel in which she was bringing bracken to her mistress's byre. Her mistress set her to beat eggs in a bowl by a closed door, and asked a farm-hand to suddenly bang the door and startle her. He did it with such effect that the bowl was dropped and shattered but the jaundice was cured. (M. M.)

He who drinks the first milk of the cow after calving will never take the Tinneas Buidhe.

DROPSY: Take Buckbean (*Menyanthes trifoliata* or Lus nan Laogh), which is found in wet, marshy ground, clean and boil the entire plant, put the juice in a bottle and drink daily. (P. C.)

WHOOPING COUGH: 'The very best thing is mare's milk.' (P. C.)

WORMS: (*a*) Pare Bog Myrtle (Roid). Boil in water to make a strong drink and take after fasting. (*b*) Salt herrings fried on red cinders (gealbhainn) should be given after fasting. Then in an hour or two as much water as the patient can drink. (P. M.)

BABY POWDER: Burn a white linen cloth and use the ash. (S. C.)

TONICS: Seal oil is used as cod liver oil and is most beneficial. Beat cockle shells to powder, boil down and take the juice as a tonic for anyone needing lime. (M. M., D. F.)

Boil the entire plant of the Centaury or Red Gentian (Ceud Bhileach) and strain. The juice is excellent for one in need of a nerve tonic or for weakness following an illness.

A SAILOR'S CURE FOR THE 'MORNING AFTER': 'Take a bunch of Sea Pinks pulled with roots. Boil for an hour or more. Leave to cool. Drink slowly and you are ready for the next night ashore.' (D. R., late Master of m.v. *Lochmor*)

# LEIGHEIS AIR CRODH (CURES FOR ANIMALS)

RED WATER—or Bun Dearg in cows: Boil the entire plant of the Tansy (Lus-na-Frainge), put the juice in a bottle and pour down the cow's throat. (A. C.)

DRY DISEASE—or Galar Tioram in cows: Boil bracken roots (rainich) and give the juice. Smash down white whelks (Gille Fionndrainn, the small white ones) and put in a bottle of cold water. Give to the cow daily. Do not cook. Slugs (seilcheag, black without shells)—give a handful alive every day. Seaweed (Feamain Chìrein or Channelled Fucus)—boil well in water and give the cow the entire contents.

# OLD CURES

CONSTIPATION: White whelks (Gille Fionndrainn), a handful pounded fine should be given to the cow every morning. The Buckbean or Lus nan Laogh is given for constipation in calves. A glassful is sufficient. (J. M.)

COLD: Give the cow a drink of hot milk with plenty of pepper in it. (P. M.)

CATARACT: For cattle or sheep, pound glass to a powder and put in the eye, covering it with a shield, and it will wear away. (J. M.)

STAGGERS: To cure a horse, cut a vein below the right ear and let so much blood away. (F. M.)

TONIC FOR COLD AND COUGH: Give seal oil, a pint at a time.

LUMP IN THE THROAT: A disease found in sheep. Take a turf (sgrath) from the roof of a thatched house and set it alight. Put the nose of the sheep over it to inhale the smoke until the nose and mouth water plentifully. This is said to cure it completely. (F. M.)

LUMP ON A HORSE: For a lump on a horse, cut it out and apply to the open wound for several days a salt and water pickle so strong that a potato will float in it. (A. G. C.)

# RECIPES FOR THE DYEING OF WOOL

★

## RECIPES FOR DYEING WOOL FROM MOSSES, FLOWERS, ROOTS, ETC.

CROTAL:
Stone Parmelia
(*Parmelia saxatilis*)
Crotal or lichen is gathered from the rocks late in the summer and is dried in the sun. A layer of crotal and a layer of wool are placed alternately on the bottom of the pot until the pot is filled. Then as much water as the pot will hold, and put on the fire. It must not be allowed to boil dry. Remove when the shade is as desired and rinse in salt water to set the colour. It is said that crotal, being plucked from the rocks, returns to the rocks, and it is shunned by fishermen. The dye is a red-brown.

FIASAG NAN CREAG:
Beard of the Rock
(*Ramilina scopu-
lorum*)
A hairy lichen growing on rocks near the sea, if used like crotal will make a pleasing orange or yellow-brown.

BARR AN FHRAOICH:
Heather tops,
Ling (*Calluna
vulgaris*)
Gather the tops when they are young and green, when growing in a shady place. Put in the pot as you would for crotal, and it will dye a lovely yellow which can also be the basis for green if combined with indigo.

SEALASDAIR:
Yellow Flag
(*Iris pseudacorus*)
Take the root when the flower is past. Clean, scrape and break up, then boil in water. It is then strained and the wool boiled with the juice for a good hour or longer, until the desired shade of blue or steel-grey (glas). A little alum is used. Sometimes the entire plant is boiled with the wool.

53

| | |
|---|---|
| SÙITH NA MÒNA:<br>Peat Soot | Put the soot in a muslin bag and boil it in water for at least an hour. Lift it, squeeze it and then put the wool in and boil for a dark yellow-brown or auburn shade. |
| FEANNTAG:<br>Nettle<br>(*Urtica dioica*) | Pluck them out of the ground, root and stem. Clean and boil. The juice is then strained and boiled with wool to make a greenish-yellow. A little alum is necessary. |
| BUADHGHALLAN BUIDHE:<br>Yellow Ragwort<br>(*Senecio Jacobaea*) | Take the tops and put in a muslin bag and boil. Then remove bag and put in wool and boil. The shade will be 'yellow gru' or blackish-yellow. Use a little alum to set colour. |
| SEALBHAG:<br>Sorrel<br>(*Rumex acetosa*) | Clean and boil the roots with a little indigo. It makes a lovely blue which will not lose its colour. In the winter use the root and in summer the entire plant. Use a little alum to set colour. If used alone it makes a red. |
| CAIRT-LOCHA:<br>Water Lily root<br>(*Nymphae alba*) | (Called in Glendale Gucagan Bàite). Clean and break up the long roots and boil them with a little copperas or alum. Strain and boil the wool in the juice to make a splendid black. The root must be boiled a long time—several hours. 'Many a time I saw my mother knit the stockings first and then dye them in the juice.' A special raft was made to go out on the lochs to gather the roots, which are always in treacherous mud and most difficult to lift. |
| NEÒINTEAN BUIDHE:<br>Corn Marigold<br>(*Chrysanthemum segetum*) | Take the flowers and put in a muslin bag and boil. Then add wool and boil until the desired shade. A little alum is required and it makes a bright, clear yellow. |
| RUIN:<br>Lady's Bedstraw<br>(*Gallium verum*) | Take the root of the plant and use as with Corn Marigold. The colour is orange-red. |
| ROID:<br>Bog Myrtle<br>(*Myrica gale*) | Use the entire plant, filling the pot with it, cover with water and boil until the colour shows on a peeled stick or bit of wool. Strain and return the dye to the pot with a tablespoon of alum and the wool which has been rinsed in hot water. Boil until the desired shade of a fine clear yellow. |

★

## TO DYE INDIGO BLUE

Save the household urine until sufficient in a big clean tub beside the fire. The temperature must be about 85° to 90° and must not vary. Put the indigo in a little bag of muslin and steep it in the urine. Every three days squeeze it, rubbing it with the hands to take the colour out. An ounce of indigo to a pound of wool, but as the strength varies, take what you think will do.

Take Sorrel (Sealbhag—*Rumex acetosa*), gather the root and stem, wash and clean it but do not break it. Boil this plant, a pound to a pint, until the juice is strong. Strain it and add to the urine. This is the mordant and makes the colour adhere to the wool. Remove the indigo bag when this is done.

Now put the wool in clean hot water, rinse it and put in the urine tub. Put a top on the tub and leave for three days. But every day lift and squeeze the wool and put back again, remembering that the temperature must always be the same.

After three days again put back the 'blue' bag and make and add the sorrel juice as before. Repeat every three days until the colour is right. For medium blue it may take a week, for dark blue a month. When the colour is as you want it lift out the wool and wash thoroughly in soft water and with a soap that will not make the fibres brittle. In Uist the water in the streams is particularly soft from the peat and most suitable, or else use rain water. Dry in the open on the heather or the clean grass.

It is most essential that the wool be well scoured before dyeing, as it will not take the colour if not truly clean.

(Miss Peigi MacRae, North Glendale.)

*Note:* A four-gallon iron pot was used for these dyes and though it is difficult to give exact measurements the pot was half-filled with the plants such as Lady's Bedstraw, Corn Marigold and Ragwort and water added to the top. Alum was added to the juice after straining and before the wool was added. The amount varied but never exceeded four ounces to a pound of wool. With light shades a little cream of tartar was added. The wool was dyed in the fleece after being thoroughly scoured, and rinsed in hot water just before being put in the dye pot.

# RECIPES FOR SPECIAL DISHES

★

CAIRGEIN or CARRAGEEN (*Chondrus crispus*). Sometimes called Irish Moss. It is used to make a hot drink or blancmange. Gather it at the spring tides, for it can be found only at very low water. It is spread on clean grass until it is washed by the rain and bleached by the sun until, from a dark purple when gathered, it becomes white with pink edges. Store it when dry in a bag or box. Take a handful, wash it in cold water and put it in a pan of milk, a quart, bring to the boil and then put off the fire to barely simmer for some twenty minutes, or until the spoon is coated. Pour through colander or strainer into bowl, to stand in a cool place until firm. A very little sugar and a flavouring can be added. It should be of the same consistency as curds. It is eaten with milk or cream, delicious if the latter be slightly turned. It is most nourishing and an excellent diet for invalids or those recovering from feverish illness.

FUARAG. At Hallowe'en oatmeal is mixed in a basin of thick or beaten cream and the thimble, sixpence, button and ring put in. The guests sit around the basin, each with a spoon, and eat it until a reward is found in a mouthful.

DEOCH-MHINEADH. A pail of cold water with a few handfuls of oatmeal added makes a refreshing drink when working outside in warm weather.

STAPAG. A drink made of whisky, sugar or honey, oatmeal and hot water. Made very strong and very hot it is a soothing and relaxing drink to take after a hard day in the hills.

GRUTH. A cream cheese made by milk being allowed to thicken in gentle heat. It is strained through a cloth and the curd is then mixed with a little salt and sour cream or fresh butter and shaped to form a cake.

57

# RECIPES

## STRUTHAN NA H-'ÉILL MICHEIL

Ceithir làn truinnseir beag do mhin eòrna, rud beag beag do shoda arain, agus fliuch le uisge. Dean an uair sin bannag air agus cuir air a' ghreideal e.

Dà ugh, dà làn spàineadh do 'shyrup', dà làn spàineadh do uachdar. An uair sin cuir a h-uile sian comhla agus cuir air a' bhannach e le badag itean. Dhà na trì do chòtaichean, fad na h-ùine 'ga chumail air bhialaibh an teine, agus 'ga chur mu chuairt, agus mu chuairt, gus am bi e bruich.

## THE RECIPE FOR THE MICHAELMAS CAKE

Four saucerfuls of barley, a pinch of baking soda, enough water to make a dough. Knead and shape into a bannock and bake on a girdle.

Coating for bannock: 2 eggs, 2 tablespoonfuls of syrup, 2 tablespoonfuls of cream. Beat together and then spread on one side of bannock with a feather, holding it in front of the fire to bake. Then turn and do the same on the other side. While putting on the coating keep turning the bannock wheel-wise and put on several coats.

(Mrs. Alasdair Currie, Ewan River, South Lochboisdale.)

In the olden times it was the custom to make the cake of all the cereals grown on the farm. A dent was made with the knuckles in the centre and a beaten egg was brushed on with a feather while it was held before the fire.

Now the 'strùthan' is generally made of a pound of flour, a teaspoonful of baking soda, salt, enough sour milk to make a dough, with carraway seeds, currants or raisins. It is baked on a girdle, turning as it bakes. When ready, the following mixture is spread first on one side and baked and then on the other: 3 tablespoonfuls of treacle, 1 tablespoonful of sugar, 2 tablespoonfuls of milk, and as much flour as will make a dough that will adhere to the bannock. It can be done on the girdle or in a not too hot oven.

## DULSE SOUP

To make dulse soup, cut the dulse in wee wee pieces so that it will melt away. Boil it in fresh milk with a little butter, pepper, and a wee thing flour, and a taste of sugar. You don't need to strain it. You eat your finger after it—so good!

(Peggy MacRae.)

# STORIES

★

Seonaidh Caimbeul was the story-teller of the Glen. His conversation was a source of unending entertainment, for he was a most gifted raconteur. He did not go in for telling the long, complex, fantastic tales which have survived, alone in Europe, in the Outer Hebrides and the West of Ireland; but he had a vast store of shorter stories and anecdotes with which he gave his friends great pleasure.

I give translations of a few of them below. The originals were taken down by my husband in November 1935. The Gaelic texts of 'The Shepherd's Wife', 'The Laird, the Priest and the Fool' and 'Thomas the Rhymer, Son of the Dead Woman' appeared in a little book called *Sia Sgialachdan* (Six Stories), published in a small edition of 250 copies in 1938.

★

## 'I AM NOT A SCHOLAR, AND I DON'T WANT TO BE'

### ANIMAL FABLE

The fox had a terrible hatred for the wolf. He didn't know how he could get the better of him because the wolf was the stronger. Now the wolf had schooling, but the fox had no schooling at all. One day when they were going together they saw a big horse, and when they were passing the horse the fox said to the wolf, 'Can you read the name that is on the horse's shoe?' 'I don't know,' said the wolf. 'Is there a name there?' 'Yes,' said the fox, 'but since you have education, see if you can read the name that is written on it.' They both went on as close as they could to the horse, and they were waiting, every time the horse lifted his foot, to see if the wolf, who was getting closer and closer to the horse, could read what name was on the horse's shoe. At last the horse lifted his foot and kicked him and knocked him a good piece away. 'Oh,' said the fox, '*I* am not a scholar and I don't want to be.' There was nothing for it but the fox had got the better of the wolf.

(Aarne Thompson, Type 47B)

59

# 'LET EVERY MAN TAKE HIS OWN SHAGS FROM THE CLIFF'

'Biodh a ch-uile duine toirt sgairbh a creig dha fhéin'

### ANECDOTE ILLUSTRATING PROVERB

Once upon a time there were people living in St. Kilda, and they used to go to the cliffs there to get shags. They kept up this practice until they left the island (in 1932). One time two men went to the cliff to get shags. One of them held the top end of the rope, and the other went down the cliff on the other end; and he collected a lot of shags, killed them and put their heads under his belt. The man above said, 'You've got enough.' 'Let every man take his own shags from the cliff,' replied the man below. Impatient as he was, he forgot his own situation.

'Well,' said the man above, 'if that's the way things are to be, let every man be at the top of his own rope,' and he flung the rope away and let the other down the cliff, himself and his shags.

★

# THE SHEPHERD'S WIFE

Once upon a time there was a man called the Cooper Bàn, or the fair-haired Cooper, who belonged to Uist, and was earning his living coopering on the mainland somewhere. At this time he was going home after spending a spell working away.

In those days one had to walk as far as the boat called the *Packet*, which was the only certain ferry that used to come to Uist then, and which sailed between Dunvegan and Lochmaddy. Well, one evening, as the Cooper was getting very tired he happened to come to a house, and he told himself that he was very lucky, since he had got so tired, and that if he got leave to stay the night he would stay. When he reached the house he went up to the door, which was shut. He knocked at the door and a woman came to open the door. 'Come in,' she said, 'it is God himself who sent you on the road to-night.' 'Well, I hope it is,' said he, and he went in. 'I am in great trouble to-night,' she said. 'Indeed? What is the matter? Is that a bier I see there?' said the Cooper. 'Yes. My husband died to-day and there is nobody here with me, so I am very pleased that you have come.' 'Well, here I am anyway,' he said. 'We are far from other houses here,' she said. 'Would you prefer to go to get men or to sit here alone with the body?' 'Well, though I were to go and get men I don't know where I would find them, so I would much rather stay,' he said. 'The dead man won't trouble me.' 'Oh, all right,' she said, 'I may as well go.' She went away without offering him drink or food.

He looked around and got some peat and he made a good fire. And he sat down by the fire and every now and then he was giving a glance over his shoulder at the man who was on the bier. One time he looked at him he saw he was moving. 'There you are,' said the man who was on the bier. 'Yes,' said the Cooper, 'but you stay where you are or else I will give you one with the little adze.' (He had his cooper's adze with him.) 'Oh, don't do that at all,' said the man who was on the bier. 'Don't be frightened. I am just as much alive as you are. Come over here and untie the cords around me, and I will get up and join you at the fire.' The Cooper went over and untied him, and the man who was on the bier got up and joined him. 'Well,' he said to the Cooper, 'I am certain that you don't need talk just now so much as food. You didn't get a bite since you came here.' 'No,' said the Cooper.

The man who had got off the bier began to prepare food. Then he and the Cooper had the food. And after they had eaten, the man from the bier said: 'Now I will tell you why I was on the bier. I am a shepherd and my wife and I are alone here; and she has started to make up to another man and that business has been going on some time now. And to-day,' he said, 'when I came home from the hill we had words about it—about the other man—and she hit me with a piece of wood,' he said, 'and I fainted and she thought I was dead, and before my senses returned to me she had me tied up on the bier where you saw me. I didn't let on that I wasn't dead, and I don't believe that she was very unhappy thinking I was. I know very well that the man she had been making up to is the man who will come with her to-night. His house is not the nearest to this house at all, so it will be a good while before they come. When they do come,' he said, 'I shall go back to the bier again as I was before and you spread the shroud over me again.'

So they talked there until the Shepherd said to the Cooper that they ought not to be very far away now. Then he went back to the bier and got the Cooper to put the shroud over him as it had been before, and he got a good stick and put it beside him on the bier, and he said: 'You will see that there will be a big, red-haired man who comes with her,' and they went on talking then until they heard them coming. The wife arrived with the very man the Shepherd had described along with her. When they came in she said: 'Were you finding the time long?' 'Oh no,' said the Cooper, 'I was warm enough at the fire. I was not at all afraid of the man who was with me.' The wife started then to make food and the red-haired man and the Cooper began to talk. And when the food was ready she invited the red-haired man to go to the other room and she didn't ask the Cooper to join them at all.

The Cooper remained by the fire. After they had been a while at their food the man who was on the bier began to move. 'Now,' he said to the Cooper, 'if I get the worst of it, you'll help me?' 'Yes,' said the Cooper, and he, the Shepherd, burst through the door; and when the red-haired man saw him he tried to get out, and the Shepherd gave him a blow with the stick and knocked him down. Then he started on him with the stick until he had put him out of the door. The Cooper didn't have to interfere. After that the Cooper remained with them until the day dawned. Then he got ready to go. 'Well, I am sure,' said the Shepherd, 'it would be much better for me to go along with you though I can't do it. But maybe you will hear yet what happens to us.'

And the Cooper parted with them and I never heard another word about what happened to them.

(Aarne Thompson, Type 1510. Cp. *The Shadow of the Glen* by Synge, obviously based on an Irish version of this story.)

61

# STORIES

## THE LAIRD, THE PRIEST AND THE FOOL

Once upon a time there was a big Laird who had a large estate, and on his estate lived several priests, for the estate was so large that it comprised several parishes: and the oldest of the priests was called Fr. John. Now what occurred to the Laird but that they were nothing but useless people, the priests, and that it would be better for him to get rid of every one of them. But he thought that if any of them were any use at all it would be Fr. John, because he was the oldest of them: and he decided to send for Fr. John and put three questions to him, and if he could solve these questions he would admit there was some use in them after all. So he sent for Fr. John, and Fr. John arrived at his house, and he asked him inside.

'I've sent for you,' said the Laird, 'to ask you three questions; and if you can solve them I'll know that you and the other priests are of some use; but unless you solve the questions I put to you,' he said, 'I shall give orders for you to be put to death, whatever happens to the others. So you come here on such and such a day and I'll put the questions to you.' That's how it was, and Fr. John returned home then.

Now Fr. John was a man who was very cheerful in his manner and always very happy; but after this day he was not nearly so cheerful as usual. And he had a brother living with him, who was somewhat simple compared with other people, and a lot of people used to call him the Fool. He noticed that his brother Fr. John was not as cheerful as usual. And when he met Fr. John outside he said, 'I don't believe you've been well for some time.' 'Oh, no,' said Fr. John, 'I'm all right, there's nothing wrong with me.' 'There must be something unusual the matter with you,' said the Fool. 'Oh, no,' said Fr. John. 'Oh indeed there is; tell me what is worrying you.' 'Oh,' said Fr. John, 'don't you know that there is many a thing on my mind that isn't suitable for telling to people like you?' 'True enough,' said the Fool, 'but I'm not trying to find out about such things at all: I'm only trying to find out what has made you so worried for the past few days. Many people besides myself would see that you have become unusually worried lately.' 'Oh,' said Fr. John, 'everyone says you are only a fool, and it wouldn't be any use telling you what is worrying me.'

'Well,' said the Fool, 'even if I am a fool, I'm your brother, and I think you should tell me anything worrying you that can be told before you tell it to anyone else.' 'Well,' said Fr. John, 'my good fellow, you're quite right, and seeing that's so, I'll tell you what's worrying me.' And he told him everything the Laird had said to him. 'And it looks as if I'll lose my life anyway. I fear very much,' said Fr. John, 'I won't be able to answer the questions he'll put to me.' 'Indeed,' said the Fool. 'Well, Fr. John, only a person who knows us both very well could tell us apart if I had on your clothes: and if that were to happen, my death would be a lesser loss than yours; the Laird won't know that it isn't you.' 'Oh, neither you nor anyone else will go in my place,' said Fr. John. 'If I'm to be killed I won't let anyone else be killed in my place.'

The Fool said no more, but went away to do some turn or other of work, and left Fr. John. However, he knew the day Fr. John had to be at the Laird's house, and when that day came he got up very early in the morning and went quietly to Fr. John's room and took Fr. John's clothes away secretly, and put them on, and went to the Laird's house. And when Fr. John got up, and found the clothes were gone, he understood very

62

well what had happened, and that the Fool had gone: and he thought that even if he went after him he could only spoil the business now, and it would be better to leave things as they were.

The Fool arrived very early at the Laird's house, and walked up and down outside it until the Laird got up. The Laird was told that Fr. John had arrived, and he sent a man out to bring him in. 'You've come early, Fr. John,' he said. 'Wasn't that what you wanted?' 'Very well,' said the Laird, 'I may as well put the questions to you before I take my breakfast, and get them off my mind.' 'I don't mind when you put them to me,' said the Fool.

'Well,' said the Laird, 'the first question I'm going to ask you is, where is the middle of the world?' The Fool had a stick in his hand, and he got up and looked around the room, and put the stick in the centre of the room. 'That's the middle of the world,' he said. 'How do you make out that the middle of the world's there?' asked the Laird. 'Oh,' said the Fool, 'I know that's the middle of the world.' 'I can't believe that unless you give me a better proof of it than that.' 'Well,' said the Fool, 'measure the distance from the western edge of the world to the stick, and from the eastern edge, and then from the south and then from the northern edge; and if the stick isn't at the middle of the world, I'll be willing to be contradicted about it.'

'Well,' said the Laird, 'I can't do that, and no more either can I say if you're right or wrong, but I'll have to accept it and say that that's one of the questions solved. The next question I'm going to ask you is, how much is my life worth?'

'I'll tell you that too. Your life is worth twenty-nine pieces of silver.' 'What do you mean, when I've more pocket money than that every day of my life?' 'Oh, it doesn't matter how much pocket money you have; that's what your life is worth.' 'Prove it, before I believe you.' 'I will. Our Saviour was sold for thirty pieces of silver and he was worth at least one more than you.' 'Well, yes,' said the Laird, 'that's right. That's two of the questions you've solved; but I've still the hardest one to put to you yet. Guess what I'm thinking now.' he said. 'Oh, that's the easiest one of all. You're thinking that it's Fr. John who's speaking to you, but it isn't—it's his brother the Fool.' 'Well,' said the Laird, 'I'm the fool, not you: you've solved all the questions. Tell Fr. John to come here when you go home, so I can have a longer talk with him than I had the last day we met.' That was how it happened to them.

(This story is well known in international folklore. Aarne Thompson, Type 922. See Stith Thompson, *The Folktale*, p. 161.)

★

# THOMAS THE RHYMER, SON OF THE DEAD WOMAN

As I heard about it, there was once upon a time a tailor. In those days, as I remember myself, tailors used to go round the houses making clothes. And this tailor came to the house of a certain man who had three sons and one daughter; and the tailor was making suits for the three sons. And the girl told him she needed some clothes too and that she would be very glad if he would make them before he departed, after he had made the sons' clothes. The tailor replied that he couldn't wait to make clothes for her. 'Well,' she said, 'I want you to make clothes for me very much, and I'll pay you for them separately from the others.' 'What will you pay me?' said the tailor. 'Anything you like, as long as you make the clothes.' 'Will you give me leave to spend a night with you?' said the tailor. 'Make you the clothes,' said she, 'and you'll get that.'

So when the tailor had finished making the sons' clothes, he made the girl's too, and he did not ask her for any payment; he had only been joking with the girl anyway. He went away not long afterwards, and a little time later the girl fell ill and died, and that was all there was to it. But one night when the tailor was coming home, he met the girl after her death. He recognized the girl very well and he spoke to her and she replied to him. 'Well,' she said, 'I never paid you what I promised for making the clothes.' 'Oh,' said the tailor, 'I never expected to get such payment, though I suggested it at the time.' 'Oh,' she said, 'what I promised must be done, or else I shall follow you everywhere.' So it was. 'Now,' she said, 'nine months after to-night you come to my gravestone, and you will find a baby boy on my gravestone, and he will be half above the earth and half under it, and,' she said, 'you will call him Thomas; and you will find a red book beside him on the gravestone, and you are not to give it to him until he is fourteen years old.' They parted after this conversation and the tailor went home.

At the end of nine months the tailor went to the graveyard, as he had promised, and he found the baby boy as she had told him, and the red book. And the boy was half above the earth and half beneath it. The tailor took him home and gave him to a wet nurse, and put away the book, which he later showed to many a learned man, such as might be likely to be able to read it, but none of the learned men to whom he ever showed it was able to make out a word in it. When the boy was fourteen years old, the tailor gave him the book, and there was not a word in it he could not read as well as if he had been studying it all the time.

Then his father started to teach him tailoring. He used to go around the houses with his father. One time, an old man in the village had died, and the tailor was asked to make a shroud for the body. And he and his son went to the house where the dead man was and when they went in they found that the people there were making no great lamentation over the departed; but when Thomas came in after his father, he began to cry. And he was crying and lamenting all the time they were making the shroud, and his father was ashamed that he was making such a lamentation for such a man whom the bereaved relations themselves were not lamenting very much. But that did not stop Thomas from lamenting. Well, when they had finished, they went home, Thomas and his father.

Not long afterwards, another old man in the neighbourhood died, and Thomas and his father were asked to make his shroud too. They were sent for, and when they reached the house they found everyone lamenting the departed with much sorrow; but when Thomas came in he began to rejoice and no one could keep up with his rejoicing and delight; and if his father was ashamed on the first night, he was utterly ashamed to-night, what with Thomas rejoicing in the middle of the household while everyone else was so sorrowful lamenting the dead man. But the tailor said to himself, 'There must be some explanation for his behaviour and before I go home to-night I'll know what this means.'

When they had finished, they went home and as they were going home, 'Alas, alas,

Thomas,' said his father, 'how you made me ashamed to-night. What did you mean, laughing all the time while everyone else was so unhappy lamenting the man who had gone from them? Tell me what you meant before we go any further.' 'Oh,' said Thomas, 'it doesn't take much to make the likes of me laugh. I was only thinking about all the things I had seen.' 'That wasn't it, tell me what you meant, and don't prevaricate.'

Thomas was putting it by, and didn't want to tell, but this would not suit his father, but he must tell. 'Well,' said Thomas, 'if you let me be until I'm sixteen years old I'll tell you then; and I'll be with you and with everyone I see in the world until the Day of Judgement, but if you make me tell you to-night you'll never see me again.' At this his father thought he was only prevaricating, and he insisted on being told. 'Well, I'll tell you,' said Thomas, 'and it won't surprise you when you hear what made me behave as I did. The first house we went to to make the shroud for the dead man, there wasn't much lamentation there for him, he wasn't worth it. When I looked around the house,' he said, 'there was nothing to be seen but a crowd of demons waiting to tear the dead man's soul apart between them; and no one inside saw that but myself. Do you wonder now why I was sorrowful and lamented when I saw that? And the house where we went to-night,' he said, 'the people there were very sad lamenting the man who had left them, and well they might lament him. Much thicker than the demons in the first house were the angels waiting for the dead's soul to-night, around the house; and was that not a great joy to me when I saw it? Didn't I have good cause to rejoice compared with the night when we were in the other house? And now,' said Thomas, 'I shall part with you, and you'll never see me again.' And his father never did see him again. Then it was that his father repented, and realized that Thomas had been telling him the truth from the beginning.

★

# THE FORTUNE OF LORD DUNEEL

Once upon a time there was a blacksmith who was married and had an only son. The smith gave the boy the best education he could. After he had come home from his schooling, his father told him that it would be a pity for a young man as well educated as himself to sit at home doing nothing. So his son decided that he would go away to earn his living. And he told his father of his decision. 'Well,' said his father, 'I think that's right, especially since you didn't learn my own craft. I haven't much I can give you,' he said, 'but I have one cow and I will sell her and you will get half the money she makes.' So the smith sold the cow and got nine pounds for her and he gave five pounds to the youth, and kept four pounds himself.

Then the son said good-bye to his parents and left the country. And he kept on travelling to find work, until he reached London, where he got a lodging in a hotel and then looked around for something to do. At the end of the third day he thought he had better pay his bill at the hotel and after he had paid his bill he had only ten shillings left. So he went then to a tailor's shop and he asked the tailor to make him a suit of the best cloth in the shop. The tailor said he would do it and that he could get it midday to-morrow if it were ready. Then the smith's son went and called at a joiner's shop and asked for a walking-stick to be made for him. The joiner made the walking-stick for him and he paid two shillings for it. He left the joiner's shop and then called at a watchmaker's shop and asked the watchmaker to put a knob of silver on top of the walking-stick and to write the name Lord Duneel on it; and he paid three shillings for it. After that he had only a crown, five shillings, left.

He was walking up the street thinking what he would do and he went into a shop and bought a crown's worth of writing paper and stamps. When the merchant was wrapping this up for him two ladies came into the shop. The parcel was wrapped for him, and he paid a crown for it. Then he went out and he left the walking-stick standing against the counter as if by mistake. After he had gone out the two ladies saw the stick there and they started to examine it and they saw the name that was on the top of the walking-stick. One of them went after him with the walking-stick and as he was only a short distance up the street she didn't call after him at all but touched him with her hand. He looked round and she asked him was it he who left the walking stick. He said it was and he gave her many thanks for the trouble she had taken coming after him with the stick. She said that it had been no trouble and they stood talking for a while and then she said to him that it surprised her very much to see a young man like him buying so much paper and stamps. 'Oh,' he said, 'there's many a place from where I am getting letters and to where I'm writing, too. They won't last as long as you think.' 'Well,' said she, 'it surprises me very much, a young man like you doing so much writing. Are you certain,' she said, 'that you are not in need of anything? Are you sure you are not short of money?' 'Oh, many thanks,' he said, 'I am not without money at all, and money won't be long in coming to me.' 'Oh,' said she, 'if you are short of money at all I would lend you a little.' 'Oh, many thanks,' he said, 'I am not short of money at all—well, not very short.' And she put her hand in her bag and took out her purse and gave him fifty pounds. And he was not willing at all to take it but he said that for fear of hurting her feelings he would accept it from her, and she said then that she would be very pleased if he would call at their house if he got the chance and he said he would, seeing how kind she had been to him. Then she gave him her address and he told her he would write to her or pay a call, and they said good-bye and she went home.

He went back to his hotel, and after a few days wrote to her and said he would call on such and such a day. He sent for a coachman—there were no cars in those times—he got the suit he had ordered from the tailor, and afterwards the coachman came to the hotel where he was staying. They went together with the horses to a smith and he asked the smith to make two silver horse-shoes and to write the name Lord Duneel on both of them, which the smith did. Then they went to call on the lady at her father's house. Now he had asked the smith to put only one nail in each of the silver horse-shoes and he asked the coachman to go slowly with the horses until they reached the gates in front of the house. And the gate was shut when they arrived; and he asked the coachman to make a turn with the coach, and where the horses turned they lost the two silver horse-shoes, so when the gate-keeper came to the gate he found two silver horse-shoes. When the lady heard what had happened she wrote him that she was terribly sorry that he had found the gate shut, but that if he came again they would put a carpet beneath his feet from the gate to the front door. He sent a letter to her saying that he accepted her apology and would call again, which he did the next day and the carpet was laid down before him. After the call was over he accepted their invitation to come to dinner on a certain day.

And he came with the coach on the day he promised. There were many friends and relations at dinner with them and everyone was very happy. But during the dinner the girl fell ill and had to go to her bed and nobody knew what was wrong with her and they had to send for a doctor. The doctor came and asked her what she felt. And she said she didn't know what was wrong with her. 'Unless I'm wrong,' said the doctor, 'you have fallen in love with someone.' Oh, she was not at all willing to agree with that, but eventually she admitted to the doctor that that was what had happened. The doctor asked her father if anything had happened to the girl recently. Her father then went to her room and asked her what was the matter with her. She was not willing to say. 'You're my only child,' said her father, 'and it can't be that you won't tell me what is troubling you. If you have fallen in love with anyone who was at the dinner we will try to put that right.' 'Yes,' she said, 'I have fallen in love with Lord Duneel.' 'Very good,' he said, 'unless he is married already.' 'Oh, he isn't,' she said, 'I know he isn't married at all.'

Then her father went down to the company who were at the dinner and they asked him about the girl. Her father said that she was better. Then they began to ask each other whether, if there were a man with whom the girl had fallen in love, though he was not in love with her himself, should he let her die of a broken heart rather than marry her. One man said that he would not care whether she died of a broken heart or not, and another man said that he would not let her die of a broken heart but would marry her, even if he were not in love with her. The same question was asked of Lord Duneel, and Lord Duneel replied that it would be a very hard thing to let anyone die if there was a way of preventing it, and that he himself would not let a girl die of a broken heart for him, but would marry her, even though he were not in love with her at all. 'Very good,' said the girl's father. 'My daughter has fallen in love with Lord Duneel.' 'Is that how it is?' said Lord Duneel. 'I am terribly sorry to have put so much trouble on the household. I had sooner have lost a large sum of money than have come near the house.' 'Oh, you mustn't say that,' said the girl's father. When the company dispersed, Lord Duneel had to stay behind; and before he went away they agreed that he and the girl should get married. But he said that before he got married he would like to send word to his father and mother and be sure that they approved. 'Well,' said the girl's father, 'that is perfectly all right. I will send my own butler to take word and tell your father and mother about it and he will bring back news how things are at your home. He'll go to-morrow.'

Lord Duneel saw the butler and told him to come to see him before he went away and he would give him directions about the road he was to take. The next day the butler left and stopped to see Lord Duneel at his hotel. 'You are on your way now?' said Lord Duneel. 'Yes,' said the butler.

Well, eventually the butler arrived at the blacksmith's house and when he reached the house he went in and the blacksmith and his wife were at their dinner at that moment and what they had for dinner was potatoes and herrings. And they asked the stranger to come in and join them at their dinner, which he did. And while they were at their dinner there were nine goats tied up in the smithy beside them and the skins that they took off the potatoes they were giving to the goats. The plate on which the potatoes were was a piece of wood. Anyway, they had their dinner, and the butler with them. The smithy was like every smithy I ever saw, so full of holes that the holes could not be counted.

Then the butler told them the errand on which he had come.

'Oh indeed,' said the smith, 'we had been told long ago that he would be hanged, and this is the way it is going to happen.' 'Oh, don't worry yet about this occasion,' said the butler. And the butler bade them good-bye and said he had to go back at once. And he returned to London and went to see Lord Duneel at his hotel.

'Here you are,' said Lord Duneel. 'Yes,' said the butler. 'Well now,' said Lord Duneel, 'tell me what you saw just as if you were telling it to your master.' 'I will do that,' said the butler. 'When I reached your father's house it happened that I arrived at dinner-time and your father and mother had just sat down to dinner,' he said. 'And as they had only just sat down, they invited me to have my dinner with them. And the table of your father and mother—the Lord Mayor hasn't got its like, and I never saw one like it myself. And while we were at dinner there were nine servants waiting at the table, the like of which is not to be seen at the table of the Lord Mayor of London, while he is at his dinner. And I think that the best clerk in London would take a long while before he counted how many men there are in your father's house. And I was very happy while I was with them and I am sorry I couldn't stay longer.' 'Very good,' said Lord Duneel. 'You keep on that tack and you will be very well off if I am alive.'

The butler then went home and told his master exactly what he had told Lord Duneel. His master was very pleased to hear this news, and it was arranged that Lord Duneel and the girl should be married without any further delay. So they were married and the girl's father was the Lord Mayor of London, and he was very rich.

Well, in due course of time they had a baby boy. When the boy had grown up so that he could take care of himself his mother told Lord Duneel that he should be going to see his grandfather and grandmother. And Lord Duneel said that was quite right but that it would be suitable to send word that they were going to come. 'Oh,' said Lady Duneel, 'quite true.'

They waited a fortnight, and at the end of the fortnight Lord Duneel wrote to his father first to make sure if it was the same man who had the nearby hotel as who had it before. If it were, he asked his father to go there and ask for a room for one month and that he and his wife were going to see him and that they would pay him—the hotel-keeper—very well. His father wrote back that it was not the same man keeping the hotel now but a stranger who had come a short time ago.

Anyway, the time came for them to go to see Lord Duneel's parents, and when they arrived there at a place near to his father's house, a man came to him and gave him a letter, and when he had read the letter he began to walk backwards and forwards without speaking a word. She kept asking him what was wrong but he didn't say anything. 'It is very strange,' she said, 'if you won't tell me what's wrong with you. If anything has gone wrong with your father or mother, or with the estate, if it can be put right we will put it right.' 'Well,' he said, 'when I went away from here and didn't seem like coming back, they took advantage of my father and mother being old and turned them out of the house where they were. Now they are in a poor little house that we cannot stay at.' 'Well,' she said, 'my uncle is a colonel in the army and if this can be put right without trouble his regiment is not far away.' 'Oh,' he said, 'without going to that trouble we will try to do as well as we can.' 'All right,' she said. And then they went to the hotel together. And he got a chance to speak to the hotel-keeper and told him how things were, and said that if he could go for a month to the hotel and let him use the hotel, he would be well paid for it. And he and the hotel-keeper came to an agreement and the hotel-keeper said that he would go somewhere else for a month and that Lord Duneel could go there as if the house belonged to him. And he did that and then he went to get his father and mother and dress them up to come to the hotel along with himself and his wife, and they were there for a month. At the end of the month Lord Duneel and his wife returned to London. He paid the hotel-keeper very well and his father and mother returned to the smithy. And that is all I heard about them.

1  North Glendale, Loch Boisdale and Beinn Choinnich from the west

2  South Lochboisdale from the east

3*a*    Peigi and Màiri MacRae's house in North Glendale

3*b*    Mrs Angus Campbell (Bean Aonghuis Ruaidh) bringing seaweed
to spread on the fields

4a  John Morrison using the *cas-chrom*

4b  The Alasdair Currie family planting potatoes with *pleadhag* and *ràcan*

5*a*  Four agricultural implements: *pleadhag* (dibble), *treisgeir* (peat cutter),
*cas-chrom* (foot plough), *ràcan* (rake)

5*b*  Cutting peat in North Glendale: left to right, working, Seonaidh Campbell (the
bard), Donald Campbell, Aonghus Ruadh Campbell, Angus John Campbell and
Donald John Campbell. Seated: James Campbell and Donald MacRae

6a  Ronald and Mór Morrison

6b  John and Donald Currie making nets for their father's lobster creels

7a  Peigi and Màiri MacRae cutting the oats

7b  Iain Campbell (Iain Clachair) plaiting heather into rope

8   Mrs Angus Campbell (Bean Aonghuis Ruaidh) raking straw on her oat field

9   Loch Boisdale. The snow marks the drains that lie between the lazy-beds and through the oat field

10   The MacRaes' house. Màiri going to the well

11  South Boisdale. Beinn Mhór to the left

12   Digging lug worms for flounder bait on the strand at South
Glendale by the Sound of Eriskay. Barra is in the distance

13   Mrs Christina MacDonald (Ciorstaidh Ruadh)

14 The hills of South Uist from Bàgh Hartabhagh

15 Seonaidh and Peigi Campbell

16 Donald MacRae, Angus John Campbell, Màiri MacRae and James Campbell, resting while herding cattle at Rudha na h-Òrdaig

# THE SONGS

★

THE songs in this book are those that were sung in Glendale, South
Uist, at dances and weddings, at daily tasks or at the fireside. It was
the custom when friends gathered in the kitchen in the evening to ask
for songs, and almost without exception each guest would contribute
one. The songs would be mainly about love, sailing, the emigrant's longing for
home such as 'O mo Dhùthaich', or happenings in the islands. Many were the
compositions of local men. Four of the neighbours were bards: Iain Campbell,
mason, known as *Iain Clachair*, his brother Seonaidh, some of whose songs were
published by J. L. Campbell and John MacInnes in 1935, and Angus John and
Roderick, the sons of Iain. The Campbell men were gifted in composing and
they had amazing memories. They were not only familiar with the great
Gaelic poetry of the eighteenth century but could recite and sing much of it.
Iain MacCodrum, Alexander MacDonald, Duncan Ban MacIntyre were often
heard, and nothing gave these men more intense pleasure than to speak the
lines aloud. They loved their language and honoured the masters of it.

The number of songs that are extant in the Hebrides is extraordinary. For
hundreds of years poetry and story-telling have been the great popular means
of artistic expression of the Gaelic race, and their music has served as a vehicle
for the transmission of their poetry, so that Gaelic songs have existed in
thousands. The hundred-odd songs I have printed here are only a half of what
I have transcribed myself, and less than a tenth of the number that my
husband and I and our friends have recorded; and that can only be a small

part of what might have been recorded, had a Scottish Folklore Commission been in the field during the past twenty-five years.

Many of the airs to which these songs are sung are of great beauty, and some have every appearance of being very old.

The tunes have been taken down with great care after many hearings. They are of sufficient merit in themselves to be heard without additional harmony. That they would make part songs is obvious, but that is not the purpose of this book. The traditional songs of the Hebrides are never accompanied nor sung in parts. It may be that it is only on the piano that the reader can hear the tunes, but it would be nearer the truth of the air if it were sung or played on a wind instrument or violin.

Versions of many of these songs will be known throughout the Hebrides, and a reader may know of more verses, or his mother may have sung a finer air. If so, I beg him to write it down, record it, or better still to teach it to a child.

The types of song in existence include the ballad, sometimes Ossianic, dealing with wars between the Gaels and the Norsemen which took place 900 to 1,000 years ago; the *Òran Mór* or 'Great Song', usually an elegy on an important person, description of an important event, or satire in this style; songs about soldiering, sailing and hunting, love songs, laments, lullabies, fairy songs, and songs for dancing known as *Puirt-a-bial* which are sometimes the origin of pipe tunes; labour songs for work that requires a rhythm such as milking, churning, rowing, spinning, and waulking or fulling cloth. The waulking songs, known as *Òrain luadhaidh*, are of great interest for they are of a type unknown elsewhere in Western Europe. Once they were sung throughout the Highlands and the Hebrides but today they are rarely heard and Glendale is one of the few places where the genuine waulking is still held. When tweed or blanket cloth is taken from the loom it must be shrunk before it can be used and the waulking is the method of shrinking it. The process is as follows:

The ends of a length of newly woven cloth are sewn together to make it a circle, and the cloth is then placed on a long trestle table and soaked with hot urine. An even number of women sit at the table, say twelve with six a side, and the cloth is passed around sunwise, to the left, with a kneading motion. They reach to the right and clutch the cloth, draw in, pass to the left, push out and free the hands to grasp again to the right. One, two, three, four, slowly the rhythm emerges. A woman will chant—

*Far* ail ill *lò, hò* ro *hù* a

and the others will join in with:

> *Hao* ri *ò* 's na *ho* hì *iù* a
> *Far* ail ill *lò, hò* ro *hù* a

and the first woman sings alone:

> 'S *trom* mo *cheum,* cha *n-eil* mi *sunn*dach[1]

The soloist continues to sing the lines which tell the tale, and (in the case of this and some similar songs) the first line of the chorus, the other women singing the other two. The choruses of waulking songs are usually meaningless, consisting of syllables that carry the air; but they have a mnemonic significance, and must always be sung correctly. The chorus is called the *fonn* or 'ground' and is the means by which the songs are popularly identified, as different versions of the same waulking song may begin with different lines. In order to make the waulking songs last long enough to do the work, each verse or *ceathramh* (usually only a half-line, single line, or couplet) is sung twice, sometimes with a different phrase of the chorus after it the second time. When the verse has two lines or two half-lines, sometimes the second line of one verse is repeated as the first line of the following verse, sometimes the whole two-line verse is itself repeated. To sing a complete waulking song alone without anyone to take up the chorus imposes a very considerable strain on any reciter.

Possibly as many as 200 waulking songs are still extant in South Uist and Barra. This collection includes 32 of them, some of which I have only recovered as fragments in Glendale, but which survive or may survive more fully elsewhere. Waulking songs can be divided into various types according to the structure of their verses and choruses. The following are represented here:

1. Half-line verse and divided chorus: Nos. 77, 97, 98, 99, 104.
2. Single-line verse and divided chorus: Nos. 80, 81.
3. Single-line verse and three-line chorus, the first line of the chorus being usually sung by the soloist: Nos. 76, 79, 82, 83, 84, 85, 88, 89, 92, 93, 102, 103.
4. Two-line verses, the first line of each verse being the last line of the preceding verse, with three-line chorus: No. 105.
5. Same structure as (4) except that chorus has four lines instead of three: No. 100.
6. Two-line couplets and three-line choruses: Nos. 78, 86, 87, 90, 91, 94, 96, 101, 106, 107.
7. Two-line couplets and two-line chorus: No. 95.

[1] See page 219.

The words of these songs sometimes resemble ballads in the Lowland Scots sense and can be as much as 400 years old. With the longest it often happens that they are a combination of two or more songs, but one should remember that these songs must at times be lengthened in order to fulfil their purpose, and that is the time needed to shrink the cloth, and that verses and parts of other songs have been added and so included with repetition over the years. The different parts are always distinguished by the chorus that occurs between them being sung three times.

I give a list of the collections of Gaelic folk tunes which I have consulted while preparing this book. The first of these was made between 1760 and 1780 by Joseph and Patrick MacDonald, and published in 1784.[1] It is interesting to note that the collectors were even then under the impression that Gaelic folksinging was soon going to die out. The collection is an attempt to present the airs authentically, but its value is vitiated by the fact that the editor admittedly interfered with the bar-signatures and rewrote the tunes which were actually in irregular time, 'in equal bars'.

In the preface the editor, Patrick MacDonald, quotes a letter from his brother Joseph proposing to dedicate the work to Sir James MacDonald: 'If Sir James MacDonald is not prejudiced and rendered cold to the Highlands, by his corrupt English education, I hope he will duly prize it.'

The custom of Highland chiefs and gentry sending their sons to be educated in England arose after the Union of Scotland with England in 1707 and was greatly intensified after the failure of the Jacobite rising with Prince Charles Edward Stuart in 1745. It was rightly reprobated by Dr. Johnson, who asserted, when travelling in the Highlands in 1775, that no Highland chief should be educated south of Aberdeen. However, Patrick MacDonald prints an imposing list of subscribers from amongst the Highland gentry.

Like many other Gaelic publications that appeared between 1760 and 1820, Patrick MacDonald's book owes its publication to the interest aroused in things Gaelic by the controversy that followed the publication of MacPherson's *Ossian*.

After 1820 interest in *Ossian* and Gaelic literature and music died down. The second generation of Highland lairds to be educated in England became entirely anglicized. The utilitarian ideas associated with the industrial revolution and, in some parts of the Highlands, the evangelical revival of the 1820s and 1830s were alike hostile to Gaelic folklore. The compulsory education introduced by the Education Act of 1872 ignored Gaelic completely—indeed, its use was usually forbidden in the classroom on the pretext it would prevent the children's learning English. It is not surprising that Gaelic literature and

[1] See John Glen, *Early Scottish Melodies*, p. xiv, also 'Joseph MacDonald' by Miss Mairi MacDonald, *Scots Magazine*, October 1953.

music declined during the nineteenth century. The peasantry themselves, the preservers of the tradition, were harried by the evictions and impoverished by the potato famine.

Like MacPherson, whose *Ossian* is now well known not to represent the authentic texts of Gaelic Fingalian ballads, but who rearranged, added to, and embroidered them, some of the collectors of Gaelic folksong who followed the MacDonalds were also led to try to improve on the originals. Such collections have tried to make Gaelic music conform to the fashionable style— first Italian, later German, last of all the pseudo-Celtic, although modal folk-songs do not lend themselves to facile harmonization, so that sometimes the results have been unfortunate. Meanwhile, the serious study and collection of Gaelic folksongs languished under the political and social disapproval of Gaelic that existed in the nineteenth and early twentieth centuries, though in 1862 Donald Campbell made a praiseworthy effort to reproduce authentic Gaelic tunes in his *Language, Poetry and Music of the Highland Clans*. It was not until 1894, when An Comunn Gàidhealach was founded at Oban, and started annual Gaelic music festivals under the influence of the Welsh Eisteddfodau, that a revival of interest in Gaelic folksong really began, and even then the tunes were sometimes spoilt by faulty transcription or unsuitable accompaniments[1]; but the work of Henry Whyte and Malcolm MacFarlane to save songs that might have been lost deserves much praise. Most of the tunes then recovered were taken down from Argyllshire singers.

The first person to take a scientific interest in Gaelic folksong, however, was Miss Amy Murray, an American who visited Eriskay in 1905 and who is said to have taken down about 100 airs there with the help of the late Fr. Allan McDonald, whose early death in the October of that year brought to a premature close what might have become a most fruitful collaboration. Of these 100 airs Miss Murray printed 7 in the second volume of the *Celtic Review* (1906), and 26, including the original 7, in her book *Father Allan's Island*, in 1920. Fourteen more have been discovered in one of Fr. Allan McDonald's notebooks, but the others most unfortunately appear to be lost beyond hope of recovery.

Next came Miss Frances Tolmie's justly famous collection, mostly made on the Isle of Skye, printed in the *Journal of the Folksong Society* in 1911—a collection from which arrangers have not hesitated to borrow. Mrs. Kennedy Fraser, whose first visit to the Outer Isles took place in the same year as that of Amy Murray, published three volumes of *Songs of the Hebrides*, and a fourth, *From*

---

[1] See Amy Murray, *Father Allan's Island*, pp. 91-93, for a penetrating study of the weaknesses of some of these transcriptions and their departure from the authentic style of Gaelic folk-singing.

*the Hebrides*, which are internationally famous, but for serious students of folk music the airs printed in her introductions are of far more value than her arranged songs. She alone of the early collectors used recording apparatus, a primitive dictaphone recording on wax cylinders, but with the passage of years these are now mouldy and nearly inaudible. Fortunately it had been possible for my husband and myself to record good versions of a great many of the same songs, as well as scores of others, first on Ediphone (1937), then with a disc machine (1938–1947) and since 1949 with a magnetic wire recorder and more recently, on tape.

In 1931 Miss Lucy Broadwood published 20 airs, collecting in Arisaig in 1906, in the *Journal of the Folksong Society*, and in 1943 I published 12 of the songs that are printed in this book in the same journal, now appearing as the *Journal of the English Folk Dance and Song Society* and referred to as the *J.E.F.D.S.S.* throughout this book. In 1952 Professor Otto Andersson of Åbo, Finland, published a valuable study of some songs from the Isle of Lewis in *The Budkavlen*, including analyses of the modes and chorus structures. And at long last Scottish academic authorities overcame their prejudices and gave belated recognition to the study of Gaelic and Scots folksong when Mr. Francis Collinson was given a research fellowship for this purpose in 1951. Although, unfortunately, successive censuses reveal that Gaelic is dying out in Scotland and in Canada, it is to be hoped that what survives of this tradition can still be preserved through the increasing interest in folkmusic that is taking place generally in many countries of the world.

Folktunes cannot be noted down correctly unless one understands the language in which they are sung. The short and long vowels, the stressed syllables and the contractions form the length of the notes of the tune. I never heard my friends in Glendale hum or sing an old tune without words. To them the words and the air were inseparable. I once mentioned that I thought a neighbour had the air of a song, and the reply was, 'How could she have the air and not the words?'

My first lessons in Gaelic were spent in learning to read and write. My reading was the Bible, and, though it is a useful way, when read aloud, to acquire pronunciation, and is the modern language in its most classical and expressive form, it is no more the language of everyday speech than our English Bible. To speak Gaelic one must be with the people whose tongue it is, and to use the language one must acquire a knowledge of the local dialect. Contrary to appearances and sound, grammar and pronunciation follow strict rules which are reasonable. But local dialects and local words are not to be found in school grammars and dictionaries. With the help of my friends, I have tried to make the Gaelic in this book true to the speech of the reciters, without departing too far from the conventional spelling. In naming other sources where versions of the words or tunes of songs in this book have been printed, I have been greatly assisted by a card index of first lines compiled by Mr. Donald Sinclair.

The songs are grouped according to their subjects. Different versions of some of the tunes have been given to show the variations occurring in a small district. A comment some people make on first hearing Gaelic songs, is that all the tunes sound alike. This is because such people cannot accustom their ears to any other than the major and minor scales. That is why some collectors in the past have changed notes to sound more 'agreeable', or brought the final note of a tune to where they felt it should be. To this day accompaniments are being written with notes which are not in the scale of the tune. We must forget the scales to which we are accustomed, and listen anew. There are many opinions on the subject of modes in folk music: I am indebted to Mr. A. Martin Freeman, who has named the modes of the songs in this book according to Mr. A. H. Fox Strangways' system. The key to the scales is given below: the five tones (in large notes) with the variable (small notes) constitute the Pentatonic scales.

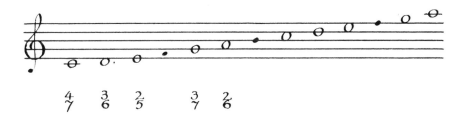

F is most often the variable note, thus:

Commencing on C ♮4:7 gives the Ionian, ♯4:7, Lydian (rare).

D ♯3:6 gives Mixolydian, ♮3:6, Dorian.

E ♯2:5 gives Aeolian, ♮2:5, Phrygian (rare).

G ♮3:♯7 gives Ionian, ♮3:♮7, Mixolydian.

A ♮2:6 gives Aeolian, ♮2:♯6, Dorian.

It is difficult to assign a definite mode to tunes in the hexatonic scale.

\* \* \*

Any small discrepancy that may occur as between the printed words and those written under the music, is due to the fact that the tunes had to be drawn before the whole of the text had been revised in proof, and it was not thought worth while redrawing a whole tune to correct one or two accents.

The Gaelic reader may also notice that a certain number of lines have extra unstressed syllables which might be omitted in a standard text: this is because the singers sang them so, and I have tried to reproduce what they actually sang, not what, perhaps, they should have said.

In the matter of accents, I have marked with accents all vowels which are pronounced long, except in the case of certain words like *till, cum,* where the vowels are long by position and well known to be so. I must apologize for any inconsistencies in the use of accents, at the same time remarking that no satisfactory standard method for their use in writing Scottish Gaelic has yet been worked out, let alone accepted.

# MOLADH UIBHIST—IN PRAISE OF UIST

## 1  O MO DHÙTHAICH

Ó mo dhùth-aich, 's tu th'air m'air-e, Uibh-ist chùmhr-aidh ùr nan gall-an,
Iar a faight-e na daoin' uaisl-e, Iar bu dual do Mhac ìc Àil-ein.
Tìr a' mhur-ain, tìr an eòrn-a, Tìr 's am pailt a h-uil-e seòrs-a,
Iar am bi na gill-ean òg-a Gabh-ail òr-an 's g' òl an leann-a,

# IN PRAISE OF UIST

1. Ó mo dhùthaich, 's tu th'air m'aire,
   Uibhist chùmhraidh ùr nan gallan,
   Far a faighte na daoin' uaisle,
   Far 'm bu dual do Mhac 'ic Ailein.

2. Tìr a' mhurain, tìr an eòrna,
   Tìr 's am pailt a h-uile seòrsa,
   Far am bi na gillean òga
   Gabhail òran 's 'g òl an leanna.

3. Thig iad ugainn, carach, seòlta,
   Gus ar mealladh far ar n-eòlais;
   Molaidh iad dhuinn Manitòba,
   Dùthaich fhuar gun ghual, gun mhòine.

4. Cha ruig mi leas a bhith 'ga innse,
   Nuair a ruigear, 's ann a chìtear,
   Samhradh goirid, foghar sìtheil,
   Geamhradh fada na droch-shìde.

5. Nam biodh agam fhìn do stòras,
   Dà dheis aodaich, paidhir bhrògan,
   Agus m'fharadh bhith 'nam phòca,
   'S ann air Uibhist dheanainn seòladh.


*Translation*

1. O my country, I think of thee, fragrant, fresh Uist of the handsome youths, where nobles might be seen, where Clan Ranald had his heritage.

2. Land of bent grass, land of barley, land where everything is plentiful, where young men sing songs and drink ale.

3. They come to us, deceitful and cunning, in order to entice us from our homes; they praise Manitoba to us, a cold country without coal or peat.

4. I need not trouble to tell you it; when one arrives there one can see—a short summer, a peaceful autumn, and long winter of bad weather.

5. If I had as much as two suits of clothes, a pair of shoes and my fare in my pocket, I would sail for Uist.

An emigrant song sung at Boisdale House by Miss Peigi and Miss Màiri MacRae and their cousin Angus MacCuish. The words were composed by Allan MacPhee, who died at Loch Carnan, South Uist. The tune is traditional. There is a similarity between it and one entitled 'Crònan Muileach' in Campbell's *Albyn's Anthology*, Vol. II, p. 60, contributed by the Countess of Compton.

Mode: Dorian 2:6.

## 2 UIBHIST NAM BEANN ÀRDA

O gur toil liom, e gur toil liom, 'S toil liom Uibh-ist nam beann àrd-a;
Tìr nan laoch bha làid-ir fur-ail Chois-inn urr-am do Chlann Ràghnaill.
Fhir a théid a null a dh'Uibh-ist 'Nad fhear tur-uis air a' bhàt-a,
Gheibh thu eachdr-aidh ann ad uidh-e, 'S gheibh thu spionn-adh ann ad shlàint-e.

*Fonn:*   O gur toil liom, é gur toil liom,
        'S toil liom Uibhist nam beann àrda;
      Tìr nan laoch bha làidir furail
        Choisinn urram do Chlann Ràghnaill.

1. Fhir a théid a null a dh'Uibhist
   'Nad fhear turuis air a' bhàta,
Gheibh thu eachdraidh ann ad uidhe,
   'S gheibh thu spionnadh ann ad shlàinte.

2. Gheibh thu daoin' ann bàidheil, fialaidh,
   'S chì thu fiamh a tha fo bhlàth orr';
Eadar Poll a' Charr' is Ìochdar,
   Cha laigh ghrian air àit as àille.

3. Do Loch Baghasdail anns an *Staffa*,
   Baile snasail, cala sàbhailt,
'S có chaidh riamh ann nach robh sona,
   'S a' sìor-mholadh a luchd àitich?

4. Chì thu Éirisgeidh nan lusan
   Chaidh a chur ann le Prionns' Teàrlach;
'S tobhta Flòraidh 'n Àirigh Mhuilinn,
   Far an d'rugadh i 'na pàisde.

5. Caisteal Ormacleit gun mhullach,
   'S tric a chluinnte guth a' bhàird ann
Togail dàn air euchd nan curaidh,
   Choisinn urram do Chlann Ràghnaill.

6. Cailean Uibhist tha iad bòidheach,
   Mar a' ghrian air òr a' deàrrsadh;
'S ged nach tuigeadh tu 'A Leòbhra'
   Bheir iad dòigheil dhut a' Ghàidhlig.

# IN PRAISE OF UIST

7. Baile maiseach tha 'n Loch Sgiobort
   Nuair bha mise greis a' tàmh ann,
   Thog mi fhìn 's mo phàisdean lurach
   Càrnan Iubailidh do'n Bhàn-righ'nn.

8. Ach ma théid thu tuath dha'n Ìochdar
   Fada sìos gu bial na tràghad,
   Nuair a bhios tu dol a null oirr'
   Fiach nach dean na tuinn do bhàthadh.

## Translation

*Chorus :*  O, I love, o, I love, o, I love Uist of the high hills:
         The land of the heroes who were strong and hospitable,
         Who won honour for Clan Ranald.

1. You who travel over to Uist by boat will find history on your route and will strengthen your health.

2. You will find men there, kindly, generous; you will see beauty there in bloom. Between Iochdar and Pollachar the sun does not shine on a more beautiful place.

3. You will go to Lochboisdale on the 'Staffa', a fair village and a safe haven. Who ever went there but was happy and constantly praising its inhabitants?

4. You will see Eriskay of the flowers, planted there by Prince Charles.[1] And the ruin at Àirigh Mhuilinn where Flora MacDonald was born.

5. Though Ormacleit Castle is roofless,[2] often the bard's voice was heard there, raising a lay to the valour of the champions who won honour for Clan Ranald.

6. The girls of Uist are pretty, like the glitter of sun on gold: though you will not understand 'a leòbhra',[3] they will address you in well-expressed Gaelic.

7. Loch Skiport is a pretty township where I myself once lived for a while; where I and my bonny children raised a Jubilee Cairn to Queen Victoria.

8. But if you go northwards to Iochdar, far north to the edge of the shore, take care when crossing (the ford) that the tide does not drown you.

This song in praise of South Uist was sung by Miss Peigi and Miss Màiri MacRae. The words were composed by Mr. A. MacIvor, schoolmaster at Loch Skiport, who afterwards emigrated to Canada and entered the ministry. The words were printed in *MacTalla*, Vol. VII, p. 224, under the name 'Aeneas'. The tune is traditional. Note the similarity to 'O No, John, No'.

Mode: Hexatonic, no 3rd (3:6).

[1] *Convolvulus maritimus* said to have been planted by Prince Charles Edward Stuart.
[2] Burnt down on the eve of the battle of Sheriffmuir, 1715.
[3] An expression meaning 'by the Book' (the Missal or possibly the Bible), used in Uist and Barra.

# ÒRAIN SEÒLAIDH—SAILING SONGS

## 3 THA GHAOTH AN IAR A' GOBACHADH

Air faill ill ó ro faill ill ó, Air faill ill ó ro éil-e, Air faill ill ù bhill ag-us ó, Na thog i ó ro éil-e.

Tha ghaoth an iar a' gob-ach-adh, 'S cha b'e mo thog-airt fhéin i; —

B'ait-e liom a' ghaoth an ear, Is las-an oirr' ag éir-igh.

*Fonn:* Air faill ill ó ro faill ill ó,
Air faill ill ó ro éile,
Air faill ill ù bhill agus ó,
Na thog i ó ro éile.

1. Tha ghaoth an iar a' gobachadh,
   'S cha b'e mo thogairt fhéin i;
   B'aite liom a' ghaoth an ear
   Is lasan oirr' ag éirigh.
   Air faill ill, *etc.*

   B'aite liom a' ghaoth an ear
   Is lasan oirr' ag éirigh,
5. Fiach an dig am bàta
   A b'àbhaist a bhith treubhach.
   Air faill ill, *etc.*

Fiach an dig, *etc.*
Uachdaran na tìr' oirre
   A Rìgh! ma dh'éireas beud dha!

Uachdaran na dùthchadh oirr',
10.  'S gu bheil mo dhùrachd fhéin leis.

A Rìgh! gur math liom fallain e,
   'S a chaisteal a bhith 'n Sléibhte.

Far am bi na fìdhlichean,
   'S na pìobanan 'gan gleusadh.

82

15. Bidh òl, bidh ceòl, bidh cosgais ann,
    Bidh tostaichean 'gan éibheach.

    Far am bi na balaich òga
    As bòidhche rachadh fo'n éideadh.

    As deas a théid air ùrlar
20.    An am a' chiùil a ghleusadh.

    Is iomadh nighean fhuranach,
    Glé luranach m'a céile,

    Dh'éireadh leat-sa, Dhòmhnaill,
    Nan rachadh tòir air Seumas.

25.    Dh'éireadh Mac 'ic Alasdair,
    'S Gleann Garadh linn le chéile.

    Dh'fhàgainn-sa mo dhùthaich
    Air chùmhnant a bhith réidh riut.

    Rachainn fhìn a Lunnainn leat,
30.    Nam biodh mo thurus réidh riut.

*Translation*

The west wind is rising and it is not to my liking; I would prefer the east wind rising in gusts, in order that the boat that was wont to be valiant may come with the laird of the land aboard her. O God, if harm should befall him! The laird of the land aboard—my good wishes are with him. O God, may he be in health! and his castle be in Sleat, where fiddles and pipes are tuning. There will be drinking, there will be music, there will be extravagance, toasts will be called; it is there are the most handsome youths that wear their (Highland) garb, the neatest who go on the dancing floor when music is struck up. There is many a courteous maiden very proud of her partner, who would rise with you, Donald, if James were pursued; MacDonell and Glengarry would rise with us together. I would leave my country on condition of being reconciled to you. I would go to London with you if my journey were agreeable to you.

From Mrs. John Currie, with the eighth verse from Miss Annie MacDonald. Versions of the words are printed in *MacTalla*, Vol. IX, p. 392, and *An t-Òranaiche*, p. 235, which are identical; and in *An Gàidheal*, Vol. VI, p. 24, where there is also a version of the tune. The circumstances of the song seem to be unknown; it may be of Jacobite significance. 'James' may be King James VIII.

Mode: Hexatonic, no 2nd.

## 4 ÒRAN *LOCH SLOY*

1. 'Sa mhaduinn mhoich Di h-Aoine 'n am sgaoil an là 's na neòil,
   A' fàgail cidhe Ghrianaig gu cianail mar bu chòir;
   A' falbh air bhòidse bliadhna, dol a' riasladh a' chuain mhóir,
   Cur cùl ri tìr nan àrdbheann far an d'fhuair mi m'àrach òg.

2. 'S i mhaduinn nach do riaraich mi, oir b'iargalt bha na neòil;
   Dol seachad sìos air Pladaidh thug am *Phantom* bhuainn an ròp,
   Is *sheat* sinn na siùil bhàna oirr' 's gum b'àrd bha iad 'sna neòil,
   'S mar chamraig gearradh sàile gu robh am bàta sin *Loch Sloy*.

3. 'S gur tric mo chadal luaineach nuair a bhios an cuan 'na ghàir',
   'S i treabhadh nan tonn uaibhreach is muir cuairteachadh fo sàil;
   Gur tric a thig mo smuaintean-sa gu tìr mo luaidh 's mo ghràidh,
   Far an robh mi òg a' buachailleachd mun dug mi ruaig gu sàil.

4. Ach tha 'n cuan mór cur eadarainn, 's neo-fhreagarrach mar thà;
   Ach slàinte 'ga mo chreidsinn-sa gu bheil sinn deas gu sàil,
   Gu bheil long mhór nan crannaibh 's i fo chanabhas gun dàil,
   'Ga stiùireadh bho Astràilia gu fearann tìr mo ghràidh.

# SAILING SONGS

*Translation*

1. In the early morning on a Friday at daybreak when clouds were dispersing, leaving Greenock quay mournfully as was fit; departing on a year's voyage to cleave the high seas, leaving behind the land of high hills where I was reared when young.

2. The morning did not please me, for the clouds were forbidding. Going south past Pladda the *Phantom* took the rope from us. We set the white sails so that they were high in the clouds. And the ship, the *Loch Sloy*, was cutting the water like cloth.

3. My sleep is often restless when the ocean roars, while the ship ploughs the proud waves and the sea eddies round the stern. Often my thoughts return to the land of my love and desire, where when I was young I tended the cattle before I took to the sea.

4. But the ocean is between us and inconvenient it is. Yet a toast to my belief that we are ready to go to sea, that the great masted ship is ready under canvas to steer home from Australia to the land of my love.

From Angus John Campbell, South Lochboisdale. The *Loch Sloy* belonged to the Loch Line, and was wrecked on Kangaroo Island in the Australian Bight. The *Phantom* in the second verse was without doubt the Clyde Shipping's Company's tug the *Flying Phantom*. The late Commodore Sir David Bone told me that he knew her in his younger days. I can find no trace of this song in books. As recovered it is probably corrupt, for good bards do not rhyme words with themselves, as occurs in the second and third verses. The metaphor in the last line of the second verse is oddly expressed, and also suggests corruption; another song about a sailing ship has a line "S i gearradh an fhairge mar siosar air caimrig' 'she cleaving the ocean as a scissor cuts cambrick,' which seems to be the idea intended here.

Mode: Mixolydian.

## 5 FAIL Ò RO MAR DH'FHÀG SINN

Fail ò ro mar dh'fhàg sinn Cur cùl ri ar càird-ean, Tha gill-ean gasd-a na dùthch-adh Cur shiùil ri cruinn àrd-a. Fail ò ro mar dh'fhàg sinn.

*Fonn:* Fail ò ro mar dh'fhàg sinn,
Cur cùl ri ar càirdean,
Tha gillean gasda na dùthchadh
Cur shiùil ri cruinn àrda.
Fail ò ro mar dh'fhàg sinn.

1. Nuair dh'fhàg sinn a mach Cluaidh,
   Gum bu luath i air sàile;
   Gun dug iad fìor-dhroch-chliù dhith
   An *criù* a rinn a fàgail.
     Fail ò ro mar dh'fhàg sinn, *etc.*

2. Nuair sheòl sinn mach a Grianaig,
   Gur cianail a bhà sinn,
   A' cuimhneachadh na h-ighneagan
   A dheanadh fiamh a'ghàire.
     Fail ò ro mar dh'fhàg sinn, *etc.*

3. Di-Ciadain rinn sinn seòladh,
   'S bu bhòidheach a bhà i:
   Trì fichead seòl 's a trì ris
   An rìbhinn a b'àille.
     Fail ò ro mar dh'fhàg sinn, *etc.*

4. Nuair dh'fhàg i fearann Éirinn
   Gun shéid i gu làidir,
   Dà *reef* againn 'na *foresail*
   'S na *royals* a b'àirde.
     Fail ò ro mar dh'fhàg sinn, *etc.*

5. Nuair dh'fhàg i 'n t-Eilein Ruadh
   Chuir sinn suas ar cuid chàbaill;
   Sin dhiùlt i dhol mun cuairt
   'S chaidh an Suaineach a bhàthadh.
   Fail ò ro mar dh'fhàg sinn, *etc.*

6. 'S gur mise a ghabh an t-uamhas
   Nuair a chuala mi chànail,
   'S gun duirt am *Mate* am Beurla:
   'Sin fhéin àit as fheàrr dha.'
   Fail ò ro mar dh'fhàg sinn, *etc.*

7. Bha sgiobair air a' *chuatar-dec*
   'S e 'g éigheach cruaidh gu h-àrd ruinn,
   'S cha b'ioghnadh liom ged liathadh e,
   Nan deanadh sìoban sàil' e.
   Fail ò ro mar dh'fhàg sinn, *etc.*

*Translation*

*Chorus:* Fal ò ro, as we departed, leaving our friends behind us; the fine lads of our country are hoisting the sails on the high masts; Fal ò ro, as we departed.

1. When we left the Clyde she was swift on the water; the crew which left her gave her a downright bad name. Fal ò ro, *etc.*

2. When we sailed from Greenock we were sorrowful, remembering the laughing girls.

3. On Wednesday we sailed and she (the ship) was beautiful, with sixty-three sails on the most handsome of women.

4. When she passed the land of Ireland it blew strongly; we had two reefs in her foresails, and in her topmost royals.

5. When she left Red Island behind we put up our cables; then she refused to go about, and the Swede was drowned.

6. Then terror took hold of me when I heard his language, and the mate said in English: 'That's the best place for him.'

7. The skipper was on the quarter-deck, shouting loudly to us aloft; I would not have wondered if he had turned grey, if salt spray would do it.

The tune and verses 1, 3, 5 and 6 from Rev. Murdo MacLeod, Dalibrog, South Uist; verses 2, 4 and 7 from Miss Kate Morrison, Loch Eport, North Uist, January 1934. A similar tune with the same chorus is printed in *Eilean Fraoich*, p. 54, with modern verses by Duncan MacDonald. See also *An Duanaire*, p. 103.

Mode: Dorian 2:6.

## 6 ÒRAN NA *POLITICIAN*

### 1

Thàinig bàt' air tìr dha'n àit'
 A dh'fhàg mise fo mhìngean,
Fhuair mi aiste dram no dhà,
 'S e sin a dh'fhàg cho tinn mi;
Mar a tha mi 'n diu cho truagh,
 Cha ghluais mi ach le dìchioll;
'S e na dh'òl mi dha'n *Spey Royal*
 Chuir am bròn air m'inntinn.

### 2

Chuala mi gun robh i ann,
 'S gu robh an t-am dhol innte;
Gu robh stuth innte gu leòr,
 Bha brògan agus sìod' ann,
Bha uisge beatha mar bha an còrr
 Gach *brand* is seòrs' bha sgrìobhte;
'S ged bha 'n ola dhubh gu h-àrd,
 Bha chuid a b'fheàrr gu h-ìseal.

### 3

Chaidh mi suas mar rinn càch
 'S gun chaith sinn pàirt a bh'innte,
Dùil liom nach biodh guth gu bràch air,
 Gu robh am bàta millte;
Ach cha b'ann mar sin a bhà
 Chaidh brath gun dàil a dh'innse,
'S ann fhuair mi sumaineadh bha garbh
 'Gam thoirt air falbh dha'n phrìosan.

### 4

'S a Loch nam Madadh chaidh sinn sìos
 'Gar cur an iarainn cinnteach;
Cha b'e seachdain 's cha b'e mìos,
 'S ann gheobhainn bliadhna phrìosan;
Bha 'n Géidseir 's *polisman* no dhà
 An àird air son ar dìteadh,
Ach a dh'aindheoin an cuid beòil
 'S ann gheobhadh Ròidseag *clear*.

88

5

Is ged a dh'fhalbhainn as a siod
    Do dh'Eilear Nis dha'n phrìosan,
'S mi nach cromadh sìos mo cheann
    Cha bhiodh dad ann do mhìchliù;
'S mur b'e cuid le luas am beòil
    'S cho deònach a bhith 'g innse,
Cha d'fhuaras greim air duine riamh
    A thug diar air tìr aist'.

6

Ach 's e dh'fhàg mi 'n diu fo ghruaim
    'S a chuir an duan air m'inntinn,
Smaointinn air na gillean truagh
    Thug a chuairt dha'n phrìosan;
Bha cho onarach 's gach àit',
    Cha chluinn' aig càch am mìomhodh,
'S nach cualas riamh gu robh iad beò
    Gu'n bhuail i stròn air tìr ann.

7

Thuirt an Géidseir an Taigh na Cùirt,'—
    'S bha diùmbadh agam fhìn ris—
Gum faigheadh iad i air falbh,
    'S nach robh an cargo millte;
'S ged bha mi fhìn air bheagan tùir,
    Co dhiù bha fios a'm cinnteach,
Nach gluaiseadh i bho'n chreig gu bràch,
    Gur h-ann 'san tràigh a chìt' i.

8

'S ge b'e choisicheas a null
    Bho'n Lùdaig 's ann a chì e—
Chì e sealladh dhith le shùil,
    'Sa ghrùnnd far bheil i sìnte;
'S e 'm *Politician* a th'ann,
    Car cam innte nach dìrich;
'S cha ghluais i as a' siod gu bràch,
    Gu'n déid i mhàin 'na pìosan.

9

Ach nam b'fhiach liom chuirinn sìos e,
    'S cha b'e briag a dh'innsinn,
Cuid a fhuair aiste gu leòr
    Dha'n h-uile seòrs' a bh'innte;
A bha stràiceil as gach dòigh,
    Is leòmach feadh na tìre;
Ach éisdibh mi, 's cha chan mi 'n còrr
    Mu'n *Pholi* chòir gu dìlinn.

*Translation*

## THE SONG OF THE *POLITICIAN*

1. A ship has come ashore in this place, which left me in distress; I got a dram or two out of her; that is what made me so ill; I am so wretched to-day that I can only move with an effort; the 'Spey Royal' I drank has made my mind sorrowful.

2. I heard she was there, and that it was the time to go into her, that there was plenty of stuff in her, there were shoes and silks, and whisky as well, of every known brand; and though there was black (fuel) oil on top, the best part was below.

3. I went up as the rest did, and we used what was in her; I thought that there wouldn't be a word about it, that the ship was a total loss; but that was not how things turned out, a report was made at once, and I got a stern summons, taking me away to prison.

4. We went down to Lochmaddy, expecting to be put in irons; not a week, nor a month, but a year's imprisonment I would get. The Exciseman and a policeman or two were out to condemn us, but in spite of their talk Ròidseag (the author) looked like getting clear.

# SONGS

5. Though I were to go thence to Inverness prison, I would not bow my head, there would be no disgrace in it; but for some people, with their careless talk and readiness to tell, not a man who took a drop out of her would have been caught.

6. What left me sad, and put the poem on my mind, was thinking of the poor lads whom the Court sent to prison; who were so well esteemed everywhere, no one was heard to say they had misbehaved, it hadn't been ever heard they were alive, until she struck her nose on land there.

7. The Exciseman said in the Court house, and I was annoyed with him for it, that they would get her away, and that the cargo was not spoilt; though I was not very intelligent myself, I knew for sure, at any rate, that she would never move from the rock, that she would (henceforth) be only seen ashore.

8. Whoever walks along from Lùdag will see, will see a sight of her with his own eyes, where she is stretched out on the bottom; the *Politician* is there, she has a bend that cannot be straightened; she'll never move from there until she goes to pieces.

9. But if it were worth my while, I would put it down, and I wouldn't tell a lie, some got plenty out of her, of every kind of thing in her, who were boastful in every way, and proud throughout the district; but listen to me, and I'll never say more about the kindly 'Polly'.

This song was made by Roderick Campbell, son of Iain Campbell (Iain Clachair), in 1942, and is a good example of how the tradition of composing popular Gaelic songs is still maintained in South Uist. The tune was transcribed from a recording made by D. J. MacKinnon, of Barra. In 1941 a merchantman named the *Politician* ran ashore on Hartamul, a small rock about a mile to the east of Eriskay and about half a mile due south of Rudha a' Mhill the south-easternmost point of South Uist. She was laden with a mixed cargo which included 32 different brands of the finest Scotch whisky, all destined for the American market—the bottles were labelled 'Federal Law forbids resale'. After she ran ashore, the crew was saved, and for several months the ship lay where she was. The impression spread, not unjustifiably, that she had been abandoned as a total wreck, and in consequence a considerable number of people busied themselves with the salvage of the most valuable part of her cargo. Eventually officialdom woke up and the local representatives of the law were instructed to take action against the salvers, some of whom were prosecuted. This was the occasion of some indignation, and was the inspiration of this song, and of others. The *Politician* was eventually moved from Hartamul and beached off Eriskay, and broken up for scrap iron. Her cargo did much to enliven South Uist (and other places) during the dark days of the war, and the whole incident was the background of the well-known novel and film *Whisky Galore*, by Sir Compton Mackenzie.

Mode: Hexatonic, no 7th.

# 7 O GUR TROM THA MO BHEAN-SA

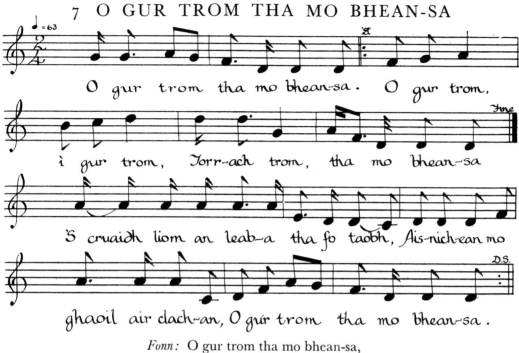

*Fonn:* O gur trom tha mo bhean-sa,
O gur trom, ì gur trom,
Torrach, trom, tha mo bhean-sa.

1. 'S cruaidh liom an leaba tha fo taobh,
   Aisnichean mo ghaoil air clachan.
   O gur trom tha mo bhean-sa, *etc.*

2. Tha mo bhean-sa air laigh-shiùbhlaidh,
   Cha dig mnathan na dùthcha faisg oirr'.

3. Bheirinn pòg a làimh an t-saoir,
   Na faicinn as ùr a mach thu.

4. 'S mi gu rachadh leat a Dhiùraidh,
   Na faighinn as ùr air ais thu.

## Translation

*Chorus:* My wife is heavy, o heavy, she is heavy,
Heavy with child is my wife.

1. Hard I think the bed that is beneath her side, the ribs of my love are on stones.
2. My wife is in childbed. The women of the country will not come near her.
3. I would give a kiss to the hand of the joiner to see you out again.
4. If I could get you back again, I would go with you to Jura.

This is an Eriskay song which the singer, Peigi Nìll MacIsaac (Mrs. John Currie), got from her father. The singer compares his fishing boat, which has been wrecked on the shore, to his wife in childbed. There is a fuller version of the words in the MSS of the late Father Allan MacDonald, Eriskay; also in K. C. Craig, *Òrain Luaidh,* p. 115; I published this song in the *J.E.F.D.S.S.,* Vol. IV., p. 194.

Mode: Dorian.

# ÒRAIN COGAIDH—SONGS OF WAR

## 8 O! GUM B'AOTROM LINN AN T-ASTAR

*Fonn:* O! gum b'aotrom linn an t-astar,
Falbh gu sunndach air bheag airtneal,
A' dol an comhdhail Bonapartaidh
A chionn bhith bagairt air Rìgh Deòrs'.

1. Ged nach biodh ann ach na Gàidheil,
   Iad gu fearail, foinnidh, làidir,
   Chuireadh iad eagal am bàis
   Air gach nàmhaid a tha beò.

2. 'S iomadh fear mu'n am seo 'n uiridh
   Bha 'na choigreach air a' ghunna,
   Fhreagras am bliadhna dha'n druma,
   Ceart cho ullamh ris an òrd.

3. 'Illean cridheil, biomaid sunndach,
   Seasamaid onair ar dùthcha;
   Fhad 's a mhaireas luaidh' is fùdar,
   Gu dé chuireas cùram òirnn?

4. Alba 's Éirinn agus Sasunn,
   An déidh cur ri chéile an ceartuair,
   Tha iad a réir an aon fhacail
   Mar fhuaim eadar clach is òrd.

5. Luchd nan adaichean croma
   'Nan sìneadh air làraich loma;
   'S e mo dhìobhail anns a' chomunn
     Nach d'fhan Abaircrombaidh beò.

6. Fhuair sinn air son deise nan Gàidheal,
   Suaicheantas bho'n Rìgh mar fhàbhar;
   Boineid ghorm is còta sgàrlaid,
     Is cocàrd a dh'it' an eòin.

7. 'S ged a dh'fhiach e fhéin 's na Frangaich
   Ri tighinn do Bhreatainn le aimhreit,
   Tillidh sinn a null gun taing thu,
     'S fheàrr dhut fuireach thall dhad' dheòin.

*Translation*

*Chorus:* O light we thought the journey, leaving happily with little sorrow, going to meet Bonaparte, because he threatens King George.

1. Though only the Gaels should be there, and they manly, handsome, strong, they would put the fear of death into every enemy alive.

2. Many a man who this time last year was a stranger to a gun, answers this year the voice of the drum as readily as the hammer (of the gun).

3. Hearty lads, let us be merry, let us uphold our country's honour; as long as lead and powder last, what shall worry us?

4. Scotland, Ireland and England, at present joined together: they are of one mind, like the sound between flint and hammer.

5. The folk of the bent hats were stretched out on the bare battlefield; my loss that of the company, Abercrombie lost his life.

6. We got for the dress of the Gaels a badge as a favour from the King; a blue bonnet and scarlet coat, and a cockade of a bird's feather.

7. Although he (Bonaparte) and the French should try to come to Britain with violence, we will drive you back willy-nilly; you had better stay over there of your own accord.

Tune and words from Miss Màiri MacRae, Angus John Campbell and Neil MacLennan, who gave the last verse. The words were composed by James Shaw, the Lochnell bard, and are printed in the Turner Collection, p. 258 (1813). This South Uist version differs considerably from the printed version in words and order and number of verses (there are fifteen in the latter). It is also printed in *Sàr-Obair nam Bàrd Gaelach*, p. 313. This song is sung to another tune in Barra, where it has been recorded by J. L. Campbell.

Mode: Hexatonic, no 6th.

# 9 THA MO DHÙIL, THA MO DHÙIL

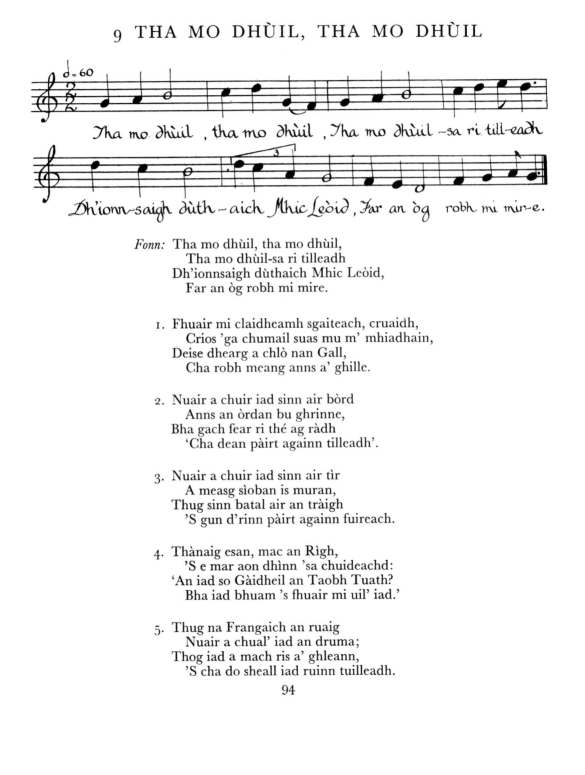

Tha mo dhùil, tha mo dhùil, Tha mo dhùil-sa ri tilleadh
Dh'ionn-saigh dùth-aich Mhic Leòid, Far an òg robh mi mir-e.

*Fonn:* Tha mo dhùil, tha mo dhùil,
　　　Tha mo dhùil-sa ri tilleadh
　　　Dh'ionnsaigh dùthaich Mhic Leòid,
　　　Far an òg robh mi mire.

1. Fhuair mi claidheamh sgaiteach, cruaidh,
　　Crios 'ga chumail suas mu m' mhiadhain,
　Deise dhearg a chlò nan Gall,
　　Cha robh meang anns a' ghille.

2. Nuair a chuir iad sinn air bòrd
　　Anns an òrdan bu ghrinne,
　Bha gach fear ri thé ag ràdh
　　'Cha dean pàirt againn tilleadh'.

3. Nuair a chuir iad sinn air tìr
　　A measg sìoban is muran,
　Thug sinn batal air an tràigh
　　'S gun d'rinn pàirt againn fuireach.

4. Thànaig esan, mac an Rìgh,
　　'S e mar aon dhìnn 'sa chuideachd:
　'An iad so Gàidheil an Taobh Tuath?
　　Bha iad bhuam 's fhuair mi uil' iad.'

5. Thug na Frangaich an ruaig
　　Nuair a chual' iad an druma;
　Thog iad a mach ris a' ghleann,
　　'S cha do sheall iad ruinn tuilleadh.

94

# SONGS OF WAR

## *Translation*

*Chorus:* I hope, I hope, I hope to return to the MacLeod's country (Skye), where I played in my childhood.

1. I got a sharp, well-tempered sword, a belt around my middle to keep it up, a red uniform of Lowland cloth—there was no fault in the lad.

2. When they put us aboard in best order, every man told his girl 'some of us will not come back'.

3. When they put us ashore, amongst the spume and the bent grass, we fought a battle on the shore and some of us remained there (*i.e.* were killed).

4. The King's son came, he was like one (of us) in the company: 'Are these the Gaels from the North? I needed them, and I have got them all.'

5. The French took to flight when they heard the drum, they took to the glen and did not face us again.

From Mrs. Seònaid Campbell (Bean Alasdair), North Glendale. There are seven verses printed in *An Duanaire*, p. 71, where the author is said to be 'Leòdach' (*i.e.* a MacLeod). Four verses with a somewhat similar tune are printed in the *Gesto Collection* without an author's name. A version of this tune was collected by Miss Lucy Broadwood at Arisaig, Inverness-shire, and printed in *J.E.F.D.S.S.*, Vol. 1, No. 3, p. 144. The date of the song is probably of the time of the Napoleonic Wars. It might refer to the expedition to Holland in 1799.

Mode: Mixolydian.

# ÒRAN FOGARRAICH—AN EXILE'S SONG

## 10 THA MI SGÌTH 'M ÒNARAN

Tha mi sgìth 'm òn-ar-an, Tha mi sgìth 's mi liom fhìn, 'S cian bho thìr m'eòl-as mi, Tha mi sgìth 'm òn-ar-an. Muigh air both-ag àir-igh ghlinn-e, 'G éisd-eachd binn-eas nan smeòr-aich-ean.

*Fonn:* Tha mi sgìth 'm ònaran,
Tha mi sgìth 's mi liom fhìn,
'S cian bho thìr m'eòlais mi,
Tha mi sgìth 'm ònaran.

### 1

Muigh air bothag àirigh ghlinne,
'G éisdeachd binneas nan smeòraichean.

### 2

Sìos is suas an Gleann Seilich
Gus na theirig mo bhrògan dhomh.

### 3

'S fada mise bho Chaol Muile,
Far 'm bi luingeas a' seòladh ann.

96

# AN EXILE'S SONG

*Translation*

*Chorus:* I am tired in solitude,
I am tired and I am alone,
I am far from my own country,
I am tired in solitude.

1

Out in the bothy of the sheiling of the glen,
Listening to the sweetness of thrushes.

2

Up and down Glen Sheilich,
Until my shoes wore out.

3

I am far from the Sound of Mull,
Where the ships are sailing.

The tune, chorus and first verse from Miss Peigi MacRae, the second and third verses from Angus John Campbell. Miss MacRae learnt the song from Miss Catriona MacIntosh while employed at Boisdale House when a young girl. There are versions of the tune printed in the following collections under the title "'S Fhad Tha Mi 'M Ònaran': Patrick MacDonald, p. 14; Finlay Dun; *Òrain na h-Albain*, p. 44; *Gesto Collection*, p. 23; *Binneas Nam Bàrd*, p. 59. The refrain and first verse are similar to the poem under the title 'Perthshire Airs, No. 91', in the John Gillies Collection (1786), p. 124; in *An t-Òranaiche*, p. 394; and in K. C. Craig's *Òrain Luaidh*, p. 101.

Mode: Pentatonic 2:6.

# CUMHAICHEAN—LAMENTS

## 11 AN GILLE DONN

*Fonn:* 'S mise tha fo mhìngean
Mu'n ghille dhonn;
Òigear nan sùil mìogach
A dh'fhàg m' inntinn trom,
'S mise tha fo mhìngean,
Mu'n ghille dhonn.

1. 'S mise tha gu galach
   Bho thoiseach an earraich,
   Thug mi gaol a mhaireas
   Do mharaiche nan tonn.

2. Mo cheist air an àrmunn,
   Làmh stiùireadh a' bhàta;
   Gheobhainn cadal sàmhach
   Leat air bàrr nan tonn.

3. Dh'fhalbh thu air an t-slighe
   Gun dùil ri thu thilleadh;
   Òigear a Chloinn Iain,
   Dh'fhàg mo chridhe trom.

98

# LAMENTS

*Translation*

Chorus: It is I that am melancholy for the brown-haired lad, the youth of the smiling eyes, about whom my mind grew sad.

1. I am tormented since the beginning of spring, I have given lasting love to the sailor of the waves.

2. I long for the hero whose hand steers the boat. I would find quiet sleep with you on the top of the waves.

3. You have gone on the voyage without hope of returning; youth of Clan Iain, (you) have left my heart heavy.

The chorus, first verse and the tune are from Miss Peigi MacRae, the second and third verses from Angus John Campbell. The complete version of this song is printed in *An t-Òranaiche*, p. 297—nine verses and chorus. It is the lament of a woman whose lover was drowned when his ship was wrecked in the Sound of Canna.

Mode: Hexatonic, no 6th.

## 12 'S ANN AIG PORT TAIGH NA H-ÀIRIGH

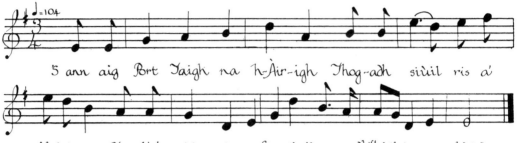

'S ann aig Port Taigh na h-Àir-igh Thog-adh siùil ris a' bhàt-a, Cha b'e'n stiùir rinn a fàg-ail, 'S ann a dh'fhàil-ig na bùird.

1. 'S ann aig Port Taigh na h-Àirigh
   Thogadh siùil ris a' bhàta:
   Cha b'e 'n stiùir rinn a fàgail,
   'S ann a dh'fhàilig na bùird.

2. 'S i dol seachad an rudha
   Thog am bàta ri siubhal,
   'S bha fear òg a' chùil bhuidhe
   'Na shuidh' air a' stiùir.

3. 'S gura mis' tha fo mhulad
   Air an fhraoch 's mi air m'uilinn:
   Chì mi 'm bàta fo h-uidheam
   A' tighinn bho Uibhist nan stùc.

4. 'S gura mis' tha gu cràiteach,
   'S mi 'nam shuidh' aig an àirigh;
   Chì mi tighinn am bàta
   'S gun thu, ghràidh, air a' stiùir.

5. 'S cha truagh liom do phiuthar,
   Ged bhiodh i daonnan 'gad chumha,
   Nuair a théid i dha'n chuideachd,
   Théid a mulad air chùl.

6. 'S gur mi tha duilich mu d' mhàthair
   A shaothraich ri t'àrach,
   Nuair nach d'fhuair i do chnàmhan
   A bhith 'gad chàradh 'san ùir.

# LAMENTS

7. Fhir nan camagan donna,
   A' mhuineil ghil 's an uchd shoilleir,
   'S mi gu rachadh 'nad choinneamh,
   Cha bu choma liom thù.

8. 'S mór am beud do chùl clannach
   A bhith 'ga reubadh 'san fheamain;
   Gun chiste, gun anart,
   Ach gaineamh a' ghrùnnd.

9. O! nan deachaidh do bhàthadh
   Nuair a chaidh mo thriùir bhràithrean,
   Bhiodh agam leisgeul, a ghràidh-ghil,
   A bhith gu bràch 'ga do thùirs.

*Translation*

1. It was at the port of the House of the Sheiling that the sails of the boat were hoisted. It was not the helm that left her but the planks that failed.

2. Going past the point the boat got well under weigh, and the young man of the yellow hair was sitting at the helm.

3. It is I that am sorrowful, leaning on my elbow among the heather. I see the boat under sail coming from Uist of the steep rocks.

4. I am in torment, sitting at the sheiling. I see the boat coming, but you, my love, are not at the helm.

5. I have not pity for your sister though she is always lamenting you; when she enters company her sorrow is forgotten.

6. I am sorry for your mother, who toiled to rear you, when she did not find your bones to bury them in the earth.

7. O lad of the brown curls, white neck and fair chest, I would go to meet you, I was not indifferent to you.

8. It is a tragedy that your curly head is being torn in the seaweed, without coffin, without shroud, but the sand of the bottom of the sea.

9. Oh! If you had been drowned when my three brothers were, my dear love, I would have had an excuse to lament you for ever.

From Angus John Campbell, South Lochboisdale, 1932. Compare the poem to 'Òran Do Ghille a Chaidh a Bhàthadh' in *An t-Òranaiche*, pp. 176-178. This song is sometimes sung with a chorus, but I give it as I got it.

Mode: Hexatonic, no 6th.

## 13 MARBHRANN DO DH'FHEAR ÀIRIGH MHUILINN

1. Aonghais òig Àirigh Mhuilinn,
   Nach cianail duilich ri innse
   Nach fhaicear tuilleadh gu bràch thu,
   Fhir a nàdur bu shìobhalt';
   'S aig an robh nàdur na h-uaisle,
   An diugh 'san uaigh 's gum b'e 'n dìobhail,
   'S an gaoirdean treun bu mhór tàbhachd,
   Cha chuir thu spàirn air 'ga shìneadh.

2. Ach Aonghais òig rìomhaich
   Gu seinnte pìob leat is bratach;
   Marcraich sunndach each crùidheach
   A ghearradh dìreach an t-astar.
   Mo chreach! do chorp cùmhraidh
   'Na laigh' air ùrlar an aigeil,
   Gun tug iad t'anam a Phàras,
   Na h-Ostail chàirich do leabaidh.

# LAMENTS

3. 'S Dia a ghléidheadh an céille
   Do na peucagan uasal
   A rinn thu fhàgail 'nad dheoghaidh,
   'S e so a' foghar a ghual iad;
   Cha robh leithid an athar
   An cliù 's am mathas 's an uaisle,
   An treas pears' 'san Roinn Eòrp' thu,
   A' suidh' an còmhlan dhaoin'-uaisle.

4. Dh'fhalbh a' chraobh 's a cuid duillich,
   Gun thuit am bun 's gun do chrìon e
   Bho'n a rinneadh do bhàthadh,
   Gur e an t-Àrd-Rìgh a b'fhianais;
   Ach bha an uair air a cumail,
   Bha gaoth is sruth mar an ciand' ann
   A chuir thairis an t-eathar,
   Mo chreach! mu leathach an lìonaidh.

5. 'S thug thu ràimh dha d' chuid ghillean,
   Cha robh tuilleadh a dhìth ort;
   Gun robh thu 'n dùil mar a b'àbhaist
   Gun robh do shnàmh mar an fhaoileag,
   Gun robh do shnàmh mar an eala
   A dh'fhalbhadh aigeannach aotrom;
   Do phearsa dìreach, deas, dealbhach,
   Gur bochd a dh'fhalbh thu gun aois bhuainn.

6. Fhir a' mhùirn 's a' chiùil-ghàire,
   Fhir thug bàrr air na ciadan
   Ann an treunad 's an gaisge,
   Gum b'fheàrr nach fhaca sinn riamh thu;
   Fhir a sheasadh na càirdean
   Nuair chuireadh càch iad gu diachainn;
   Ged bha thu ciùin ann ad nàdur,
   'S e do ghàirdean gun dìoladh.

7. Nuair a chruinnicheadh an campa
   Bu tusa ceannard nan daoine;
   An nì a theireadh tu, dhiant' e,
   Air neo dh'fhiachadh tu faobhar;
   C'àit' an robh ann an Alba
   Triath sheasadh calma ri t'aodann—
   A h-aon a labhradh riut dàna?
   'S e 'n t-eun as àirde 'sa chraoibh thu.

8. 'S bu tu sealgair a' mhunaidh,
   Le do ghunna nach diùltadh
   Air damh cròiceach nan cabar
      A leumadh aigeannach, sunndach,
   'S ged a leumadh, gu marbhadh:
   Bha thu 'd shealgair bho dhùthchas
   Ròin is eala agus earba,
      Is fiadh nan gearrchasan lùthmhor.


9. H-uile h-aon thig air astar
      Trom, airtneulach, sgìthear,
   Bheir sùil chianail air t'aitreamh
      Far na chleachd iad bhith dìreadh,
   Gu fàrdrach na fialachd,
      'S i 'n diu a' crìonadh fo'n dìle;
   Bu tric aighear le uaill ann
      'S a chuir luchd fuachd an cuid sgìos dhiubh.


*Translation*

1. Young Angus of Arivullin, how sad and difficult it is to tell that you will never be seen again, you who were of most civil disposition, who possessed also the spirit of nobility, are to-day in the grave, and what a loss! No more will you exert yourself to stretch your strong and powerful arm.

2. But, o young and beautiful Angus, for whom the pipes used to play and the standard flutter, joyful rider of well-shod horses which would speed straight the journey, alas! your fragrant body lies on the bottom of the deep, and the Apostles who prepared your bed have taken your soul to Paradise.

3. And may God preserve their senses to the beautiful and gentle children whom you left behind you. This is the autumn that has pained them. There was not the like of their father in character, in goodness and in nobility. You were the third person in Europe sitting in the assembly of noblemen.

4. Away has gone the tree with its foliage. The stock fell and withered since you were drowned, as God is witness; but the appointed hour was kept, the wind and tide were both there to overturn the vessel, alas, about the middle of the flood-tide.

5. You gave the oars to your crew, you required nothing more; you thought, as usual, you could swim like the seagull, that you could swim like the swan which would go lightly and lively, with your straight and beautiful form. Sad it is that you left us without reaching old age.

6. Lad of joy and mirth, one who excelled hundreds in strength and heroism, it would have been better if we had never seen you. You who would stand loyal to your friends when others put them to hardship; though you were gentle in your nature, it was your arm which could work vengeance.

LAMENTS

7. When the camp was mustered, you were the leader of men. Your commands were performed or else you would test your blade. Where in Scotland was there a chief who would dare to face you—where was there one who would speak boldly to you? You were the highest bird in the tree.

8. You were the hunter on the moor with your gun, which would not misfire on the antlered stag that would leap spiritedly and joyfully, and though it leapt, you would kill it. It was native to you to hunt the seals and the swans, and the roes and the agile small-footed deer.

9. Everyone who comes from afar sore, weary and fatigued will cast a sorrowful eye on your dwelling to which they used to ascend, to the hospitable dwelling to-day decaying under the rains. Often there was joy and pomp there, and therein the cold traveller threw off his weariness.

This elegy was composed by Angus Campbell (Aonghus mac Dhòmhnaill 'ic Eóghainn), known as 'Am Bàrd Sgallach' in his native island of Benbecula. Fear Àirigh Mhuilinn was Captain Angus MacDonald of Milton, South Uist, a nephew of Flora MacDonald. He was drowned in Loch Eynort in 1809 while ferrying kelp to a ship lying in the loch. His small boat was swamped and his two dogs in trying to save him were really the cause of his drowning. Angus John Campbell, who knew verses 2, 3, 4, 5 and 8, gave me the tune; the words printed here were given me by Duncan MacDonald, Peninerine.

Six verses of the song were printed, with an English translation by John Whyte, in *T.G.S.I.*, Vol. XIV, p. 168, in a paper read by Charles Fraser-Mackintosh, M.P., on 22 February 1888, the words having been taken down by the Revd. Fr. John Mackintosh, parish priest of Bornish, from Neil MacEachin in Howbeg, aged 97 in 1892. The same six verses were reprinted in *Mac Talla*, Vol. X, p. 144, in December 1901. This song is the only 'Òran Mór' in this collection.

The tune may be compared to that of *'S mi 'm shuidhe gu stolta* in the Gesto Collection, p. 27; also to that of 'An Island Sheiling Song' in *Songs of the Hebrides*, I. 32, which was taken down by Mrs. Kennedy-Fraser from Ann MacNeil (sister of the late Canon John MacNeill) in Barra, and set to words composed by Kenneth MacLeod.

Better readings from another version of the song taken down from Duncan MacDonald by his son D. J. MacDonald:

V. 1, l. 5 *Com na tuigse 's na h-uaisle* 'Heart of understanding and nobility'
V. 3, l. 4 *ghuail*
V. 4, l. 5 *cumadh*
V. 9, l. 2 *sgitheil*

Mode: Ionian 4: 7.

# ÒRAIN SEILGE—SONGS ABOUT HUNTING

## 14 SEANN-ÒRAN SEILGE—I

*Fonn:* Ho ro ì a bhi o hó,
Chall éileadh a ro hó,
Ho ro ì a bhi o hó,
Chall o ho ro bhì.

1. Mharbhainn ràc agus lacha,
Agus tarmachan creachainn,
Earba riabhach nam badan
Bhiodh 'sa mhaduinn fo fhiamh.

2. Spor thana gheur dhùbhghorm,
'N déidh a glasadh 's a dlùthadh,
Chuireadh sradag ri fùdar,
Nuair a lùbainn mo mhiar.

106

3. Bidh mi nis a' falbh dhachaigh,
   Le mo ghuanna fo m'achlais,
   Nuair a dhiùlt i orm lasadh
      Ri damh cabrach nam fiadh.

*Translation*

1. I would kill the wild drake and the wild duck, and the ptarmigan of the mountains, and the brindled young roe of the thicket which in the morning was afraid.

2. Thin, sharp blue-black flint, after being locked and brought into position, it would set a spark to the powder when I bent my finger.

3. And now I will be going home with my gun under my arm, when it refused to fire for me on the antlered stag of the deer.

From Rev. Murdo MacLeod, Dalibrog, South Uist. This hunting song is believed to have come from the north-west part of Ross-shire, but the most complete version of the poem is in *T.G.S.I.*, Vol. XXVII, p. 335 (18 verses), where it is said to be the composition of Angus Cameron, Stratherrick, Loch Ness-side. A version of the tune with seven verses is printed in the *Celtic Magazine*, Vol. III, p. 480. *An t-Òranaiche*, p. 359, contains a complete version. I published this song in the *J.E.F.D.S.S.*, Vol. IV, p. 191.

Mode: Hexatonic, no 6th.

## 15 SEANN-ÒRAN SEILGE—II

Seinn u ri bhinn o ho, Eile challuinn ho ro ho.

Seinn u ri bhinn o ho, Eile challuinn ò hì,

'S nuair a chunnaic mi 'n còmhlan 'Nan laigh' air a' mhòintich,

Bha trì fichead is còrr ann, 'S air an tòir bidh mi triall.

*Fonn:* Seinn u ri bhinn o ho,
Eile challuinn ho ro ho,
Seinn u ri bhinn o ho,
Eile challuinn ò hì.

'S nuair a chunnaic mi 'n còmhlan
'Nan laigh' air a' mhòintich,
Bha trì fichead is còrr ann,
'S air an tòir bidh mi triall.

### Translation

When I saw the company (of deer) lying on the hillside, there were sixty and more there. I will go in pursuit of them.

From Angus John Campbell, South Lochboisdale. This second tune to 'Seann-Òran Seilge' has a chorus similar to that of the *T.G.S.I.* poem, and there is a slight similarity between the ninth verse of that poem and Mr. Campbell's.

Mode: Hexatonic, no 6th, weak 3rd.

# SONGS OF LOVE

### *Translation*

*Chorus:* Heavy, heavy, curly hair; heavy, heavy, curly hair. There are yellow curly tresses around the shoulder of my sweetheart.

1. On a clear summer evening, when I was walking on the pavement, who met me but my darling, at the end of the house of the glasses (*i.e.* the inn).

2. You are going to marry, and I am going to sail on the ship of three great masts, and the parting is a sorrow to me.

3. It is your proud mother who was to blame that we did not marry; but you are my first girl since I began sweethearting.

4. Many a night we sat together in the byre, and when I sought to leave you your arm would hold me.

5. Do you remember our conversation in the little bed in the back room? The love I gave you when I was young to-day wounds me with regret.

The words and tune are from Miss Màiri MacRae, North Glendale, 1931. I published this song in the *J.E.F.D.S.S.*, Vol. IV., p. 190.

**Mode:** Hexatonic, no 6th (weak 2nd).

# 18 FHUAIR MI LIOM THU, MHÀIRI

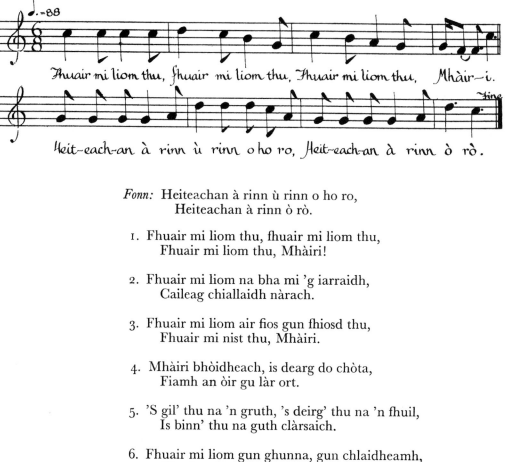

Fhuair mi liom thu, fhuair mi liom thu, Fhuair mi liom thu, Mhàir—i.

Heit-each-an à rinn ù rinn o ho ro, Heit-each-an à rinn ò rò.

*Fonn:* Heiteachan à rinn ù rinn o ho ro,
Heiteachan à rinn ò rò.

1. Fhuair mi liom thu, fhuair mi liom thu,
   Fhuair mi liom thu, Mhàiri!

2. Fhuair mi liom na bha mi 'g iarraidh,
   Caileag chiallaidh nàrach.

3. Fhuair mi liom air fios gun fhiosd thu,
   Fhuair mi nist thu, Mhàiri.

4. Mhàiri bhòidheach, is dearg do chòta,
   Fiamh an òir gu làr ort.

5. 'S gil' thu na 'n gruth, 's deirg' thu na 'n fhuil,
   Is binn' thu na guth clàrsaich.

6. Fhuair mi liom gun ghunna, gun chlaidheamh,
   Olc air mhath le càirdean.

# SONGS OF LOVE

## Translation

1. I got you for myself, I got you for myself, I got you for myself, Mary!

2. I got for myself what I was seeking, a sensible, modest maiden.

3. I got you for myself, without anyone knowing, I have got you now, Mary.

4. Beautiful Mary, red is your coat, the colour of gold to the ground on you (from head to heels).

5. You are whiter than curds, redder than blood, you are sweeter than the sound of a harp.

6. I got (her) without gun or sword, whether her relations liked it or not.

From Miss Màiri MacRae, North Glendale, 1932. The eighteenth-century bard Alexander MacDonald (Alasdair Mac Mhaighstir Alasdair) composed a song in praise of Morar to this tune and chorus. It has been printed in many collections under the title 'Fàilte Na Mórthir': the *Gesto Collection*, p. 43; *J.E.F.D.S.S.*, Vol. XVII, p. 300 (Broadwood Collection); *Coisir na Cloinne* (Alex MacLaren Publication); Kennedy Fraser, Vol. II, p. 163; Donald Campbell's *Language, Poetry and Music of the Highland Clans*, p. 273; William Matheson, *The Songs of John MacCodrum*, p. 330. In the Daniel Dow *Collection of Ancient Scots Music* (c. 1780) there is a version of this tune, entitled 'The Boatman's Song' or 'Luinnag Ferramh Bata' (*sic*).

Mode: Six note compass.

## 19 MÀIRI NIC A PHÌ

Màir-i nic a Phì, 'S toil liom fhìn a chail-eag; Tha i laghach, bòidh-each,

Cha n-eil pròis fain-ear dhith; Màir-i nic a Phì, 'S toil liom fhìn a' chail-eag.

Tha i laghach sàmh-ach Bho'n thàin-ig i 'n àit-e,

'S toil-each-as mar thà i Le bàn-ran 's le cean-ail.

*Fonn*: Màiri nic a Phì, 's toil liom fhìn a' chaileag,
Tha i laghach, bòidheach, cha n-eil pròis fainear dhith;
Màiri nic a Phì, 's toil liom fhìn a' chailcag.

1. Tha i laghach sàmhach
   Bho'n thàinig i 'n àite,
   'S toileachas mar thà i
   Le bànran 's le ceanal.

2. Nan cuirt' ann an rùm thu,
   Solus orra chùlaibh,
   Chuireadh tu na flùraichean
   Gu dlùth air anart.

3. Tha i laghach grianach,
   Cha n-eil car nach dian i,
   Cunntaidh i na ciadan
   'Gan snìomh as an ealain.

114

# SONGS OF LOVE

*Translation*

*Chorus:* Mary MacPhee, well I like that maiden.
She is sweet and bonny, she is not haughty.
Mary MacPhee, well I like that maiden.

1. She is sweet and gentle since she came here. 'Tis a joy to find her as she is with her pleasant talk and good temper.

2. If you were put in a room with a light at your back you would embroider flowers finely on linen (cloth).

3. She is sweet and sunny, she can turn her hand to anything. She can count the (threads in) hundreds, spinning them with skill.

**From Mrs. Agnes Currie, Lochboisdale.**

**Mode:** Hexatonic, no 4th.

## 20 MO GHAOL AN TÉ NACH DÌOBAIR MI

*Fonn:* Mo ghaol an té nach dìobair mi
Cho fad' 's a dhianadh fìrinn e.
Gu faithnichinn ceum na h-ìghneig miosg
Nam mìltean air a' chabhsair.
Mo ghaol an té nach dìobair mi.

I

Nuair bha mi òg 's mi 'm bhuachaille
Gun umam ach na cuaranan,
'S e dh'fhàg a' bhròg cho uallach orm
Ri cosnadh cruaidh an Fhrangaich.

2

'S nuair bha mi òg 'nam ghlasghiullan,
A' siubhal bheann is ghlacagan,
B'e 'n spòrs bu mhiann 's bu taitnich' liom,
Nuair thachradh tu 'sa ghleann rium.

3

Gun saorainn thu 's gun sòrainn thu,
Gu mionnaichinn 's gum bòidichinn
Nach d'fhuair mi sian a dh'fhòtus innt'
O'n fhuair mi eòlas cainnt oirr'.

4

Gun saorainn thu gun teagamh
Ge b'ann air bhialaibh seisein e;
Nach robh thu ball am eiseamail
Mur dug mi greis air cainnt riut.

5

Shaorainn, shaorainn, shaorainn thu,
Air m'fhacal fhéin gu faodainn e,
Nan creideadh clann nan daoine dhiom
Gu saorainn Màiri ghreannmhar.

6

Tha falt buidhe dualach ort,
'S a bhàrr a' fàs 'na chuaileinean
'S do phòg mar mhil na cuaiche liom
'S do shnuadh air dhreach an t-samhraidh.

*Translation*

*Chorus:* My love is the one who will not forsake me as long as pledge can stand. I would know the step of the maiden among thousands on the pavement. My love is the one who will not forsake me.

1. When I was young and herded cattle I only wore untanned shoes. The hard service of the French has made me wear an elegant shoe. (*Meaning doubtful here.*)

2. When I was a young man and walked mountains and glens, the sport I wished and which delighted me was when you met me in the glen.

3. I would clear you, I would not involve you, I would swear and give my oath that I found no vice in her since I knew her to speak to.[1]

4. I would clear your name without doubt, even before a Kirk Session, that you were not beholden to me except that I spoke to you for a time.

5. I would clear your name, upon my oath I could well do that. If the children of men would believe me I would clear the name of gay-hearted Mary.

6. You have curly yellow hair growing in ringlets, your kiss to me is like the honey in the combs, your complexion is like the hue of summer.

From Miss Màiri MacRae, North Glendale, 1931, who learnt it from Màiri Bhàn Dhòmhnaill 'ic Ailein while making hay at Boisdale House when a young girl. In the Stewart Collection (1804), p. 348, there is a poem entitled 'Màiri Ghreannar', and it is also in *Sàr-Obair nam Bàrd*, p. 396. The poem has nine verses and is obviously this same song. There it is said to have been composed by a 'Mr. Kenneth MacKenzie, late Tacksman of Monkcastle and Strath na Sealg, Loch Broom, Ross-shire, to his own servant girl'. Mr. MacKenzie died in 1827.

See also the collection of Gaelic poems made by Archibald Menzies (1870), p. 261, where a version with ten verses is attributed to 'Coinnich M'Choinnich'. In this version the fifth verse here is used as the refrain, and verses equivalent to the third, fourth, and sixth verses here occur.

Mode: Hexatonic, no 4th.

[1] This is obviously the meaning, as confirmed by the text printed in *Sàr Obair*: actually the reciter said 'Nach d'fhuair mi sian a dh'fhòtus ort/Gun d'fhuair mi eòlas cainnt ort.'

## 21 Ó HO NIGHEAN, É HO NIGHEAN!

Ó ho nigh-ean, é ho nigh-ean, ó ho nigh-ean a' chinn duibh àl-ainn; 'S duil-ich liom gun dug iad bhuam thu Càch a bhith 'gad luaidh gach là rium. 'S iom-adh oidhch-e, fad a' gheamhr-aidh, — Sneachd-a trom is cath-adh làir ann; Ràin-ig mi thu le deagh-dhùr-achd, 'S dh'fhàg siod gu tùr-sach gach là mi.

*Fonn:* Ó ho nighean, é ho nighean,
      Ó ho nighean a' chinn duibh àlainn;
      'S duilich liom gun dug iad bhuam thu,
      Càch a bhith 'gad luaidh gach là rium.


1. 'S iomadh oidhche fad 'a gheamhraidh,
      Sneachda trom is cathadh -làir ann;
      Ràinig mi thu le deagh-dhùrachd,
      'S dh'fhàg siod gu tùrsach gach là mi.


2. 'S cha robh car a dhianadh té 'ile
      Nach cuireadh tu fhéin do làmh ann,
      Nigheadh 's dh'fhuaighleadh tu mo léine,
      'S bhleoghnadh tu spréidh dhomh air àirigh.

3. Ach mas e 's gun d'rinn thu m'fhàgail
   'S gura h-e 'm fear ùr as fheàrr leat,
Mo mhìle beannachd gu bràch leat,
   Dh'fhàg thu mi mar uan gun mhàthair.

4. 'S ge bè 'n té a thog an naidheachd
   Na b'ann fallain nì i 'n gàire,
   'S na biodh aon neach air a bainis
   Gus an lig a leanabh ràn as.

5. 'S tric a thug mi falbh gun fhios leat,
   Mar chlaidheamh brist' air dhroch-chàradh;
   'S nuair a shaoil liom bha thu agam,
   B'fhada, 's o! b'fhada mo ghràdh bhuam.

6. Thug mi fad ràithe na bliadhna
   Dol 'gad iarraidh orra mhàthair,
   'S bho nach d'fhuair mi mar a dh'iarr mi,
   Thilg mi dhìom gach lìon 's gach bàta.

*Translation*

*Chorus:* O my maiden, é my maiden, o my maiden of the beautiful dark hair. Sad am I that they took you from me (and to hear) others praise you each day to me.

1. Many a night throughout the winter, with heavy drifting snow, I reached you with a good will and (yet) that left me sorrowful each day.

2. There is not a turn that another woman would do, to which you would not put a hand; you would mend and wash my shirt, and you would milk the cattle for me at the sheiling.

3. But if you have left me and prefer a new lover, my thousand blessings with you for ever; you have left me like a lamb without a mother.

4. Whatever woman raised the rumour, may she not be well enough for healthy laughter: let there not be one person at her wedding until (after) her infant has cried.

5. Often I went away with you secretly like a broken battered sword; and when I thought that you were mine, far, oh, far was my love from me.

6. I spent a quarter of the year going to ask your mother for you; since I did not get what I asked, I abandoned all (my) boats and nets.

From Mrs. John Currie (Peigi Nìll), North Glendale, 1932. The chorus of a love song in *The MacDonald Collection*, p. 202, is similar. This song is known in North Uist. Words were printed in the first volume of *MacTalla*.

119

# SONGS

Miss Peigi MacRae has the following additional verses:

> 7. Mise 'n seo mar chraoibh gun duillich
>    Air a tilgeadh an cùl gàraidh;
>    Dh'fhalbh an tacsa bha ri m' ghualainn,
>    Dia a lìon an cuan 's a thràigh e!
>
> 8. Ach nam faighinn mar a dh'iarrainn,
>    'N cuan an iar bhith air a thràghadh,
>    'S mi gu ruigeadh uair 'sa bhliadhna
>    Far a bheil mo chiad-ghaol gràdhach.
>
> 9. 'S nuair a théid mi gu do chistidh,
>    'S a chì mi do *phicture* àlainn:
>    Dh'fhàg siod tana glas mo chuailein,
>    'S cha n-eil dual dheth mar a dh'fhàs e.
>
> 10. 'S gur ann bhuainn a dh'fhalbh an t-iùran
>     'S gann gun lùbadh fiar fo shàilean;
>     'S ann an Cairo(?) chaidh an ùir air
>     'S dh'fhàg siod tùrsach cridh' do mhàthar.

*Translation*

7. I am here like a leafless tree thrown behind a wall; the support that was at my side has gone; 'tis God who made the sea flow and ebb.

8. But if I could get my wish, the western ocean dry, once a year I would reach the place where my beloved first-love is.

9. When I go to your chest, and see your fair picture—that has left my hair thin and grey, not a tress of it is as it first grew.

10. The splendid lad has gone from us; grass would hardly bend under his heels; he was buried in Cairo(?) which left your mother's heart sorrowful.

The last verse may be from a different song.

Mode: Mixolydian.

## 22 IAIN DUINN, BEIR ORM

Iain duinn, beir orm, Iain duinn, fàisg mi,
Iain duinn, beir orm, mun doir mi choill' orm;
Iain duinn, beir orm, Iain duinn, fàisg mi.

'S mur beir thus' orm, beiridh fear eil' orm,
Iain duinn, beir orm, Iain duinn, fàisg mi.

### Translation

Brown John, catch me, brown John, hug me,
Brown John, catch me before I make for the wood.
If you do not catch me, someone else will.

From Angus John Campbell, South Lochboisdale.

**Mode:** Six note compass.

# ÒRAIN NA FÉILLE—SONGS OF THE FAIR

## 23  AN T-EACH ODHAR

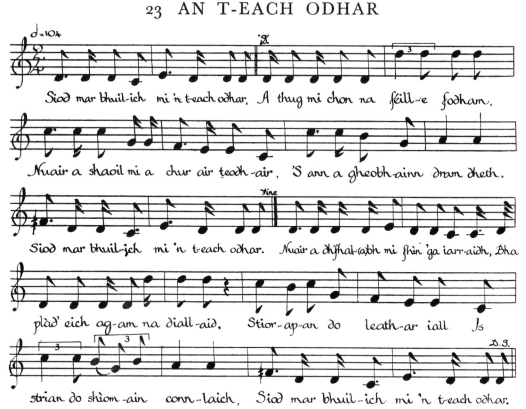

Chaidh esan chon na féille leis an each, agus a réir chollais gun chreic e an t-each 's gun a dh'òl e an t-airgiod. Bha e 'n sin a' cantail:

*Fonn:*  Siod mar bhuilich mi 'n t-each odhar,
A thug mi chon na féille fodham,
Nuair a shaoil mi a chur air teodhair,
'S ann a gheobhainn dram dheth.
Siod mar bhuilich mi 'n t-each odhar.

**1**

Nuair a dh'fhalbh mi fhìn 'ga iarraidh,
Bha plàd' eich agam 'na diallaid,
Stiorapan do leathar iall,
Is strian do shìomain connlaich.
Siod mar bhuilich mi, *etc.*

**2**

Cha robh agam far na féille
Do'n ghearran a b'fhaide leumadh,
Ach trì facail do dhroch-Bheurla,
'S bha mi fhéin a' call dheth.
Siod mar bhuilich mi, *etc.*

122

13

'Mura pàigh thu mi 'sa mhionaid
Cha bhi idir *bhòt* agad.'

14

Thànaig Marsanta na Mine:
Litrichean 'na dhòrn aige.

15

Labhair e 's a ghuth air chrith:
'Bheil dad idir dhòmhs' agad?'

16

'Mura pàigh thu an t-suim uile,
Cha n-urrainn mi an còrr thoirt dhut!'

17

Thànaig Marsanta na *Tea*,
'S da rìribh cha do chòrd e rium.

18

'Thug thu riarachadh do chàch,
Ged nach eil fàirdein dhòmhs' agad.'

19

Dh'iarr e fiachan bh'air mo mhàthair
O'n a bhà mi 'nam ògghiullan.

20

Gun dànaig Marsanta a' Chotain
Botal aig' 's gun d'òl sinn rud;

21

Ar liom gur h-e dusan not
A thuirt e rium bha còir aig' air.

22

Dh'éibh an Saor orm le cabhaig;
'Trobhad facal, òganaich!'

23

'An diu a gheall thu m'fhaicinn ceart,
Thoir tarraing air do phòcannan!'

24

Am fear thug dhòmhs' a' chruach as
Bha e tacan còmhla rium.        [t-earrach,

25

'Thoir dhomh not a gheibh am Bàillidh,
'S bheir mi dàil 'sa chòrr dheth dhut.'

26

Cha n-fhaighinn o Fhear nan Cliabh
Ach 'sìochair'' agus 'rògaire'.

27

Nuair bu mhiann liom bhith dol dhachaigh,
Nochd an Clachair 's streòdag air.

28

'Cuimhnich air beagan bha eadaruinn,
Gu bheil e deiseil dhòmhs' agad.'

29

Thànaig an Griasaiche air fhiaradh,
Is bha droch-bhial gu leòr aige.

30

Thànaig an Tàilleir a nall
'S gun d'fhuair mi dram o'n òganach.

31

'Cuimhnich air a' bheagan thasdan
Bh'agam ort o'n bhònuiridh?'

32

Thànaig an *Traveller* Gallda,
Srann aig a chuid chleòcannan.

33

Gu robh deàrrsa as a bhrollach
Agus lainnir as a bhòtainnean.

34

'S ann a thuirt e rium 'sa Bheurla:
'*You must pay the whole of it!*'

125

35
'S ann thuirt an Gobha rium le truas—
'Gur olc do thuar 's cha neònach liom.'

36
'Cha n-eil mis' an diu 'nam éiginn,
Gléidh fhéin e ma bhios còrr agad.'

37
Gun sheas a' Bhainfhigheach as mo chionn
'Thoir dhomh mo chrùn, a rògaire!'

38
Riob an Dotair mi o m' chùlaibh,
Ghabh mi null a chòmhradh ris.

39
'Leathchrùn air son banochdach Chaluim,
Is mo shalaraidh còmhla ris!'

40
Dh'fhàg mi uaislean ann an dìochuimhn',
'S cha do dh'iarr iad gròt orm.

41
Maighstir Teàrlach Ghearraidh Bhailteis,
Agus Alasdair Dòmhnallach,

42
Rob Fearghustan, Fear an Droma,
Domhnall *Clark* 's Fear Bhòirnis.

43
Fiachan o bhliadhna gu bliadhna,
Ac' air son sìol is clòimh orm.

44
Bho nach dànaig a' Bhean Ghlùine
Chuir e iùnadh mór orm.

*Translation*

*Chorus:* Hug oireann ò ro hùraibh ò, the matter is not agreeing with me, hug oireann ò ro hùraibh ò.

1. I arose early the day of the fair, heavy was my step and it was not surprising. New potatoes and a plate of shell-fish my love put on the table for me.

3. I went off with the little drab brown stirk to see if I could find a drover for him. I waited until evening. The price was not suiting me. I sat down in a little heathery glen beside one of the drovers. When I saw who was coming towards me it caused me great worry.

7. The big factor was in a hurry to claim his rights. He put the ground-officers on the watch in case I should run off from him to the moor. 'Remember to come to me to-morrow with the rent in your pocket for me, and a part of the old "arrears" along with it just as surely. Remember the Act is in my favour. No more delay will you get.'

12. The Poor-Law officer (Rate Collector) came with a little pocket-book of morocco. 'Unless you pay me this minute you will not get a vote at all.' The meal-merchant came with accounts in his hand. He spoke in a shaking voice: 'Have you anything at all for me? If you don't pay the whole sum I can't give you any more.'

17. The tea-merchant came and indeed he did not please me. 'You gave something to the rest though you have not a farthing for me.' He wanted a debt that my mother owed since I was a wee boy.

20. Then came the cotton goods merchant. He had a bottle and we drank some of it. It seems to me he said he had a right to £12.

22. The joiner shouted to me in a hurry: 'Come here for a word, young man. To-day you promised you would see me right. Give a pull on your pockets.'

24. The man that had given me a stack (of fodder) in the spring—he was a while with me. 'Give me a pound to pay the factor and I will give you delay over the rest of it.'

26. All I got from the creel-maker was 'sneak' and 'rogue'. When I wanted to go home the mason appeared, slightly under the weather. 'Remember to have it ready for me, the wee thing that was between us.' The shoemaker sidled up and he had plenty of abuse for me.

30. The tailor came over and I had a dram from the fellow. 'Remember the few shillings that you owed me since the year before last?'

32. The commercial traveller came, his cloaks a-rustling. There was a brightness on his chest and a shine on his boots. He said to me in English, 'You must pay the whole of it!'

35. The smith spoke to me in pity: 'You look bad, and no wonder. I am not in need to-day. Keep what you have if there's anything left.' Then the weaveress stood over me: 'Give me my crown, you rogue!'

38. The doctor plucked me from behind. I went across to speak to him. 'A half-crown for Calum's vaccination and my salary along with it.'

40. I forgot the gentry and they did not ask a groat from me. Mr. Charles (MacLean) of Garryvaltos and Alasdair MacDonald (his manager), Rob Ferguson tacksman of Drimore, Donald (MacLean) clerk (to the Factor), and the Tacksman of Bornish (John Ferguson). (There were) debts I owed them for seed and wool from year to year.

44. That the midwife did not come caused me great surprise.

The words and air were given by Roderick MacDonald (Ruairi am Posta), Lochboisdale. The scene of the song is the cattle-sale held at Gerinish, South Uist, and the words were composed by Ronald Laing (Raghnall Clachair), Dalibrog. It has been printed in *MacTalla*, Vol. VI, No. 14. The tune is traditional and was used by Mrs. Kennedy Fraser for 'The Hebridean Sea Reiver's Song', Vol. I, p. 118.

**Mode:** Pentatonic 2:6.

# ÒRAIN BHEAGA—LITTLE SONGS

## 25 BIDH SÌOR-CHAOINEADH—I

Bidh sìor-chaoineadh am beinn, am beinn,
Bidh sìor-chaoineadh am beinn a' cheò.
Bidh sìor-chaoineadh am Beinn Dòbhrain,
'S gaol mo chridh' am beinn a' cheò.

*Translation*

There is constant wailing in the hill, in the hill,
There is constant wailing in the hill of the mist,
There is constant wailing in Beinn Dòbhrain,
And the love of my heart in the hill of the mist.

From Angus John Campbell, South Lochboisdale. There are somewhat similar words to another tune in the Tolmie Collection, No. 11, where there is a note by Dr. George Henderson which describes the wailing as being *a' ghaoir-uisge* or *a' ghairm-uisge*, which is heard in the mountains (it is heard in Beinn Mhór, South Uist). 'A long, continuous murmuring sound, like the cry of a child in pain. It is very eerie in its rise and fall and may last for ten minutes. It is a natural phenomenon, and is a forerunner of wind and rain.' Beinn Dòbhrain is noted for this woeful cry. In an article by Mrs. Mary MacKellar called 'The Sheiling', printed in *T.G.S.I.*, Vol. XIV, p. 140, there are three verses printed which are said to belong to this song; she regards it as a cattle song sung at the sheiling. Also in K. N. MacDonald, *Puirt-a-Beul*, p. 46.

Mode: Mixolydian.

## 26  BIDH SÌOR-CHAOINEADH—II

*Bidh sìor-chaoin-eadh am beinn, am beinn, Bidh sìor-chaoin-eadh am beinn a' cheò, Bidh sìor-chaoin-eadh am Beinn Dòbh-rain. 'S gaol mo chridh' am beinn a' cheò .*

From Mrs. Iain Campbell, South Lochboisdale.

See preceding, and also a version of the air in sol-fa in an article by Calum Mac Pharlain on 'The Bagpipe and the Gael' in *Guth na Bliadhna*, Vol. V, p. 369.

Mode: Hexatonic, no 4th.

## 27 CHOLLA, MO RÙIN

Cholla, mo rùin, seachainn an Dùn,
Tha mise 'n làimh, tha mise 'n làimh;
Cholla, mo ghràidh, seachainn an t-àit',
Tha mise 'n làimh, tha mise 'n làimh.

A bhràthair ghaolaich, ghlac iad mi,
A bhràthair ghaolaich, ghlac iad mi,
A bhràthair ghaolaich, ghlac iad mi,
'S mi 'nam ònar,[1] ghlac iad mi.

*Translation*

Colla, my love, keep away from the fort,
I am a prisoner, I am a prisoner.
Colla, my love, keep away from the place,
I am a prisoner, I am a prisoner.

Loving brother, they have caught me,
Loving brother, they have caught me,
Loving brother, they have caught me,
I am alone, they have caught me.

[1] 'Ònar' was sung, though the rhyme requires 'aonar'.

# LITTLE SONGS

From Miss Mary Smith, South Boisdale, 1948. This is a pibroch (compare tune in *Gesto Collection*, p. 75, under the title 'Pibroch of Dunnybeg', 1647). *T.G.S.I.*, Vol. II, p. 20, contains six verses with a note from the Rev. Robert MacGregor, Kilmuir, Skye. J. L. Campbell also recorded it from Mrs. J. B. Johnston in Beaver Cove, Cape Breton, Nova Scotia, and from Miss Mary Morrison in Barra. The words to Miss Smith's song are slightly similar to the fifth and sixth verses of a pibroch printed with words and music in Donald Campbell's *A Treatise on the Language, Poetry and Music of the Highland Clans*. His note on the tradition is that this pibroch was played by the piper to Colla Ciotach (MacDonald), who 'landed in a party on Islay in an advance expedition from Ireland with instructions to take the Castle of Dun-a-berty by surprise, should he find the Campbells off their guard'. But the Campbells were warned, and captured the party, hanging all but the piper. He asked leave to play his pipes, and the Campbell chieftain, being fond of music, permitted him. His pibroch gave a warning to the expedition of what had happened, and though the Campbell chieftain, realizing what had been done, stabbed the piper, the MacDonalds in their birlinns who had waited for the word to go ashore heard the warning and made their escape. Also in *Celtic Monthly*, III, p. 188.

Mode: Six note compass.

## 28 DÀ LÀIMH 'SA PHÌOB

Dà làimh 'sa phìob, làmh 'sa chlaidheamh,
Dà làimh 'sa phìob, làmh 'sa chlaidheamh,
Dà làimh 'sa phìob, làmh 'sa chlaidheamh,
'S truagh an diugh bhith gun trì lamhan!

*Translation*

Two hands to the pipe, and a hand to the sword,
Two hands to the pipe, and a hand to the sword,
Two hands to the pipe, and a hand to the sword,
Sad to-day that I am without three hands!

Miss Annie MacDonald (Lochboisdale), Canna, 1948. This tune is said to have been played by the piper who endeavoured to explore through an uncharted cave while accompanied by his dog. This story is well known throughout the west. The dog emerges at the far opening hairless and the piper is never seen again. But at one stage of his journey a woman above the ground hears him playing this air under the earth. See the Tolmie Collection, pp. 157-160, for songs entitled 'Uamh an Òir'. Also in K. N. Mac-Donald, *Puirt-a-Beul*, pp. 44 and 47.

Lord Archibald Campbell in his *Records of Argyll*, p. 173, says that this tune was played on the pipes by a MacDougall at the Battle of Allt Dearg between the Campbells and the MacDougalls in the thirteenth century.

Mode: Hexatonic, no 6th.

# LITTLE SONGS

## 29 MO THAOBH FODHAM

Mo thaobh fodham, m'fheòil a' lobhadh, Daol 'nam shùil, daol 'nam shùil:
Dà bhior' iar-uinn 'gan sìor-shiar-adh Na mo ghlùn, 'na mo ghlùn.

Mo thaobh fodham, m'fheòil a' lobhadh,
Daol 'nam shùil, daol 'nam shùil,
Dà bhior iaruinn 'gan sìor-shiaradh
'Na mo ghlùn, 'na mo ghlùn.

*Translation*

My side under me, my flesh rotting,
A beetle in my eye, a beetle in my eye,
Two sharp iron points always piercing
Into my knee, into my knee.

From Mrs. Agnes Currie, Lochboisdale.

In Lord Archibald Campbell's *Records of Argyll* there is an article by Alexander Carmichael entitled 'Beothail, Nighean Rìgh Lochlann' concerning the Island of Lismore. Beothail was the daughter of the king of Scandinavia, and she died at Lismore of a broken heart when her lover was killed in battle in the north. She composed a lament to ask that she be taken to Norway to be buried beside her lover among her own people, and this was eventually done. Dr. Carmichael collected nine couplets of this lament, of which two are similar to these printed here. In the *Gesto Collection*, Part 2, p. 29, is an air entitled 'Uamh an Òir' with two verses, and two lines of the second verse are similar to the first two lines printed here. It is the same type of tune. Miss Annie Johnston of Castlebay, Barra, an authority on Hebridean music and folklore, told me that 'Mo Thaobh Fodham', 'Cholla, mo Rùin' and 'Dà Làimh 'sa Phìob' are all associated with the 'Uamh an Òir' (the Piper's Cave) folk tale.

Mode: Five note compass, no 4th or 6th.

133

## 30 DÌRIDH MI STÙC NAN CREAG

*Fonn:* Dìridh mi stùc nan creag,
Teàrnaidh mi stùc nan creag,
Dìridh mi stùc nan creag,
'S muladach thà mi.

1. Chaidh an t-each fairis ort,
Chaidh an t-each fairis ort,
Chaidh an t-each fairis ort,
Phronn e do chnàmhan.

2. Och nan och, leag iad thu,
Och nan och, leag iad thu,
Och nan och, leag iad thu,
'N eabar a' ghàraidh.

3. 'S truagh nach e mise bh'ann,
'S truagh nach e mise bh'ann,
'S truagh nach e mise bh'ann,
'S bata math làidir.

### Translation

*Chorus:* I climb the pinnacle of the crag, I descend the pinnacle of the crag,
I climb the pinnacle of the crag, and melancholy am I.

1. The horse went over you, he crushed your bones.

2. Alas, alas, they threw you down in the mire of the enclosure.

3. It is a pity that I was not there, with a good strong stick.

# LITTLE SONGS

From Miss Peigi MacRae, North Glendale. The words are a fragment of a lament said to have been composed, with the tune, by Lady MacIntosh, whose husband was killed by being thrown from his horse on their wedding day. The poem is printed in Campbell's *Albyn's Anthology*, p. 42, and also in the *Killin Collection of Gaelic Songs*, p. 46, with a tune that is similar to the theme or *ùrlar* of the pibroch 'MacIntosh's Lament'. In a note in the introduction Mr. Stewart says: 'The lament is said to have been composed on the death, in the year 1526, of Lachlan, the fourteenth laird of MacIntosh. . . . The traditionary account is that this Lachlan MacIntosh possessed a black horse of great power and beauty, but which, it was predicted, would be the cause of its master's death. He rode it towards the church on his marriage day; but as it proved singularly unmanageable, he drew his pistol and shot it dead. Another horse—a piebald—was at once brought to him. On the return, the bride and her party went first, the bridegroom and his friends following; hence her lament that she was not present when the fatal accident occurred. When passing the body of the black horse the piebald shied so badly that MacIntosh was thrown and killed on the spot.' The first verse of Miss MacRae's is not in either of the other collections and her tune may well be a very early version. See also *Carmina Gadelica*, Vol. V, p. 346.

Mode: Hexatonic, no 6th.

## 31 CHUIR IAD MISE A DH'EILEIN LIOM FHÌN

Chuir iad mise a dh'eilein liom fhìn,
Chuir iad mise a dh'eilein liom fhìn,
Chuir iad mise a dh'eilein liom fhìn,
Eilein mara fada bho thìr.

Eilein mara fada bho thìr,
Eilein mara fada bho thìr,
Eilein mara fada bho thìr,
Fada, fada, fada bho thìr.

*Translation*

They sent me to an island by myself; an island in the sea far from land.
An island in the sea far from land; far, far, far from land.

Sung by Miss Peigi MacRae, at Boisdale House, January 1932. See also the poem with lines similar which is given in a paper to the *T.G.S.I.*, Vol. XXV, p. 334, by Mr. Alexander MacDonald on the subject of 'Poetry and Folklore of Lochness Side'. Though Miss MacRae sang this as a *crònan*, I also heard a similar song with many lines sung as a waulking song, near Pollachar, South Uist. The air is obviously a pipe tune.

Mode: Ionian in C.

# TÀLAIDHEAN—LULLABIES

## 32  CHA BHI MI 'GAD THÀLADH

O bà, o bà, o bà, o ì,
O bà, o bà, o bà, o ì,
O bà, o bà, o bà, o ì.

Cha bhi mi 'gad thàladh
Bho'n shàraich thu mi.

*Translation*

O bà, o bà, o bà, o ì, I will not rock you to sleep, since you have worn me out.

From Miss Peigi MacRae, North Glendale, who described it as the sleepiest song she knew. A very similar tune, with different words, 'Chuir iad mise ghleann falaich' ('They sent me to a hidden glen'), was published by Miss Amy Murray in her book *Father Allan's Island*, p. 38. Fr. Allan McDonald had previously taken down the words from Mrs. R. O'Henly, Rudha Bàn, Eriskay, on 10th October 1896. Miss Murray's version of the air is also used in *Òrain Dà Ghuthach*, p. 7, for a modern song called 'Linn An Àigh'. See also K. N. MacDonald, *Puirt-a-Beul*, p. 43.

Mode: Aeolian.

## 33 'S E DIÙRAM, 'S E DIÙRAM

'S e Diùr-am, 's e Diùr-am, 's e Diùr-am hó ró, 'S e Diùr-am, 's e Diùr-am, 's e Diùr-am hó ì, 'S e Diùr-am a hù ri ri, ù ro bho ró, 'S e Diùr-am an t-uas-al Mac Ru-air-i nan ar(a)m. 'S e Diùr-am mac Iain 'ic Loch-lainn 'ic Ru-air-i, Air an d'fhàs an cùl clann-ach, 's e gu sleamh-uinn m'a ghual-ainn. Nuair a chì mi thu tigh-inn bidh mo chridh' air mo ghual-ainn, Ri Diùr-am mac Iain 'ic Loch-lainn 'ic Ru-air-i.

*Fonn:* 'S e Diùram, 's e Diùram, 's e Diùram hó ró,
    'S e Diùram, 's e Diùram, 's e Diùram hó ì,
    'S e Diùram a hù ri ri, ù ro bho ró,
    'S e Diùram an t-uasal, Mac Ruairi nan arm.

# LULLABIES

1. 'S e Diùram mac Iain 'ic Lochlainn 'ic Ruairi,
   Air an d'fhàs an cùl clannach, 's e gu sleamhuinn m'a ghualainn;
   Nuair a chì mi thu tighinn bidh mo chridh' air mo ghualainn,
   Ri Diùram mac Iain 'ic Lochlainn 'ic Ruairi.

2. Thug mise seachd bliadhna 's mi siubhal nam beann,
   Gun chù, gun ghille, gun duine ri m' làimh,
   Mi siubhal 's a' sireadh, bad breacain 'nam làimh,
   'S mi feitheamh ri tighinn Mhic Ruairi nan arm.

## Translation

*Chorus:* 'Tis Diùram, 'tis Diùram, 'tis Diùram,
     'Tis Diùram, the nobleman, MacRury of the weapons.

1. 'Tis Diùram, son of John, son of Lachlan, son of Roderick,
   Whose hair grew in ringlets, smoothly about his shoulders;
   When I see you coming my heart rises
       For Diùram, son of John, son of Lachlan, son of Roderick.

2. I spent seven years walking the hills,
   Without a dog, without a servant, without anyone at my hand,
   I walking and searching, a ragged plaid in my hand,
       Waiting for the coming of MacRury of the weapons.

The tune and chorus with two verses are from Mrs. John Currie (Peigi Nìll), North Glendale, 1933. My husband recorded a version of this song with both tune and words somewhat similar in Antigonish, Nova Scotia, sung by Angus MacDonald, known as 'Angus the Ridge'. The meaning of the title word 'Diùram' is unknown. Compare *Carmina Gadelica*, Vol. V, p. 330.

Mode: Ionian.

## 34  GILLE BEAG Ó, GILLE LAG Ó—I

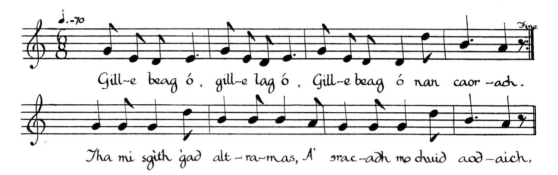

Gille beag ó, gille lag ó,
Gille beag ó nan caorach,
Gille beag ó, gille lag ó,
Gille beag ó nan caorach.

Tha mi sgìth 'gad altramas
    A' sracadh mo chuid aodaich.

Nam bu mhac duin' uasail thu
    Gu faighinn luach mo chaorach.[1]

*Translation*

Little lad ó, feeble lad ó,
Little lad, ó, of the sheep.

I am tired nursing you
Tearing my clothing.

If you were the son of a nobleman
I would get the value of my sheep.

From Mrs. Agnes Currie, Lochboisdale, 1947.

Mode: Pentatonic 3:6.

[1] 'Luach mo chaorach' is what the singer says, and insists on, although one might expect 'luach **mo** shaothrach' 'reward of my labour'.

## 35 GILLE BEAG Ó, GILLE LAG Ó—I!I

Gill-e beag ó -, gill-e lag ó, Gill-e beag ó nan caor-ach,

Gill-e beag ó -, gill-e lag ó Tha mi sgìth 'gad alt-ra-mas, A'

srac-adh mo chuid aod-aich. Gill-e beag ó —

From Mrs. Iain Campbell, South Lochboisdale.

For a version or relative tune in print of these three songs entitled 'Gille Beag Ó' see the Simon Fraser of Knockie Collection, No. 9, p. 14, entitled 'Giullan nam Bó' or 'The Cowboy'.

Mode: Hexatonic, no 3rd.

## 36 GILLE BEAG Ó, LEANABH LAG Ó

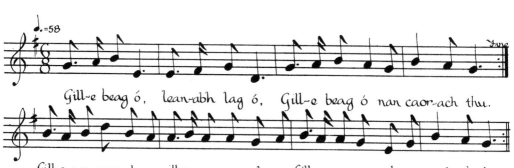

Gill-e beag ó, lean-abh lag ó, Gill-e beag ó nan caor-ach thu.

Gill-e nan caor-ach-an, gill-e nan caor-ach-an, Gill-e nan caor-ach-an, gaol-ach thu.

Gille beag ó, leanabh lag ó,
Gille beag ó nan caorach thu;
Gille beag ó, gille lag ó,
Gille beag ó nan caorach thu.

Gille nan caorachan, gille nan caorachan,
Gille nan caorachan, gaolach thu.

*Translation*

Little boy ó, weak little babe ó,
You are the little boy of the sheep.

Little boy of the sheep, little boy of the sheep,
Little boy of the sheep, my darling you are.

From Miss Peigi MacRae, North Glendale, 1947, who learned it from her mother.

Mode: Hexatonic, no 4th.

## 37  BÀ, BÀ, MO LEANABH BEAG

Bà, bà, mo lean-abh beag, Bidh tu mór ged tha thu beag,

Bà, bà, mo lean-abh beag, Cha n'urr-ainn mi 'gad thàl-adh.

Dé, a ghaoil, a nì mi ruit, Gun bhainn-e cìch-e a-gam dhut?

Eag-al orm gun gabh thu crup Le buig-ead a' bhun-tàt- a

Bà, bà, mo leanabh beag,
Bidh tu mór ged tha thu beag,
Bà, bà, mo leanabh beag,
   Cha n-urrainn mi 'gad thàladh.

Dé, a ghaoil, a nì mi riut
Gun bhainne cìche agam dhut?
Eagal orm gun gabh thu crup
   Le buigead a' bhuntàta.

*Translation*

Bà, bà, my little babe,
You will be big although you are wee,
Bà, bà, my little babe,
   I am not able to soothe you.

What, love, will I do for you,
For I have no breast milk for you?
I fear that you will get the croup
   From the softness of the potatoes.

The tune and words from Mrs. Agnes Currie, Lochboisdale, and Miss Peigi MacRae. This lullaby may have been composed at the time of the potato famine in 1848, when conditions in the Highlands and the Isles were nearly as dreadful as in Ireland. For a nearly identical tune see 'Mo Ghille Dubh' (old Skye air) in the *Gesto Collection*, part 2, p. 8. Another version of the tune set to words by Henry Whyte under the same title is in *Òrain a' Mhòid*, Vols. I and VIII. See also *Carmina Gadelica*, Vol. V, p. 134.

Mode: Pentatonic 4:7.

## 38 O BÀ, MO LEANABH, O BÀ, O BÀ

O bà, mo lean-abh, o bà, o bà, O bà, mo
lean-abh, o bà, o bà, O bà, hi rì, hill ù, ill
o ro, Gun thill na fear-a chaidh bhuainn gu sàil.

O, 's iom-adh cruaidh-fhort-an bha lor-(o)g nam brathan, 'S gu robh mo
chuid-sa dheth 'na mo làimh; Mo lean-abh gun bhaist-eadh, 's mi
fhìn fo'n uir-eas, O, 's iom-adh sgial duil-ich r'a sheinn, r'a sheinn.

*Fonn:* O bà, mo leanabh, o bà, o bà,
O bà, mo leanabh, o bà, o bà,
O bà, hi rì, hill ù, ill o ro,
Gun thill na feara chaidh bhuainn gu sàil.


O, 's iomadh cruaidh-fhortan bha lorg nam brathan,
'S gu robh mo chuid-sa dheth 'na mo làimh:
Mo leanabh gun bhaisteadh, 's mi fhìn fo'n uireas,
O, 's iomadh sgial duilich r'a sheinn, r'a sheinn.

144

# LULLABIES

*Chorus:* O bà, my baby, o bà, o bà; o bà, my baby, o bà, o bà;
O bà, hi rì hill ù, ill o ro; the men who went away from us to sea have
returned.

Many a hard fortune follows women, and I have had my share of it;
My baby unbaptized, and I in want; o, there is many a sad tale to
tell.

A lullaby from Mrs. John Currie (Peigi Nìll), North Glendale, October 1935. There
is a similarity between this song and 'Ba-ba, Mo Leanabh' in Miss Tolmie's Collection,
No. 8. Also compare the tune of the same title in Captain Fraser of Knockie's Collection,
No. 79; Dr. K. N. MacDonald's *Puirt-a-Beul*, p. 43, where it is called a 'Lochaber Lullaby'.
See also the words printed in *An Gàidheal*, Vol. 2, p. 168; *MacTalla*, Vol. IV, No. 36.
I published this song in the *J.E.F.D.S.S.*, Vol. IV, p. 155.

Mode: Aeolian.

## 39  O BÀ O Ì, Ó MO LEANABH

O bà o ì, ó mo lean-abh, Ba, o ì, ó – mo ghaol,

Chaid-il thus-a shùgh mo chéill-e, Gum-a slàn a dh'éir-eas tu.

Gal-ar dubh-ach deur-ach bròn-ach, Ead-ar a léin-e 's a còt-a,

Air an té thug bhuam-sa 'n t-òig-ear, Gur e mi fhìn a b'fheàrr còir air

*Fonn:*  O bà o ì, ó mo leanabh,
　　　　  Bà o ì, ó mo ghaol,
　　　　  Chaidil thusa shùgh mo chéille,
　　　　  Guma slàn a dh'éireas tu.

1. Galar dubhach, deurach, brònach,
   Eadar a léine 's a còta,
   Air an té thug bhuam-sa 'n t-òigear,
   Gur e mi fhìn a b'fheàrr còir air.

2. Galar dubhach 'sa cheann-adhairt
   'S e bhith tighinn daonnan 'ga tadhal,
   Air an té thug bhuam mo raghainn
   'S mi fhìn seachd bliadhna 'ga thaghadh.

3. Galar a bhios air na mucan
   Nuair a bhios 'ad làn dha 'n t-saill,
   Siod a bhith air bean mo leannain
   'San fhìor-aineoil[1] fada thall.

[1] *Sic*, though one would expect *'San tìr aineoil*, the pronunciation of which would be different in South Uist dialect.

146

# LULLABIES

*Translation*

*Chorus:*  O bà o ì, ó my babe, bà o ì, ó my darling,
Thou hast slept, my dearest,
Healthy thy waking be.

1. Miserable, wretched, tearful disease between her shirt and coat
   On the one who lured the young man to whom I had better right.

2. Black disease on the pillow and (it) always attacking
   The one who lured my chosen one whom I chose for seven years.

3. The disease that affects pigs when they are full of fat,
   May that afflict the wife of my lover, and she far away in a strange land.

From Mrs. Agnes Currie, Lochboisdale. A mother curses her rival who has taken away the father of her child. There is a similarity between this tune and 'Òran Cadail na Bothan-Àirigh', p. 103, in *Father Allan's Island* (Eriskay), collected there by the author, Miss Amy Murray.

Mode: Six note compass.

# 40 THÀLAIDHINN THU

Nam bu liom fhìn thu, thàlaidh-inn thu, Nam bu liom fhìn thu, thàlaidh-inn thu, Nam bu liom fhìn thu, thàlaidh-inn thu, Thàlaidh-inn, thàlaidh-inn, thàlaidh-inn thu, Nam bu liom fhìn thu, lean-abh mo chìch-e — Nam bu liom fhìn thu, thàlaidh-inn thu, Thàlaidh-inn, thàlaidh-inn, thàlaidh-inn thu.

Nam bu liom fhìn thu, thàlaidhinn thu,
Nam bu liom fhìn thu, thàlaidhinn thu,
Nam bu liom fhìn thu, thàlaidhinn thu,
Thàlaidhinn, thàlaidhinn, thàlaidhinn thu.

Nam bu liom fhìn thu, leanabh mo chìche,
Nam bu liom fhìn thu, thàlaidhinn thu,
Thàlaidhinn, thàlaidhinn, thàlaidhinn thu.

### Translation

If you were mine own I would soothe you
I would soothe, I would soothe, I would soothe you.

If you were mine own, babe of my bosom,
If you were mine own I would soothe you,
I would soothe, I would soothe, I would soothe you.

# LULLABIES

From Miss Peigi MacRae, who learnt it from her mother. I published this song in the *J.E.F.D.S.S.*, Vol. IV, p. 154. There is a more modern version of the tune with the same chorus and two verses printed in *Modern Gaelic Bards*, p. 241, with the note that it was contributed by Henry Whyte (Fionn), who got it from Sheriff Nicolson, who again got it from the Rev. John MacDonald at his manse in Harris in 1865. 'The *tàladh* is supposed to have been sung by a good fairy, who having entered a house found a baby sleeping in a cradle, its mother having evidently deserted it.' This same modern tune is printed in *Coisir a' Mhòid*. Another tune very similar to Miss MacRae's is printed in *Eilean Fraoich*, p. 34, under the title 'Banaltrum Shunndach', also a lullaby. There is sometimes a weak hiatus audible in 'thàlaidh'inn' which might be two or three syllables.

Mode : Pentatonic 3:6.

## 41 THA MÌLE LONG AIR CUAN ÉIRINN

1. Tha mìle long air cuan Éirinn,
   Tha mìle long air cuan Éirinn,
   Tha mìle long air cuan Éirinn,
   'S truagh nach robh mi fhìn air té dhiubh.

   *Fonn:* Ho bà ba é, ho ba a bà e,
   Ho bà ba é, ho ba bà e,
   Ho bà ba é, ho ba a bà e,
   Ho bà, ho bà, bà é, bà e.

2. Ho ì ho à, crodh an tàilleir: *(trì uairean)*
   Siosar is miaran is snàthad.

3. Cha tuit iad an toll no 'm féithe, *(trì uairean)*
   Ma thuiteas, gun tog e fhéin iad.

# LULLABIES

4. Gur binn guth eòin 'san deagh-mhaduinn *(trì uairean)*
   Gu cur a' ghille òig 'na chadal.

5. Tog dhìom do làmh, tha i fuar liom, *(trì uairean)*
   Rìgh! gur beag orm fear fuadain.

*Translation*

1. There are a thousand ships on the Irish Sea,
   Pity that I were not on one of them.

2. Ho ì ho à, the tailor's cattle
   (Are) scissors, thimble and needle.

3. They will not fall into a hole or bog,
   And if they do he will lift them out himself.

4. Sweet is the voice of a bird on a fine morning
   For putting the little boy to sleep.

5. Lift your hand from me, it is cold to me,
   O King, little I care for a stranger.[1]

The tune, chorus and first three verses from Miss Peigi MacRae and the last two verses from Mrs. Agnes Currie. See Mrs. Kennedy Fraser's *Songs of the Hebrides*, Vol. IV, Introduction, p. viii, for slightly similar tune entitled 'Hero Keening'.

Mode: Pentatonic 4:7.

[1] or, Light o' love.

## 42 TÀLADH CHOINNICH ÒIG

Fail iù fail eò hi ù ho ró, Fail iù fail eò, hill-inn o ho, Ho hi ho ró, ho hi ibh ó A Mhac Coinn-ich, na biodh gruaim ort, Cha do ghlac do mhàth-air buar-ach, No plaid-e bhàn air a h-uachd-ar; Ach sìod-a dearg is stròl uain-e.

*Fonn:* Fail iù fail eò hi ù ho ró,
Fail iù fail eò, hillinn o ho,
Ho hi ho ró, ho hi ibh ó.

1. A Mhac[1] Coinnich, na biodh gruaim ort,
   Cha do ghlac do mhàthair buarach,
   No plaide bhàn air a h-uachdar,
   Ach sìoda dearg is stròl uaine.

2. 'S e Mac Coinnich fhuair an urram[1]
   A miosg nam morbhairean uile.
   Cheannaicheadh e fìon Baile Lunnainn,
   Each is dìollaid fo chuid ghillean.

3. A Mhac[1] Coinnich mhóir a Brathann,
   Mhic an t-seòid nach fhuiligeadh masladh:
   Cheannaicheadh tu fìon dha t'eachaibh
   'S crùidhean dha'n òr a chur fo'n casan.

[1] *Sic.*

# LULLABIES

4. Cha n-eil an Coinneach òg ach leanabh,
   Cha do rànaig e aois a sheanar—
   Marbhaiche 'n fhéidh air na beannaibh,
   Is coilich dhuibh air bàrr nam meangan.

## Translation

1. MacKenzie, do not be downcast, your mother never handled a cow fetter, or wore a white plaid[1], but red silk and green satin.

2. MacKenzie has gained honour amongst all the lords; he used to buy the wine of London town, and his servants rode on saddled horses.

3. Great MacKenzie of Brahan, son of the hero who would not endure contempt, you would buy wine for your horses and shoe their feet with horseshoes of gold.

4. Young Kenneth is but a babe. He has not reached the age of his grandfather—the killer of the deer on the mountain peaks and the black cock on the tops of the branches.

From Miss Peigi MacRae, North Glendale, who learnt it from her father, who was born on the Isle of Pabbay in the Sound of Harris, but whose people came from Kintail, the MacRae country. Compare the verses printed in *T.G.S.I.*, Vol. VII, p. 118, and the Glasgow University Magazine *Ossian*, where a version containing nine verses as well as these four is printed by Mr. Angus Matheson, M.A., from the Dornie MS. Mr. Matheson says the song was 'apparently composed by his nurse, probably a MacRae, to Coinneach Òg, son of Colin MacKenzie of Kintail'. Coinneach Òg was born in 1569. See also *T.G.S.I.*, Vol. XLI, pp. 318–320.

Mode: Dorian.

[1] 'The ancient dress wore by the women, and which is yet wore by some of the vulgar, called arisad, is a white plaid, having a few small stripes of black, blue, and red. It reached from the neck to the heels, and was tied before on the breast with a buckle of silver or brass, according to the quality of the person.'

Martin Martin, *A Description of the Western Islands of Scotland*, c.1695.

## 43 TÀLADH AR SLÀNAIR

Mo ghaol, mo ghràdh, is m'fheud–ail thu,
M'ionnt–as ùr is m'éibhn–eas thu, Mo mhac–an
àl–ainn ceut–ach thu, Cha n-fhiù mi fhéin bhith 'd dhàil.
A – le – lu – ia, A – le – lu – ia,
A – le – lu – ia, A – le – lu – ia.

**1.**

Mo ghaol, mo ghràdh, is m'fheudail thu,
M'ionntas ùr is m'éibhneas thu,
Mo mhacan àlainn ceutach thu,
Cha n-fhiù mi fhéin bhith 'd dhàil.
  Aleluia, Aleluia, Aleluia, Aleluia.

**2.**

Ged as leanabh dìblidh thu,
Cinnteach 's Rìgh nan Rìghrean thu,
'S tu 'n t-oighre dligheach, fìrinneach
Air Rìoghachd Dhé nan Gràs.

**3.**

Bu mhór sòlas agus ioghnadh
Buachaillean bochda nan caorach,
Nuair chuala iad na h-ainglean glaodhaich,
'Thàinig Slànair thun an t-saoghail.'

**4.**

'S tusa grian gheal an dòchais,
Chuireas dorchadas air fògairt;
Bheir thu clann-daoin' bho staid bhrònaich
Gu naomhachd, soilleireachd, is eòlas.

**5.**

Hosanah do Mhac Dhàibhidh,
Mo Rìgh, mo Thighearna, 's mo Shlànair,
'S mór mo shòlas bhith 'gad thàladh,
'S beannaichte am measg nam mnài mi.

# LULLABIES

1. My love, my dear, my darling Thou,
   My new treasure and my joy art Thou,
   My beautiful fair Son art Thou,
   I am unworthy to be near Thee.
   Alleluia, Alleluia, Alleluia, Alleluia.

2. Although Thou art a helpless babe,
   'Tis certain Thou art the King of Kings,
   Thou art the true and rightful heir
   To the Kingdom of the God of Graces.

3. Great was the wonder and the joy
   Of the poor shepherds of the sheep
   When they heard the angels proclaiming,
   'A Saviour has come into the world!'

4. Thou art the white sun of hope
   Who will banish darkness from us;
   Mankind Thou wilt redeem from sorrow
   To sanctity, light and knowledge.

5. Hosannah to the Son of David,
   My King, my Lord and my Saviour.
   Joyfully to sleep I lull Thee,
   Blessed amongst women am I.

This hymn is sung at Midnight Mass on Christmas Eve in South Uist and Eriskay. The words were written by Father Ranald Rankin, C.C., and given by him to the children of his congregation in Moidart when he was parting with them for Australia in 1855. The song has twenty-nine verses and was printed in the *Transactions of the Gaelic Society of Inverness*, Vol. XV (1889), and in the *Northern Chronicle*, 24 April 1889. It was also in the collection of Gaelic hymns that Father Allan McDonald had printed privately in 1893. The tune is like a waulking song of which the first line in some versions is 'An cuala sibh mar dh'éirich dhomh-sa?' Fr. Allan McDonald calls the tune of this hymn 'Cumha Mhic Àrois'.

Mode: Six note compass.

## 44 DIAN CADALAN

Dian cadalan, a shùgh mo chéille,
Dian cadalan ó, chagarain ó.
'S e 's fhaide liom gun iad réidh rium,
Dian cadalan, a shùgh mo chéille.

'S e 's fhaide liom bhith 'gad thàladh;
T'athair ag ràdh nach leis fhéin thu,
Dian cadalan, a shùgh mo chéille.

*Translation*

Go to sleep, my dearest darling, go to sleep, o little love. Weary am I that they are at enmity with me; go to sleep my dearest darling.

I feel it long soothing you, your father saying that you do not belong to him. Go to sleep, dearest darling.

From Mrs. Iain Campbell, South Lochboisdale, 1948. This was a difficult tune to write down, and it is not easy to revive it from paper. Mrs. Campbell sang it almost quickly and with lightness, a sad and beautiful little *crònan*.

Mode: Mixolydian.

# ÒRAIN BHLEOGHAINN—MILKING SONGS

## 45 'S E M'AGHAN FHÌN THU

'S e m'agh-an fhìn thu, 'S e m'agh-an fhìn thu, 'S e m'agh-an fhìn thu, 'S e m'agh-an donn. Nuair bhios buar-ach air crodh na dùthch-a, Bidh buar-ach ùr air m'agh-an donn.

*Fonn:* 'S e m'aghan fhìn thu,
'S e m'aghan fhìn thu,
'S e m'aghan fhìn thu,
'S e m'aghan donn.

Nuair bhios buarach air crodh na dùthcha
Bidh buarach ùr air m'aghan donn.

Nuair bhios buarach air crodh na tìre
Bidh buarach shìoda air m'aghan donn.

*Translation*

*Chorus:* Thou art my own little heifer,
My brown heifer.

When the cattle of the countryside are fettered
There will be a new fetter on my little brown heifer.

When the cattle of the land are fettered
There will be a fetter of silk on my little brown heifer.

From Mrs. Angus Currie (Anna Ruadh), South Lochboisdale. In Rev. T. Sinton's *Poetry of Badenoch*, p. 17, there is a poem slightly similar on the same theme; see also Mrs. Mary MacKellar's paper 'The Sheiling', published in the *T.G.S.I.*, Vol. XV, where there are four verses and an interesting note; *An Gàidheal*, Vol. II, p. 371, where there are three verses and the same chorus. The *buarach* or fetter is the rope that ties the hind legs of a cow to prevent her from kicking the pail when being milked.

Mode: Pentatonic 4:7.

# 46  A BHÓLAGAN, A BHÓ CHIÙIN

A Bhó-lag-an, a bhó chiùin, A Bhó-lag-an, a bho chiùin.

A bhó chridh-eag 'sa bhó ghràdh-ag. Cridh-eag nam bà, gabh ri d' laogh.

'N oidhch-e bha buach-aill' muigh Cha deach-aidh buar-ach air boinn,

Cha deach-aidh nuall a ceann laoigh, A' caoin-eadh buach-aill' a' chruidh.

*Fonn:*  A Bhólagan, a bhó chiùin,
A Bhólagan, a bhó chiùin,
A bhó chridheag 's a bhó ghràdhag,
Cridheag nam bà, gabh ri d' laogh.


1.  'N oidhche bha buachaill' muigh
Cha deachaidh buarach air boinn,
Cha deachaidh nuall a ceann laoigh
A' caoineadh buachaill' a' chruidh.


2.  'S e mo chuilean m'aghan fhìn;
Na faighinn mo shaghach làn,
Cha b'uilear a mhnaoi do chuim
Buachaille cuimichte ri sàil.


3.  'S iomadh buaile, bó gun laogh,
Cha déid dhachaigh, bó gun laogh,
Théid air chreachaibh, bó gun laogh,
Leum i 'n gàradh, bó gun laogh.

158

# MILKING SONGS

*Chorus:* Bólagan, gentle cow, Bólagan, gentle cow,
Dear little cow, beloved little cow,
Dearest of cows, take to your calf.

1. The night (the) herdsman was outside
   No fetter was put on a cow,
   No calf uttered a low
   Lamenting the herdsman of the cattle.

2. My own little heifer is my darling,
   If I got my milk-pail full,
   A female of thy form would need
   A careful herdsman at her heel.

3. 'Many a fold' is the calfless cow,
   'Won't go home' is the calfless cow,
   'Goes a-reiving' is the calfless cow,
   'Leapt the dyke' is the calfless cow.

A milking song from Mrs. Agnes Currie, Lochboisdale. The first verse is printed in Lord Archibald Campbell's *Records of Argyll*, p. 395, where the song was contributed with other milking songs of South Uist by Dr. Alexander Carmichael. See also *Carmina Gadelica*, Vol. I, pp. 266–7, and Vol. IV, pp. 56, 60.

Mode: Six note compass.

## 47 GAOL A' CHRUIDH

Gaol a' chruidh, gràdh a' chruidh, Gaol a' chruidh, 's lioms' thu,

Gaol a' chruidh, gràdh a' chruidh, Gaol a' chruidh, 's lioms' thu,

Gaol a' chruidh, gràdh a' chruidh, Gaol a' chruidh, 's lioms' thu,

Théid sinn a màir—each Gu àir—igh ni'n Fhionn—laidh.

Ged tha crodh chàich a muigh Cha robh m'agh donn-s'ann,

Ged tha crodh chàich a muigh Cha robh m'agh donn-s'ann,

Ged tha crodh chàich' a muigh Cha robh m'agh donn-s'ann,

Fuir(i)ghidh m'agh, fan-aidh m'agh, Fuir(i)ghidh m'agh riùm-sa.

# MILKING SONGS

*Fonn:* Gaol a' chruidh, gràdh a' chruidh, gaol a' chruidh 's liom-s' thu,
Gaol a' chruidh, gràdh a' chruidh, gaol a' chruidh 's liom-s' thu,
Gaol a' chruidh, gràdh a' chruidh, gaol a' chruidh 's liom-s' thu,
Théid sinn a màireach gu àirigh ni'n Fhionnlaidh.

Ged tha crodh chàich a muigh cha robh m'agh donn-s' ann,
Ged tha crodh chàich a muigh cha robh m'agh donn-s' ann,
Ged tha crodh chàich a muigh cha robh m'agh donn-s' ann,
Fuirghidh m'agh, fanaidh m'agh, fuirghidh m'agh rium-sa.

## Translation

Darling of the cattle, love of the cattle,
Darling of the cattle, you are mine.
We will go to-morrow to the sheiling of Finlay's daughter.

Though the rest of the cattle are outside,
My brown heifer is not there.
My heifer will wait, my heifer will stay,
My heifer will wait for me.

From Mrs. Iain Campbell, South Lochboisdale.

Mode: Ionian.

## 48  TILL AN CRODH, FAIGH AN CRODH—I

Till an crodh, faigh an crodh,
Till an crodh, Dhòmhnaill,
Till an crodh, faigh an crodh,
'S gheibh thu bean bhòidheach.

Till an crodh, laochain!
'S gheibh thu bean ghaolach,
Till an crodh, laochain!
'S gheibh thu bean bhòidheach.

*Translation*

Turn the cattle, go find the cattle, turn the cattle, Donald, and you will get a beautiful wife.

Turn the cattle, my lad, and you will get a loving wife, turn the cattle, my lad, and you will get a beautiful wife.

A milking song from Mrs. Agnes Currie, Lochboisdale, 1948.

Mode: Six note compass.

# 49 TILL AN CRODH, FAIGH AN CRODH—II

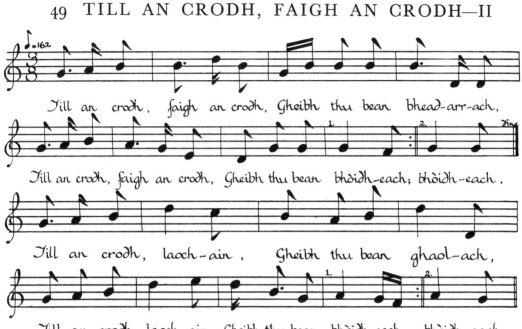

Till an crodh, faigh an crodh, Gheibh thu bean bhead-arr-ach,

Till an crodh, faigh an crodh, Gheibh thu bean bhòidh-each; bhòidh-each.

Till an crodh, laoch-ain, Gheibh thu bean ghaol-ach,

Till an crodh, laoch-ain, Gheibh thu bean bhòidh-each. bhòidh-each.

*Fonn:* Till an crodh, faigh an crodh,
Gheibh thu bean bheadarrach,
Till an crodh, faigh an crodh,
Gheibh thu bean bhòidheach.

Till an crodh, laochain,
Gheibh thu bean ghaolach,
Till an crodh, laochain,
Gheibh thu bean bhòidheach.

*Translation*

Turn the cattle, get the cattle,
You will get a playful wife.
Turn the cattle, get the cattle,
You will get a beautiful wife.
Turn the cattle, my lad,
And you will get a loving wife.
Turn the cattle, my lad,
And you will get a beautiful wife.

Mrs. Mary Ann Currie, South Lochboisdale.

Mode: Mixolydian.

## 50 TILL AN CRODH, FAIGH AN CRODH—III

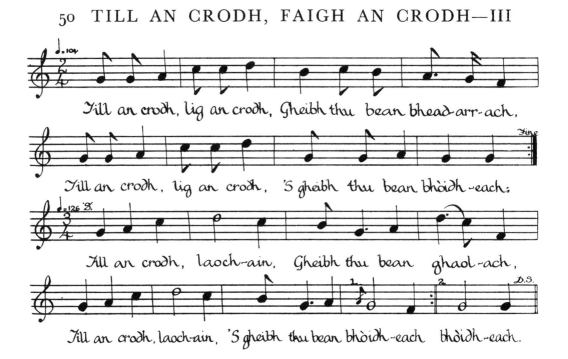

Till an crodh, lig an crodh, Gheibh thu bean bheadarrach,

Till an crodh, lig an crodh, 'S gheibh thu bean bhòidheach;

Till an crodh, laochain, Gheibh thu bean ghaolach,

Till an crodh, laochain, 'S gheibh thu bean bhòidheach bhòidheach.

From Miss Peigi MacRae, North Glendale.

Three versions of this tune. It is very well known that no two people sing it alike. The same type of tune with words nearly similar, except with 'Dhunnachaidh' for 'Dhòmhnaill', is printed in the Tolmie Collection, No. 28. See also D. Campbell's *Language, Poetry and Music of the Scottish Clans*, p. 275. Father Allan McDonald, Eriskay, collected the words from Angus MacInnes, Smerclet, South Uist, in 1896, and with it this note: 'A pipe tune. It is said to have been composed on the night when young Glengarry had gone to marry the MacKintosh's daughter. As everything was being got ready for the wedding feast word was brought that the cattle lifters were busy driving away the MacKintosh's cattle. The gentlemen at once started in pursuit of the reivers, and young Glengarry (Dòmhnall) distinguished himself. They brought back the cattle and went on with the marriage feast.'

Mode: Six note compass.

# ÒRAIN SHÌDHE—FAIRY SONGS

## 51 MO CHÙBHRACHAN

### I

O, shiubhail mi bheinn o cheann gu ceann, Bho thaobh gu taobh, gu taobh nan allt, O, shiubhail mi bheinn o cheann gu ceann, Ge tà, cha d'fhuair mi 'n cùbh-rach-an.

Mrs. Iain Campbell

52

### II

Fhuair mi lorg-(o)g an dòbhr-àin duinn, An dòbhr-ain duinn, an dòbhr-ain duinn. Fhuair mi lorg-(o)g an dòbhr-ain duinn, Cha d'fhuair mi lorg-(o)g mo chùbh-rach-an

Mrs. John Currie

165

53

III

Fhuair mi lor(o)g na lach' air an lòn, Na lach' air an lòn, na lach' air an lòn, Fhuair mi lor(o)g na lach' air an lòn, Cha d'fhuair mi lor(o)g mo chùbh-rach-ain.

Miss Màiri MacRae

1. O, shiubhail mi bheinn o cheann gu ceann,
   Bho thaobh gu taobh, gu taobh nan allt.
   O, shiubhail mi bheinn o cheann gu ceann,
   Cha d'fhuair mi lorg mo chùbhrachain.

2. Fhuair mi lorg an dòbhrain duinn,
   An dòbhrain duinn, an dòbhrain duinn,
   Fhuair mi lorg an dòbhrain duinn,
   Cha d'fhuair mi lorg mo chùbhrachain.

3. Fhuair mi lorg na h-eal' air an t-snàmh,
   Na h-eal' air an t-snàmh, na h-eal' air an t-snàmh,
   Fhuair mi lorg na h-eal' air an t-snàmh,
   Cha d'fhuair mi lorg mo chùbhrachain.

4. Fhuair mi lorg na lach' air an lòn,
   Na lach' air an lòn, na lach' air an lòn,
   Fhuair mi lorg na lach' air an lòn,
   Cha d'fhuair mi lorg mo chùbhrachain.

5. Fhuair mi lorg an laoigh bhric, dheirg,
   An laoigh bhric, dheirg, an laoigh bhric, dheirg,
   Fhuair mi lorg an laoigh bhric, dheirg,
   Cha d'fhuair mi lorg mo chùbhrachain.

6. Fhuair mi lorg na bà 'sa pholl,
   Na bà 'sa pholl, na bà 'sa pholl,
   Fhuair mi lorg na bà 'sa pholl,
   Cha d'fhuair mi lorg mo chùbhrachain.

7. Fhuair mi lorg a' cheò 'sa bheinn,
   A' cheò 'sa bheinn, a' cheò 'sa bheinn;
   Fhuair mi lorg a' cheò 'sa bheinn,
   Cha d'fhuair mi lorg mo chùbhrachain.[1]

*Translation*

1. O, I searched the hill from end to end, from side to side, to the edge of the streams. O, I searched the hill from end to end, I did not find my Cùbhrachan.[2]

2. I found the track of the brown otter, the brown otter, the brown otter; I found the track of the brown otter, I did not find my Cùbhrachan.

3. I found the track of the swimming swan, I did not find my Cùbhrachan.

4. I found the track of the wild duck on the pond, I did not find my Cùbhrachan.

5. I found the track of the spotted red fawn, I did not find my Cùbhrachan.

6. I found the track of the cow in the bog, I did not find my Cùbhrachan.

7. I found the track of the mist on the hill, I did not find my Cùbhrachan.

The cradle song is well known throughout the Highlands and Islands. It is sung by a mother whose child has been stolen by the fairies. I have given the three tunes from Mrs. Iain Campbell, Mrs. John Currie and Miss Màiri MacRae to show the contrast of the same song from the three near neighbours; the desperation of the first, the forlorn hope of the second and the despair of the third. There is a version of the tune with four of the verses printed in *Coisir na Cloinne*, p. 18, noted by M. N. Munro from Mrs. Malloch at Crianlarich. There is also a version in the Tolmie Collection, No. 12. The poem is printed in *An Duanaire*, p. 94, under the title 'An Còineachan', and there is an excellent version of ten verses printed in *The MacDonald Collection*, p. 326, with a note.

Mode: Mrs. Campbell—Irregular, no 4th or 6th.
      Mrs. Currie—Mixolydian.
      Miss MacRae—no 6th or 7th.

[1] Miss MacRae always ended her verse 'Ge tà, cha d'fhuair mi 'n Cùbhrachan' = 'And yet I did not find the little fragrant one.'
[2] Mo Chùbhrachan = My little fragrant one, a term of endearment for a little child.

## 54 CRODH CHAILEIN

Gun doir - eadh crodh Chail - ein am bainn - e do m'
ghaol , 's gun doir - eadh crodh Chail - ein am bainn - e do m' ghaol , 's gun
doir - eadh crodh Chail - ein am bainn - e do m' ghaol , Air
mull - ach a' mhun - aidh gun luinn - eag , gun laogh .

[1]1. Gun doireadh crodh Chailein am bainne do m' ghaol,
   'S gun doireadh crodh Chailein am bainne do m' ghaol,
   'S gun doireadh crodh Chailein am bainne do m' ghaol,
2. Air mullach a' mhunaidh gun luinneag, gun laogh.

   Air mullach a' mhunaidh gun luinneag, gun laogh, (*trì uairean*)
3. Crodh riabhach, breac, ballach air dhath nan cearc fraoich.

   Crodh riabhach, breac, ballach air dhath nan creac fraoich, (*trì uairean*)
4. Crodh lìonadh nan cuman 's crodh a thogadh na laoigh.

   Crodh lìonadh nan cuman 's crodh a thogadh na laoigh, (*trì uairean*)
5. Crodh Chailein, crodh Chailein, crodh Chailein mhic Cuinn.

   Crodh Chailein, crodh Chailein, crodh Chailein mhic Cuinn, (*trì uairean*)
6. 'S gun dugadh crodh Chailein am bainn' air an fhraoich.

[1] Each first line to be sung three times.

# FAIRY SONGS

*Translation*

1. Colin's cattle would give their milk to my beloved,

2. On the top of the moor without milking song or calf.

3. Brindled, speckled, spotted cattle, the colour of the grouse.

4. Cattle that would fill the milk pails and rear the calves.

5. The cattle of Colin, son of Conn.

6. Colin's cattle would give their milk on the heather.

From Miss Màiri MacRae, who learnt it from her mother, who came from the Island of Bernera in the Sound of Harris. Her story of the song was that Colin was a fairy whose cattle were the deer. His mortal sweetheart composed this song for their milking. In Mrs. Mary MacKellar's interesting papers entitled 'The Sheiling' which were published in *T.G.S.I.*, Vol. XV, p. 159, she says: 'The fairy race were said to milk the deer on the mountain tops, charming them with songs composed to a fairy melody.' I printed this song in the *J.E.F.D.S.S.*, Vol. IV, p. 152.

There are many versions of this tune, which is found in most collections of Gaelic or Highland songs, but the one most similar to Miss MacRae's is in the Kennedy Fraser Collection, Vol. IV, p. 114, entitled 'A Skye Milking Song'.

Many cows will not give their milk unless they are sung to during the milking and have their calf beside them. This explains the phrase 'gun luinneag, gun laogh' = without (milking) song or calf.

Mode: Six note compass.

## 55 A' GHAOIL, LIG DHACHAIGH GU M' MHÀTHAIR MÌ

*Fonn:* A ghaoil, lig dhachaigh gu m' mhàthair mi,
A ghràidh, lig dhachaigh gu m' mhàthair mi,
A ghaoil, lig dhachaigh gu m' mhathair mi,
Air tòir a' chrodh-laoigh a thàna mi.

1.

'S ann a raoir a chuala mi
Mo ghaol a bhith air a chuartachadh;
Ged thachair thu 'n iomall na buaile rium,
A ghràidh, lig dhachaigh mar fhuair thu mi.

2.

Ged bheireadh tu crodh agus caoirich dhomh,
Ged bheireadh tu eachaibh air thaodaibh dhomh
Ged bheireadh tu sin agus daoine dhomh,
A ghràidh, lig dhachaigh mar fhuair thu mi.

# FAIRY SONGS

*Translation*

*Chorus*: My love, let me home to my mother,
My love, let me home to my mother,
My love, let me home to my mother,
I had come to seek the milk-cattle.

1. It was last night that I heard
That my love had been surrounded;
Though you met me at the edge of the cattlefold,
My love, let me home as you found me.

2. Though you were to give me cattle and sheep,
Though you were to give me horses on halters,
Though you were to give me servants besides,
Love, let me home as you found me.

From Miss Peigi MacRae, North Glendale. Originally, the second line of verse 1 was probably 'gam chuartachadh' = 'visiting me' or 'searching for me'. This line varies in each version.

There is a version of this song in the *Gesto Collection*, p. 25, under the title 'Òran Sùgraidh', 'Courting Song'. My husband found a better version in the papers of the late Rev. George Henderson in Glasgow University Library, apparently taken down by Dr. Henderson in Uist about sixty years ago. This is called 'Còmhradh eadar Nighean Òg agus Each-Uisge' (a conversation between a young girl and a water-horse). As this version is more intelligible, I reproduce it with acknowledgment to Dr. Henderson:

*Fonn:* Ho ró, lig dhachaigh gu m' mhàthair mi (*trì uairean*)
'S ann a dh'iarraidh chrodh-laoigh a thàinig mi.

*Ise:* Gur h-ann a raoir a chuala mi
Mo ghaol a bhith ri buachailleachd,
'S ged fhuair thu'n iomall na buaile mi,
A ghaoil, lig dhachaigh mar fhuair thu mi!

*Esan:* Ged 's ann a raoir, *etc.*
Cha lig mi dhachaigh, *etc.*

*Ise:* 'S mi dìreadh ris na gàraidhean,
'S a' teàrnadh ris na fàirichean,
Gun d' thachair fleasgach bàidheil rium,
'S cha d'fheuch e bonn g'a chàirdeas rium.

*Esan:* 'S tu, *etc.*

*Ise:* Trodaidh mo phiuthar 's mo bhràthair rium,
Trodaidh mo chinne 's mo chàirdean rium,
Trodaidh m'athair 's mo mhàthair rium,
Mur déid mi dhachaigh mar thàinig mi.

*Esan:* Ged throdadh, *etc.*

171

# SONGS

## Translation

*Chorus:* Ho ró, let me home to my mother (*three times*),
'Twas to look for milk cattle that I came.

*She:* It was last night I heard
My love was a-herding,
And though you have found me beside the cattlefold,
My love, let me home as you found me!

*He:* Though it was last night that you heard
That your love was a-herding,
And though I have found you beside the cattlefold,
My love, I will not let you home as I found you.

*She:* I am climbing by the stone walls,
I am descending by the ridges,
A pleasant youth has met me
And has not shown me any friendship.

*He:* You are climbing, *etc.*

*She:* My sister and my brother will scold me,
My relations and my friends will scold me,
My father and my mother will scold me
Unless you let me home as I came.

*He:* Though your sister and your brother scold you,
Though your relations and your friends scold you,
Though your father and your mother scold you,
I will not let you home as you came.

The dialogue version of this song is almost certainly the correct traditional form. The girl has been sent to bring home the cattle for milking; possibly she expected to meet her own lover; a water-horse in human form has met her at the cattlefold, and is preventing her from returning home, detaining her against her will. In this context the second verse sung by Miss Peigi MacRae ought probably to be put in the mouth of the fairy lover. See also *Carmina Gadelica*, Vol. V, p. 162. A version of the air is printed in Seumas Munro's *Am Filidh* (1840) on p. 10 of the Appendix.

Mode: Mixolydian.

# PUIRT A BIAL—VOCAL DANCE MUSIC

## 56  A CHAORAIN, A CHAORAIN!

A chaor-ain, a chaor-ain, buail-idh mi 'sa chlaig-ionn thu, A chaor-ain, a chaor-ain, cnag-aidh mi 'sa cheann thu. A chaor-ain, a chaor-ain, buail-idh mi 'sa chlaig-ionn thu, Buail-idh mi 'sa chlaig-ionn thu mur-a las thu 'n lamp-a!

A chaorain, a chaorain, buailidh mi 'sa chlaigionn thu,
A chaorain, a chaorain, cnagaidh mi 'sa cheann thu,
A chaorain, a chaorain, buailidh mi 'sa chlaigionn thu,
Buailidh mi 'sa chlaigionn thu mura las thu 'n lampa!

*Translation*

Little peat, little peat, I will knock your crown for you,
Little peat, little peat, I will crack your head for you,
Little peat, little peat, I will knock your crown for you,
I will knock your crown for you if you don't light the lamp.

From Miss Annie MacDonald, Lochboisdale.

Mode: Major.

## 57  A' CHAORA CHROM

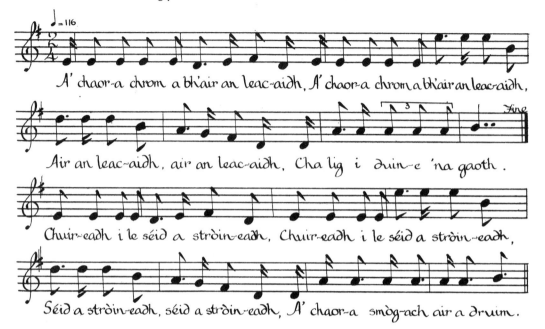

1. A' chaora chrom a bh'air an leacaidh,
   A' chaora chrom a bh'air an leacaidh,
   Air an leacaidh, air an leacaidh,
     Cha lig i duine 'na gaoth.[1]

2. Chuireadh i le séid a stròineadh,
   Chuireadh i le séid a stròineadh,
   Séid a stròineadh, séid a stròineadh,
     A' chaora smògach air a druim.[2]

3. Tha bainn' aig na caoirich uile,
   Tha bainn' aig na caoirich uile,
   Caoirich uile, caoirich uile,
     Galan aig a' chaora chruim.

4. Tha uan aice urad ri gamhain,
   Tha uan aice urad ri gamhain,
   Tha uan aice urad ri gamhain,
     'S e cho sleamhain ris an im.

[1] 'na gaoth = 'na còir, near her.
[2] smògach = pet name meaning clumsy or big-pawed.

# VOCAL DANCE MUSIC

*Translation*

1. The crooked-horned ewe which was on the flat rock, she will not let a man near her.

2. She would put with a snort from her nose the clumsy-footed ewe on her back.

3. All the sheep have milk, but the crooked-horned ewe has a gallon!

4. She has a lamb as big as a stirk, and as slippery as butter.

From Miss Peigi MacRae, North Glendale. The tune has some resemblance to 'An t-Each Odhar' in this book. The words date from the time when ewes' milk was taken. Poems with a verse or line similar have been published in the following: *MacTalla*, Vol. V, p. 222; *An Gàidheal*, No. 6, p. 204; *T.G.S.I.*, Vol. XIX, p. 84, where the 'Caora Chrom' has another meaning—a whisky still—and Vol. XXI, p. 32, of the same society.

Mode: Hexatonic, no 6th, weak 3rd.

## 58 CAS NA CAORA HIORTAICH, Ò!

Cas na caor-a Hiort-aich ò! Hiort-aich Hiort-aich, Hiort-aich ò! Cas na caor-a Hiort-aich ò! B'e siod a' chas sgiob-alt-a Siod a' chaor-a bha grinn Dh'fhàs-adh an dath air a druim. Cha n-iarr-adh i crot-al no suith Ach snìomh na clòimh gu briog-ais-ean.

*Fonn:* Cas na caora Hiortaich, ò!
Hiortaich, Hiortaich, Hiortaich, ò!
Cas na caora Hiortaich, ò!
B'e siod a' chas sgiobalta.

1. Siod a' chaora bha grinn,
Dh'fhàsadh an dath air a druim.
Cha n-iarradh i crotal no sùith
Ach snìomh na clòimh gu briogaisean.

2. Siod a' chaora bha luath
Nuair a thigeadh i mun cuairt,
Cha robh h-aon anns an taobh tuath
An uair sin chuireadh it' aisde.

3. Chaidh an t-uan leis fhéin
Null ann an siod leis an spréidh,
Sin nuair a chaidh ise 'na béist,
Nuair theann a séin ri gliogadaich.

176

4. Siod a' chaor' anns an robh sgèan[1]
Cha do chleachd i bhith air sliabh;
'S ann aig baile bha i riamh,
'S grinn am fiar a dh'icheadh i.

*Translation*

*Chorus:* The foot of the Hirta[2] sheep, ò!
Hirta, Hirta, Hirta, ò!
The foot of the Hirta sheep, ò!
That was the nimble foot.

1. That was the elegant sheep, the colour would grow on her back. She would require neither lichen nor soot (for dyeing), but to spin the wool for trousers.

2. That was the sheep that was swift, whenever she would come around not one on the north country could 'pull a feather out of her' (keep up with her).

3. The lamb went by himself over yonder with the cattle, that is when she became violent, when her chain began to rattle.

4. That is the sheep that was angry, she was not accustomed to be on the hill. She was always at home and lovely would be the grass she would eat.

From Miss Peigi MacRae, North Glendale, 1948. There is a pipe tune in the Gesto Collection, p. 30, entitled 'Òran Hirteach' or 'St. Kilda Song', with chorus in imitation of birds. The first eight measures are obviously this same song. It has a note that it is 'Miss Cameron's Set'. In the Kennedy Fraser *Songs of the Hebrides*, Vol. IV, introduction, p. xx, there is a love-song of four measures from the Isle of Eigg which is closely related to this tune.

The Caora Hiortach of the song is the Soay sheep, which is the St. Kilda local breed of sheep. They look like a cross between a deer and a goat, having long legs, a long neck and a shorter tail than the mainland sheep. They are very swift and can leap great heights—so the praise in the song of the 'nimble foot'. As they are too wild to gather, dogs were trained to catch hold of them, and the St. Kildan, instead of clipping, plucked the fleece by hand. The wool is fine and soft and of a light brown colour known as 'moorit'. As the song says, it would require no dye, only to spin it for the trousers.

Mode: Dorian.

[1] 'She was wild (angry) after being shifted to the hill from the low ground,' explained the reciter.
[2] Hirta = St. Kilda.

## 59 OCH, OCH, OCH, OCH, OCH, MAR A THÀ MI

Och, och, och, och, och, mar a thà mi,
Ged tha mise 'sa chùil dhuibh, cha n-ann air son na meàirle,
Och, och, och, och, och, mar a thà mi,
Am flùr a bh'air an truinnsear, 's an t-im a bh'air an t-sàbhsair,
Och, och, *etc.*
An coileach dubh 's an coileach geal 's an coileach a bha àlainn,
An dithist a bha eireachdail a dh'eireagan a' Ghàidseir,
Nan cuireadh iad dha'n phrìosan mi, cha b'ann air son na meàirle.

*Translation*

Och, och, och, och, och, alas for my condition,
Though I am in a dark corner, it is not for theft,
The flour that was on the dish, and the butter that was on the saucer,
The black cock and the white cock and the beautiful cock,
The handsomest pair of pullets that belonged to the Exciseman,
If they would put me in prison, it wasn't for theft.

# VOCAL DANCE MUSIC

The tune and first two lines from Miss Peigi MacRae, 1954. The last three lines were noted in Benbecula, from Mrs. Patrick MacCormick, the same year. The song is supposed to be made by a cat, who was suspected of having stolen the food and poultry mentioned.

Mode: Six note compass, no 7th.

# 60 AN RÀCAN A BH'AGAINNE

An ràc-an a bh'ag-ainn-e, Na meàrl-aich a thach-air ris, An
ràc-an a bh'ag-ainn-e. 'S e Chall-uinn thug am bàs dha.

Chaidh e null air an lòn, Chaidh e shuir-(i)gh' air na h-eòin,

Thug mi sgrìob air a thòir, 'S gòr-ach a bhà mi.

'S iom-adh rud a rinn e riamh, Creid-idh mi gu robh e fìor,

Tunn-ag-an a chaidh am fiadh, 'S iad-san a shàbh-ail e.

*Fonn:* An ràcan a bh'againne,
Na meàrlaich a thachair ris,
An ràcan a bh'againne,
 'S e Challuinn thug am bàs dha.

 1. Chaidh e null air an lòn,
Chaidh e shuirgh' air na h-eòin;
Thug mi sgrìob air a thòir,
 'S gòrach a bhà mi.

180

2. 'S iomadh rud a rinn e riamh,
   Creididh mi gu robh e fìor,
   Tunnagan a chaidh am fiadh,
      'S iadsan a shàbhail e.

3. Chaidh e null air an loch,
   Chaidh a phunndadh 'sa *spot*,
   Lùbadh e a's a' phoit,
      Phlodadh gu bàs e.

4. Gheibh sinn dìnneir a nochd
   Nach do rinneadh leithid am poit;
   'N crotal thug mi far na cloich'
      'S clòimh na caora Spàintich.

## *Translation*

*Chorus:* The drake we used to have, thieves happened on him; the drake we used to have, Hogmanay was the occasion of his death.

1. He went over across the pond, he went courting the birds; I took a turn looking for him. 'Tis foolish that I was.

2. Many a thing that he ever did; I believe it was true that the ducks that went wild, 'tis they that saved him.

3. He went over across the loch, he was pounded on the spot, doubled up inside the pot, and finished off by being boiled.

4. We'll get a dinner to-night, the like of which was never made in a pot; crotal I got off the rocks, and wool from the Spanish sheep.

From Miss Peigi MacRae, North Glendale. A dance tune with words to commemorate a drake whose gay life was ended by thieves for the feast of Hogmanay.

Mode: Hexatonic, no 6th.

## 61 BODACHAN A MHILL ANNA

Bodachan a mhill Anna, mhill Anna, mhill Anna,
    Bodachan a mhill Anna, bidh e air an daoraich.

Bidh e air an dallanach, an dallanach, an dallanach,
    Bidh e air an dallanach a bharrachd air an daoraich.

Cha n-fhaic thu trì gearrain a' treabhadh a' sgrìob earraich,
    An t-iomlan air druim Annaig 's i tarraing a' mhaoraich.

# VOCAL DANCE MUSIC

*Translation*

The old man that Anna spoilt, that Anna spoilt, that Anna spoilt,
The old man that Anna spoilt, he is always drunk.

He is blind, blind, blind drunk,
Blind drunk as well as foozled!

You will not see three geldings ploughing the spring furrow,
(But) the burden on Anna's back carrying shellfish.

From Mrs. Agnes Currie, North Lochboisdale. *Cf.* K. N. MacDonald, *Puirt-a-Beul*, p. 19.

Mode: Mixolydian.

## 62  DANNS' A BHRIGI, DANNS' A BHOCAI!

Danns' a bhrig-i, danns' a bhoc-ai, Danns' a bhrig-i, a chait bhàin,

Danns' a bhrig-i, danns' a bhoc-ai, Bha thu raoir an taigh Iain Bhàin.

Danns' a bhrig-i, danns' a bhoc-ai, Danns' a bhrig-i, a chait bhàin.

Ù a hu a, ù a hu a, 'S geal do shùil-ean, a chait bhàin.

Danns' a bhrigi, danns' a bhocai,
Danns' a bhrigi, a chait bhàin!
Danns' a bhrigi, danns' a bhocai,
Bha thu 'n raoir an taigh Iain Bhàin!

Danns' a bhrigi, danns' a bhocai,
Danns' a bhrigi, a chait bhàin!
Ù a hu a, ù a hu a,
'S geal do shùilean, a chait bhàin!

Danns' a bhrigi, danns' a bhocai,
Danns' a bhrigi, a chait bhàin!
Danns' a bhrigi, danns' a bhocai,
Bidh thu nochd an taigh Iain Bhàin!

# VOCAL DANCE MUSIC

*Translation*

Dance the breeks, dance the bucks,
Dance the breeks, white cat!
Last evening you were at fair John's house.

Dance the breeks, dance the bucks,
Dance the breeks, white cat!
Ù a hu a, ù a hu a,
Bright are your eyes, white cat!

Dance the breeks, dance the bucks,
Dance the breeks, white cat!
To-night you will be at fair John's house.

From Mrs. Agnes Currie, Lochboisdale, 1948.

Mode: Mixolydian.

## 63 DO CHROCHADH A THOILL THU

Do chroch-adh a thoill thu, thoill thu, Do chroch-adh a
thoill thu, Mhàir-i;  Do chroch-adh a thoill thu, thoill thu,
Rinn thu rud nach d'rinn do mhàth-air.  Dh'òl thu 'm bainn-e
bha a's a' mhios-air, Bhrist thu 'm miod-ar 's a' mhias sàbh — a,
'Sa dh'ain-dheoin 's na shùigh an t-ìvl-ar, Bha lùin an cùil a' bhun-tà-ta.
Uig-ead-ar, ag-ad-ar, o-thoill, o-thoill. Uig-ead-ar, ag-ad-ar, o-thoill, o-thoill,
Uig-ead-ar, ag-ad-ar, o-thoill, o-thoill, Dh'òl thu 'm bainn-e raoir, a Mhàir-i.

# VOCAL DANCE MUSIC

1. Do chrochadh a thoill thu, thoill thu,
   Do chrochadh a thoill thu, Mhàiri;
   Do chrochadh a thoill thu, thoill thu,
   Rinn thu rud nach d'rinn do mhàthair!

2. Dh'òl thu 'm bainne bha a's a' mhiosair,
   Bhrist thu 'm miodar 's a' mhias sàbha;
   'S a dh'aindheoin 's na shùigh an t-ùrlar,
   Bha lùin an cùil a' bhuntàta.

3. Uigeadar, agadar, othoill, othoill,
   Uigeadar, agadar, othoill, othoill,
   Uigeadar, agadar, othoill, othoill,
   Dh'òl thu 'm bainne raoir, a Mhàiri.

*Translation*

1. You deserved, you deserved to be hanged!
   You deserved to be hanged, Mary!
   You deserved, you deserved to be hanged!
   You did something your mother never did!

2. You drank the milk that was in the dish,
   You broke the churn and the gravy plate:
   And in spite of what the floor sucked up
   There were pools in the potato corner.

3. Uigeadar, agadar, othoill, othoill,
   You drank the milk last night, Mary.

From Mrs. John Currie, North Glendale.

Mode: Hexatonic, no 3rd.

187

## 64 M'ITEAGAN IS M'EÒIN IS M'UIGHEAN

M'iteagan is m'eòin is m'uighean,
Mo chrodh-laoigh ri taobh mo thaigh';
Le m'iubhair, le m'archair, le m' bharrgha dubh ciarach,
Gu siubhlainn an oidhche fo bhrìgh nam beann àrda
Le m'àilleagan cùmhraidh,
Ho ró, m'ulaidh, hé, m'ulaidh, cead torrach troighlich.
A Ruairi, bu chorrach thu;
A liùbhan, a leòbhan, bha uair a ghabhainn òran,
A liùbhan, a leòbhan, cha ghabh mi nochd ach gnòmhan.

188

*Translation*

My little feathers, my birds, and my eggs, my breeding cattle beside my house; with my bow, with my [                    ], with my black dusky spear-point [?], I would walk the night under the mountain [?] of the high hills with my sweet jewel, ho ro my treasure, he my treasure [                                              ]. Rory, you were quick-tempered; alas, alas, once I used to sing, alas, alas, to-night I can only groan.

From Mrs. John Currie, North Glendale. Obscure; possibly corrupt.

The late Mrs. Neil Campbell, sister of Angus MacLellan ('Aonghus Beag'), Frobost, who died in 1970 at the age of 102, told my husband, who recorded many old songs from her, that this song was the *crònan* (croon) made by the well-known seventeenth-century poetess Mary MacLeod (Mairi nighean Alasdair Ruaidh) on the *maide bhuinn* (threshold) when she was forbidden to make songs inside or outside the house. (12/6/63).

## 65 FACA SIBH OIGHRIG?

1. 'Faca sibh Oighrig?'
   Ars an Gob, ars an Gob.

2. 'Có bha 'ga foighneachd?'
   Ars an Gob, ars an Gob.

3. 'An té a bh'air na h-éibhlean,'
   Ars an Gob, ars an Gob.

4. 'Teapot Oighrig!'
   Ars an Gob, ars an Gob.

*Translation*

1. 'Have you seen Euphemia?' said the Spout,[1] said the Spout.

2. 'Who was asking for her?' said the Spout, said the Spout.

3. 'The one that was on the hot embers,' said the Spout, said the Spout.

4. 'Euphemia's teapot!' said the Spout, said the Spout.

From Miss Peigi MacRae, North Glendale, 1947.

Mode: Pentatonic 4:7.

[1] Nickname for a woman with a long nose.

# 66 Ó EADAR AN DÀ CHRAICIONN!

Ó! eadar an dà chraicionn, eadar an dà bhalg!
Eadar an dà bhoicionn, dà chraicionn, dà bhalg!
Thug e 'm boicionn leis a' chraicionn,
'S thug e 'n craicionn leis a' bhalg,
Thug e 'm boicionn leis a' chraicionn,
Leis an drip a bh'air a' falbh.

*Translation*

Ó! between the two skins, between the two bags!
Between the two hides, two skins, two bags!
He took the hide with the skin,
He took the skin with the bag,
He took the hide with the skin
With his hurry to be away.

From Mrs. John Currie (Peigi Nìll). See note to Hogmanay Ballads, p. 23.

Mode: Four note compass.

## 67 Ó M'ULAIDH, M'ULAIDH ORT

Ó m'ul-aidh, m'ul-aidh ort, Cha nfhaigh a h-uil-e té do phòg.

Ó m'ul-aidh, m'ul-aidh ort, Cha nfhaigh a h-uil-e té do phòg.

Ó m'ul-aidh, m'ul-aidh ort, Cha nfhaigh a h-uil-e té do phòg.

J ho ro mo Niall-ach-an, An gabh thu 'm bliadh-na nigh-ean 'n Òir,

J ho ro mo Niall-ach-an, An gabh thu 'm bliadh-na nigh-ean 'n Òir.

J ho ro mo Niall-ach-an, An gabh thu 'm bliadh-na nigh-ean 'n Òir.

J ho ro mo Niall-ach-an, An gabh thu 'm bliadh-na nigh-ean 'n Òir.

Ó m'ul-aidh, m'ul-aidh ort, Cha nfhaigh a h-uil-e té do phòg.

# VOCAL DANCE MUSIC

Ó m'ulaidh, m'ulaidh ort,
Cha n-fhaigh a h-uile té do phòg;
Ì ho ro mo Niallachan,
An gabh thu 'm bliadhna nighean 'n Òir?

*Translation*

O my treasure, my treasure art thou,
Not every woman would get your kiss;
Ì ho ro my little Niall,
Will you take the wealthy maid this year?

From Miss Peigi MacRae, North Glendale.

Mode: Mixolydian.

## 68  Ó HO NA RIBEINEAN

Ó ho na ribeinean,
Na ribeinean, na ribeinean,
Ó ho na ribeinean,
    A thug an gille ruadh dhomh.

Faca sibh an currac ud,
Fasan th'air a' mhullach aic'?
'S ann tha fàth a' mhulaid aig
    An té nach urrainn fhuasgladh.

*Translation*

Ó ho, the ribbons, the ribbons, the ribbons,
Ó ho, the ribbons that the red-haired laddie gave to me.

Did you see that cap, the fashion which is on her head?
The woman who cannot undo it has cause for grief.

From Miss Peigi MacRae, North Glendale, 1935.

Compare tune in *Coisir nan Cloinne*, p. 12, entitled 'Dòmhnall Bàn nan Gobhar'.

Mode: Hexatonic, no 6th.

# 69 'S COMA LIOM BUNTÀTA CARRACH

'S coma liom buntàta carrach gus an déid a sgrìobadh,
'S coma liom buntàta carrach gus an déid a sgrìobadh,
'S coma liom buntàta carrach gus an déid a sgrìobadh,
'S coma liom an déidh a phronnadh gus an déid an t-ìm air.

*Translation*

I don't like scabby potatoes until they have been scraped,
I don't like them mashed until there is butter on them.

From Miss Annie MacDonald, Lochboisdale.
Last line, 'phronnadh' was sung, but metre suggests the form originally used was 'phrannadh'.

Mode: Hexatonic, no 6th.

## 70 THA T'ATHAIR AIR AN DAORAICH

Tha t'athair air an daoraich,
'S mo ghaol an gille beag ruadh.

'S e mo ghille laghach, laghach,
'Se mo ghille laghach, ruadh.

# VOCAL DANCE MUSIC

*Translation*

Your father is drunk, my love is the little red laddie;
He's my nice, nice laddie, my nice auburn-haired laddie.

From Miss Peigi MacRae, North Glendale.

Mode: Mixolydian.

# 71 THUIRT AN GOBHA 'FUIRICHEAMAID'

Thuirt an gobh-a "fuir-ich-eam-aid" Thuirt an gobh-a "fal-(a)bh-am-aid",

Thuirt an gobh-a ris a' ghobh-a, 'S a bhean an dor-us an t-sobhail.

Hill i ò am min-im bó am, 'S ann a chaidh i iom-(a)-rall.

Gheall o hó min-im bó am, Bó hann-a, bó hann-a, bó am.

Gheall o hó min-im bó am, Bó hann-a bó hill-e-an.

Mur-a faigh sinn car-(a)bh-an-aich, Mur-a faigh sinn car-(a)bh-an-aich,

Mar sin is liùgh-ag-an glas-a Chum-as an dubh-an ó'n fheam-ainn

Bheir-ea-maid greis air an tarr-ainn, Na mair-eadh na duir-(a)gh dhuinn,

# VOCAL DANCE MUSIC

Gheall a hó min-im bó am, Bó hann-a, bó hann-a bó am

Gheall o hó min-im bó am, Bó hann-a bó hill-e-an

1. Thuirt an gobha 'fuiricheamaid',
Thuirt an gobha 'falbhamaid',
Thuirt an gobha ris a' ghobha,
'S a bhean an dorus an t-sobhail;
Hill i ò am minim bó am,
'S ann a chaidh i iomrall.
Gheall o hó minim bó am,
Bó hanna, bó hanna bó am,
Gheall o hó minim bó am,
Bó hanna bó hillean.

2. Mura faigh sinn carbhanaich,
Mura faigh sinn carbhanaich,
Mar sin is liùghagan glasa
Chumas an dubhan o'n fheamainn,
Bheireamaid greis air an tarrainn,
Na maireadh na duirgh dhuinn.
Gheall o hó minim bó am,
Bó hanna, bó hanna, bó am,
Gheall o hó minim bó am,
Bó hanna bó hillean.

*Translation*

1. The smith said, 'Let us stay'; the smith said, 'Let us go',
The smith said to the smith, with his wife in the door of the barn;
Hill i ò am minim bó am, 'tis how she went astray,
Gheall o hó minim bó am, bó hanna, bó hanna, bó am
Gheall o hó minim bó am, bó hanna bó hillean.

2. Unless we get bream, unless we get bream,
And likewise little grey lythe that will keep the hook from the seaweed,
We would spend a while pulling them in, if our handlines would last.
Gheall o hó minim bó am, bó hanna, bó hanna bó am
Gheall o hó minim bó am, bó hanna bó hillean.

From Miss Peigi MacRae, North Glendale, 1934.

I have heard other versions in South Uist and Barra, some of which J. L. Campbell has recorded. See also K. N. MacDonald, *Puirt-a-Beul*, p. 12.

Mode: Dorian.

## 72 THOGAIL A' BHUNTÀT'!

1. Orra[1] bhuinneagan, a ghaoil,
    Orra bhuinneagan, a ghràidh,
   Orra bhuinneagan, a ghaoil,
    Théid thu thogail a' bhuntàt.'

2. O, cha lig mi thu dha'n tobar,
    O, cha lig mi thu dha'n tràigh,
   O, cha lig mi thu dha'n tobar,
    Ach a thogail a' bhuntàt'.

[1] Orra = air do (Uist dialect).

3. Hé, orra bhonna, bhonna,
    Hé, orra chorra-chnàmh,
    Hé, orra bhonna, bhonna,
    Théid thu thogail a' bhuntàt'.

*Translation*

On your little feet, my love, on your little feet, my darling,
On your little feet, my love, you will go to lift the potatoes.

O, I won't let you go to the well, o, I won't let you go to the shore,[1]
O, I won't let you go to the well, but to lift the potatoes.

Hé! on your feet, hé on all fours,
Hé! on your feet, you will go to lift the potatoes.

From Miss Peigi MacRae, North Glendale, 1934.

See Kennedy Fraser, *Songs of the Hebrides*, Vol. IV, p. 16; also the tune in the *Gesto Collection*, p. 142, where it is called 'Miss Jessie MacLeod's Favourite'; *An Gàidheal*, June, 1954.

Mode: First and third parts Pentatonic 3:7; second part Hexatonic, no 3rd.

[1] *I.e.* to collect shellfish.

# ÒRAIN SNÌOMHAIDH—SPINNING SONGS

## 73 CUIGEAL NA MAIGHDIN

1. Cuigeal na maighdin,
Cuigeal na maighdin,
Stocain air bhiorain,
An t-snighe 'ga froighneadh.
Cuigeal na maighdin,
Cuigeal na maighdin.

2. Caidil, a leanabain,
Caidil, a leanabain,
Cha n-eil mir' agam-sa
Am pòca no 'm balgaibh.
Caidil, a leanabain,
Caidil, a leanabain.

3. Caidil, a leanabain,
Caidil, a leanabain,
Cha do shnìomh thu 'n clò bàn,
'S tu 'nad thàmh fad na h-oidhche;
Caidil, a leanabain,
Caidil, a leanabain.

# SPINNING SONGS

1. The distaff of the maiden, the distaff of the maiden,
   A stocking on knitting pins, while sooty drops ooze
     (from the rafters).

2. Sleep, little baby, sleep, little baby,
   Not a morsel have I in bag or in sacks.

3. Sleep, little baby, sleep, little baby,
   You did not spin the white cloth, you were asleep the night long.

From Mrs. Agnes Currie, Lochboisdale.

A song for spinning with the distaff. Peat soot gathers in the black houses, which are those with the fire in the centre of the floor and which have no chimney. The vent was built not directly over the fire, which would allow the rain to put it out, but to the side. Consequently in certain weather when the smoke would not be drawn it would hang about the rafters, and the soot in time became like soft tar. The *snighe* of the song are the drops of this.

Mode: Pentatonic 3:7.

## 74 HO RÓ GUN TOGAINN AIR ÙGAIN FHATHAST

*Fonn:* Ho ró gun togainn air ùgain fhathast,
Hó hi ù mun déid mi laighe,
Ho ró gun togainn air ùgain fhathast.

1. Cha robh pluc, no meall, no gaog ann,
No gìog chaol, no sliasaid reamhar.

2. Beannachd aig an làimh a shnìomh e,
'S i rinn gnìomh na deagh-bhean-taighe.

*Translation*

*Chorus:* Ho ró, I would raise an 'ùgain' on it yet,
Hó hi ù, before I go to rest,
Ho ró, I would raise an 'ùgain' on it yet.

1. There was in it not a knot, or lump, or thin yarn,
Or small prickle of teasle, or thick, coarse thread.

2. A blessing on the hand that spun it,
It did the work of a good housewife.

From Miss Peigi MacRae, North Glendale, who sang it as she spun. The chorus and two verses are from the well-known waulking song by Duncan Ban MacIntyre, see Angus MacLeod's edition, p. 146.

Mode: Mixolydian 3:6.

## 75  ÒRAN SNÌOMHAIDH

O hi rì, hó ro bho o hug ó, O hi rì, hó ro bho o hug ó.

O hi rì hi rì bhù Ai li ri bhi o ro bhó, O hi rì, ho ro bho ho, o hug ó.

A spinning lilt from the Rev. Murdo MacLeod, Dalibrog, South Uist. He heard it in his youth in Skye. I published this tune in the *J.E.F.D.S.S.*, Vol. IV, p. 196.

Mode: Hexatonic, no 3rd, weak 6th.

# ÒRAIN LUADHAIDH—WAULKING SONGS

The Waulking Songs in this book are given in the order in which they might naturally be sung at a waulking. For classification according to structure of chorus and verse, as well as a description of waulking itself, see pages 6 and 72–4.

## 76 CLÒ NAN GILLEAN

Iom-air o hó, clò nan gill-ean, Iom-air o hó, clò nan gill-ean, Iom-air o hó, clò nan gill-ean. Bho dhòrn gu dòrn, clò nan gill-ean. Iom-air o hó.

*Fonn:* Iomair o hó, clò nan gillean,
Iomair o hó, clò nan gillean,
Iomair o hó, clò nan gillean.

1. Bho dhòrn gu dòrn, clò nan gillean,

    Luaidheam gu luath, clò nan gillean,

    Luaidheam le sunnd, clò nan gillean,

    Seinn le gaol, clò nan gillean,

5. Cuir an roladh, clò nan gillean.

# WAULKING SONGS

*Translation*

*Chorus:* Waulk, o hó, the cloth of the lads. (*three times*)

1. From hand to hand, the cloth of the lads,

   Let me waulk quickly, the cloth of the lads,

   Let me waulk with joy, the cloth of the lads,

   Sing with love, the cloth of the lads,

5. Put into a roll, the cloth of the lads.

From Miss Peigi MacRae, North Glendale, and Miss Annie MacDonald, Lochbois-dale.

The tune, chorus and first two verses from Miss Peigi MacRae; the last two verses from Miss Annie MacDonald. There are lines of this song under this title in the Tolmie Collection, No. 65. See also the Kennedy Fraser Collection, Vol. I, p. xxiv of introduction, for similarity in tune.

Mode: Six note compass, no 7th.

# 77 ÉILEADH 'S NA HÙRAIBH O HO!

*Fonn:* Éileadh 's na hùraibh o ho, a hu o ho.

1. Fliuch an oidhche, a hu o ho,
   Éileadh 's na hùraibh o ho,
   Nochd 's gur fuar i, a hu o ho,
   Éileadh 's na hùraibh o ho,
   Nochd 's gur fuar i, a hu o ho,
   Éileadh 's na hùraibh o ho,

2. Cha n-eil cùram, a hu, *etc.*,   orm na buaile, a hu, *etc.*,
   No cùram cruidh   laoigh ri uallach,
   Ach do chùram-s'   ghaoil, a Ruairi.

5. Thug am bàta   bàn an cuan oirr',
   Mo leannan air   bòrd a fuaraidh,
   Làmh air an stiùir   air bàrr stuaghan,
   Làmh cheangal nam   ball 's g'am fuasgladh;
   Cha b'fhear cearraig   bheireadh bhuat i,

10. No fear làimheadh   deise 's fuachd air,
    No lasgaire   do dhuin' uasal.
    Guma slan dha'n   t-saor a dh'fhuaigh i,
    Dh'fhàg e dìonach   làidir luath i,
    Aigeannach gu   siubhal cuan i,

15. 'S iomadh sgeir dhubh   air na bhuail i,
    Agus liathagan   liath a ghluais i,
    Agus duileasg   donn a bhuain i,
    Agus bàirneach   ghlas a ghluais i.

# WAULKING SONGS

*Translation*

1. Wet is the night and cold, it is not the care of the cattlefold, nor care of herding cows with calves that weighs upon me, but anxiety about you, Roderick, my love. 5. The white boat has put to sea with my love on her weather-board. His is the hand to grasp the rudder on the crest of the waves, his the hand for tying and loosening the ropes. 9. It is no left-handed man who would take it from you, nor is it a right-handed man who feels the cold, nor a sprig of a nobleman. 12. Well may it go with the carpenter who nailed her together. He made her watertight, strong and swift; and spirited to traverse the sea. On many a black reef has she scraped, many a grey tangle root has she stirred; many (a tuft of) brown dulse has she reaped; many a grey limpet has she dislodged.

From Mrs. Iain Campbell, Miss Mary Smith and Miss Peigi MacRae. There is a closely related tune in 3/4 time with chorus and with nine lines similar in the Tolmie Collection, No. 76. The poem is also printed in *The MacDonald Collection*, p. 263, and in K. C. Craig's *Òrain Luaidh*, p. 43.

Mode: Five note compass.

## 78 CHA DÉID MI LIOM FHÌN 'NA MHÒINTICH

*Fonn:* Hug ó ro nan ho ì a bhó,
Cha déid mi liom fhìn 'na mhòintich,
Hug ó ro nan ho ì a bhó.

1. Cha déid mi liom fhìn dha'n bhuailidh,
   Cha robh siod 'na bhuanachd dhòmhsa.

2. Latha dhomh 's mi falbh na Leacaich,
   Thachair an lach' is na h-eòin rium.

3. Fhir mhóir nan calpannan geala,
   Rinn thu mo mhealladh 's mi gòrach;

4. Chuala mi gu robh do mhàthair
   'Gam chàineadh, cha n-e mo shòlas.

5. Ach ged ghabh thu ormsa seachad
   Chunntadh m'athair crodh òg dhut.

6. Dìridh mi mullach na beinne,
   Chì mi 'n t-eilein am bheil thu còmhnuidh.

7. 'S gura mise tha fo mhulad
   Tha leann-dubh orm an còmhnuidh.

210

# WAULKING SONGS

## Translation

*Chorus:* Hug ó, *etc.* I will not go alone to the moor.

1. I will not go by myself to the cattlefold; that was not any benefit for me. 2. The day that I was walking on the stony hillsides I came across the wild duck and the ducklings. 3. O tall man of the white calves, you deceived me when I was foolish. 4. I heard that your mother was abusing me; that was no pleasure for me. 5. But though you passed me by, my father would have counted young cattle for you. 6. I shall climb to the top of the mountain, I shall see the island where you dwell. 7. And I am sorrowful, melancholy dwells with me always.

From Miss Màiri MacRae and Miss Annie MacDonald. The chorus and eight lines of this song are similar to the poem in K. C. Craig's *Òrain Luaidh*, p. 16.

Mode: Pentatonic 2:6.

## 79 DH'ÉIRICH MI RO' BHIAL AN LATHA

*Fonn:* Hi rì rì ill ù ill o ro,
É hoireann ó, ho ro eile,
Hi rì rì ill ù ill o ro.

Dh'éirich mi ro' bhial an latha
A choimhead an eòrna bh'aig m'athair,
Chunna mi grùnn mór do dh'aighean.

*Translation*

I arose before the dawn
To watch my father's barley,
I saw a great herd of heifers (? hinds) there.

From Mrs. Mary Steele, Kildonan, South Uist, 1948. A fragment. Compare lines with those in poem in *The MacDonald Collection*, p. 261. There is a complete version of the words in the papers of the late Fr. Allan McDonald, and a shorter one in K. C. Craig's *Òrain Luaidh*, p. 45. In both cases the opening line is 'Fliuch an oidhche nochd 's gur fuar i'.

Mode: Hexatonic, no 3rd.

# 80 'S E MO LEANNAN CALUM GAOLACH

'S e mo leann-an Cal-um gaol-ach, Hoir-eann ó ho ri ho ró,

'S e mo leann-an Cal-um gaol-ach, Hoir-eann ó ho ri ho ro ho.

'S e mo leannan Calum gaolach,
Hoireann ó ho ri ho ró,
'S e mo leannan Calum gaolach,
Hoireann ó ho ri ho ro ho.

Cha do laigh e 'n raoir fo m' aodach,

Cha laigh e nochd ann ma dh'fhaodas,

Fhad 's a chumas clach is aol e,

'S e mo leannan Calum gaolach.

### Translation

Beloved Calum is my sweetheart. He did not lie under my bedclothes last night. He will not lie there to-night if stone and lime (the walls) will keep him out. Beloved Calum is my sweetheart.

From Miss Peigi MacRae, North Glendale. Fragment only. Compare with No. 68 in the Tolmie Collection. Each line sung twice followed by a different phrase of the chorus.

Mode: Hexatonic, no 7th.

## 81 'S MULADACH MI 'S MI AIR M'AINEOIL

*Fonn:* Illean ó ró ho ró.
    É ho ù hi ri ó,
    Thog a bhó, illean ó ró ho ró.

1. 'S muladach mi 's mi air m'aineoil (*soloist*)
    Illean ó ró ho ró.[1] (*chorus*)

2. Latha dhomh 's mi falbh a' ghleannain,
    É ho ù hi ri ó, (*soloist*)
    Thog a bhó, illean ó ró ho ró. (*chorus*)

    Latha dhomh 's mi falbh a' ghleannain,
    Illean ó ró ho ró.

3. Thachair ormsa còmhlan fhearaibh
    É ho ù hi ri ó,
    Thog a bhó, *etc.*

    Thachair ormsa còmhlan fhearaibh,
    Illean, *etc.*

    Dh'fhoighneachd iad dhìom có dhiu leanainn?
5. Leanaidh mi Mac Fir-a'-Bhaile
    Dh'an do lùb mi glùn gu talamh,
    'S dh'an do shil mo chìochan bainne,
    Sealgair geòidh thu, ròin is eala,
    'S a' bhric a nì leum 's an fhéidh nì langan.

[1] Occasionally this line of the chorus is sung twice.

214

# WAULKING SONGS

*Translation*

Sad am I and I in a strange place,
One day as I went through the little glen,
I met a company of men,
They asked of me which of them I would follow?
I will follow the son of the Tacksman
For whom I bent my knee to the ground,
And for whom my breasts gave milk,
Hunter of the wild goose, the seal and the swan,
The leaping trout and the bellowing deer.

From Miss Màiri MacRae, North Glendale. There is a similarity between this tune and that of No. 60 of the Tolmie Collection entitled 'Illean ò, ro Mhaith hò!' For the words see *An Duanaire*, p. 128, under the title 'Fear Bhreacain Bhallaich'—for words of the chorus and four lines similar; also *The MacDonald Collection*, p. 270; and K. C. Craig's *Òrain Luaidh*, p. 82, for an excellent version. Each line is repeated with a different part of the chorus after it.

Mode: Dorian.

## 82 GURA MISE THA FO ÉISLEIN

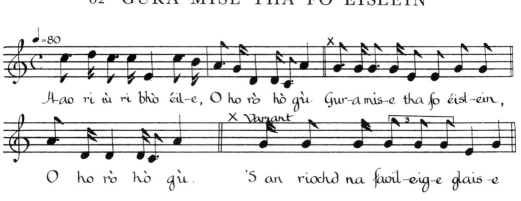

*Fonn:* O ho rò hò gù,
Hao ri iù ri bhò éile,
O ho rò hò gù.

1. Gura mise tha fo éislein
Moch 'sa' mhaduinn 's mi 'g éirigh,
Dol a bhuachailleachd na spréidhe,
Chì mi 'n eilid 's a céile,
5. 'S iad a' mire ri chéile,
Rìgh! gur buidhe dhaibh péin siod!
Cha n-ionann 's mar dh'éirich
Dhomhs' 's do Dhòmhnall mac Sheumais;
'S ann a thug iad mi air éiginn
10. Mach a ghleannan an t-sléibhe,
Mach a ghleannan na géige,
'Nam bhanachaig ri spréidhe,
Chon na Baintighearn' òig cheutaich',
Bhean a bheathaich na ceudan
15. Do luchd sgrìobhaidh is leughaidh,
Do luchd Laidinn is Beurla,
Do luchd Fraingeis is Gréigis.

'S truagh nach robh mi fad seachdainn
'N riochd a' gheòidh no na laçhann,
20. 'S an riochd na faoileige glaise,
'S mi gu snàmhadh an cuan farsainn,
'S mi gu streapadh an caisteal,
'S mi gum bristeadh na glasan
Gus a faighinn a mach thu.

216

25. Fear as òig' a chloinn Lachlainn,
    'S tu nach iarradh crabhata
    Mar a bhitheadh 'san fhasan;
    Dh'fhóghnadh gilead do chraicinn.
    Agus deirgid do leacainn,
30. Agus bòidhchead do phearsa,
    Di-Dòmhnaich 'sa chlachan.

*Translation*

1. I am sad arising early in the morning, going to herd the cattle. I see the hind and her mate playing together. 6. O God, they are fortunate! It is not so that befell me and Donald, son of James. They took me by force out to the little glen of the hills, out to the little glen of branches (to be) the dairymaid of the cattle. 13. (They took me) to the young, graceful lady, the lady who fed hundreds of people who could read and write, of people who knew Latin and English, of people who knew French and Greek. 18. It is sad that I was not for the length of a week in the form of a wild goose or a wild duck, in the form of the grey seagull. 21. I would swim the broad ocean, I would climb the castle, I would break the locks until I would get you out. 25. Youngest of Clan Lachlan, you would not want a cravat as was the fashion. 28. The whiteness of your skin would suffice, and your ruddy cheeks, and the beauty of your person in the church on Sunday.

From Mrs. Mary Steele and Miss Màiri MacRae.

Compare this tune with that in the Kennedy Fraser Collection, Vol. IV, p. xl, entitled 'A Sleat Dairy Maid'. Also the chorus of No. 63 of the Tolmie Collection, 'Chaidh na Fir a Sgathbhaig', bears a resemblance. For words compare K. C. Craig's *Òrain Luaidh*, p. 47. I published this song in the *J.E.F.D.S.S.*, Vol. IV., p. 153.

Mode: Hexatonic, no 6th.

## 83 CHAIDH MI DHA'N BHEINN

*Fonn:* Hoireann ó ho ri ho ró,
Hoireann ó ho ri ho ró,
Hoireann ó ho ri ho ró.

Chaidh mi dha'n bheinn oidhch' as t-fhoghar
Leis an òigear sheòlta, sheaghach.

### Translation

I went to the hill one autumn night
With the cunning, clever young man.

A fragment from Miss Annie MacDonald and Mrs. Agnes Currie, Lochboisdale, May 1948.

The two lines are similar to the first and third lines of No. 68 in the Tolmie Collection entitled 'Òran Teannachaidh' (a song for tightening the cloth). See K. C. Craig's *Òrain Luaidh*, p. 99, for two similar lines in a different song.

Mode: Six note compass.

# 84 'S TROM MO CHEUM, CHA N-EIL MI SUNNDACH

Farail ill ló, hó ro hù a,
Hao ri ò 's na ho hì iù a,
Farail ill lò, hó ro hù a.

1. 'S trom mo cheum, cha n-eil mi sunndach,
   'S trom an sac a th'air mo ghiùlain,
   'S e 'n sac a tha 'n sin, cridhe brùite,
   Cudrom dhà is cudrom triùir ann,
5. Tha cudrom cheathrar mas e 's mù ann.
   Gura h-e mo cheist an cùirteir,
   Chaidil thu raoir air mo chùlaibh.
   An dig thu nochd, no 'm bi mo dhùil riut?
   'N dian mi an dorus mór a dhùnadh?
10. 'N dian mi siod, no 'n caisg mi an cù dhut?

*Translation*

1. Heavy is my step, I am not joyful. Heavy is the burden which I bear. The burden I bear is a broken heart. 4. It is a burden enough for two people, a burden for three. It is a burden sufficient for four people, which is greater. 6. My love is the courtier. Last night you slept at my back. 8. Will you come to-night, or shall I expect you? Shall I close the outer door? 10. Shall I do that, or shall I tie up the dog for you?

From Miss Peigi MacRae, North Glendale, and Miss Mary Smith, Boisdale. This is an incomplete version.

See *A Choice Collection of Gaelic Poems*, p. 150; also Kennedy Fraser, Vol. I, p. 145, where in 'Flora MacDonald's Love Song' are two lines similar; and in K. C. Craig's *Òrain Luaidh*, p. 7, there are four lines similar.

Mode: Hexatonic, no 6th.

## 85 ALASDAIR ÒIG MHIC 'IC NEACAIL

Hill-ean ó ho ì ho ró, Na huill ir-inn ó ho ì o ro hó; 'S mul-ad-ach, 's mul-ad-ach a thà mi, Hill-ean ó ho ì - ho ro hó.

*Fonn:* Hillean ó ho ì ho ro hó       (*soloist*)
Hillean ó ho ì ho ró,       (*chorus*)
Na huill irinn ó ho ì o ro hó.    ( ,, )

1. 'S muladach, 's muladach a thà mi,
   Dìreadh na beinne 's 'ga teàrnadh;
   'S nach fhaic mi tighinn am bàta
   Ris an togte na siùil bhàna,
5. Bha m'athair oirr' s mo thriùir bhràithrean,
   'S mo leannan fhìn air ràmh-bràghad,
   Alasdair na gruaige bàine.

   Alasdair òig, mhic 'ic Neacail,
   B'fheàrr liom fhìn gum beirinn mac dhut,
10. Dhà no trì dhiubh, sia no seachd dhiubh,
    Cóigear no sianar no seachdnar;
    Bheirinn cìoch is glùn dhaibh an asgaidh,
    Bheirinn ciùird a làimh gach fear dhiubh;
    Fear 'na dhiùca, fear 'na chaiptin,
15. Fear 'na dhròbhair mór air martaibh.
    Fear air a' luing mhóir a' Sasunn,
    Fear 'na cheannard air sluagh feachdach.

220

# WAULKING SONGS

*Translation*

1. Sad, sad am I, mounting and descending the hill; and I do not see the boat coming, on which the white sails were hoisted. 5. My father was in her, and my three brothers, and my sweetheart himself at the bow oar, 7. Alasdair of the fair hair. Young Alasdair, son of Nicolson, would that I should bear thee a son, two or three to you, six or seven to you, five or six or seven sons. 12. I would nurse them for nothing; I would give a trade to the hand of each of them. 14. One a duke, one a captain, one a mighty drover of cattle, one on a great English ship, one a leader of an armed host.

This is a well-known waulking song in South Uist and was given me by Miss Peigi and Miss Màiri MacRae, Miss Màiri Smith and Miss Annie MacDonald. There is a poem in *The MacDonald Collection*, p. 265, where a few lines are similar, and it is there said to have been composed in the Isle of Skye. Compare also poems with some lines similar in *T.G.S.I.*, Vol. VII, p. 73, and Vol. XXVII, p. 395; K. C. Craig's *Òrain Luaidh*, p. 8; and an interesting comparison in *Éigse*. Mr. Angus Matheson has drawn my attention to *Éigse, A Journal of Irish Studies*, Vol. II, pp. 2–3, where an Irish keen collected by Professor Séamus O'Duilearga has a resemblance.

Mode: Hexatonic, no 7th.

## 86  GUR TU MO NIGHEAN DONN BHÒIDHEACH

O ù ho ro hù ò, Gur tu mo nighean donn bhòidh-each, O
ù ho ro hù ò. 'S mis-e tha gu mul-ad-ach Air
m'uil-inn anns an t-seòmb-ar

*Fonn:*  O ù ho ro hù ò,
Gur tu mo nighean donn bhòidheach,
O ù ho ro hù ò.

1. 'S mise tha gu muladach
    Air m'uilinn anns an t-seòmbar.

2. Mise muigh air cùl na tobhta,
    Is tusa staigh a' còrdadh.

3. Do shlios mar chailc as àille dreach,
    Mo chreach! mur faigh mi còir ort!

4. Shiubhlainn leat an ear 's an iar
    Gun each, gun strian, gun ròpa.

5. Rachainn gu Cinn-Tìre leat,
    'S dha'n tìr 'san robh mi eòlach.

6. Rachainn ro' Chaol Muile leat
    Gun fhuireach ri mo bhrògan.

7. Rachainn leat a dh'Uibhist,
    Far am buidhicheadh an t-eòrna.

8. Rachainn do na runnagan,
    Nam biodh do chuideachd deònach.

9. Rachainn-sa dha'n ghealaich leat,
    Nan gealladh tu mo phòsadh.

# WAULKING SONGS

*Translation*

*Chorus:* O ù ho ro hù ò, you are my beautiful brown-haired maiden.

1. I am sorrowful, reclining in my room. 2. I am outside behind the house while you're inside being betrothed. 3. Your side is like chalk of fairest hue, alas if I can't get you! 4. I would go with you to east and west without horse, without bridle, without halter. 5. I would go to Kintyre with you, the land that I knew well. 6. I would go with you through the Sound of Mull without waiting to put on my shoes. 7. I would go with you to Uist, where the barley ripens golden. 8. I would go to the stars, if your people were willing. 9. I would go with you to the moon if you promised to marry me.

From Mrs. Iain Campbell and her daughter Mary (Mrs. Angus James MacLeod), South Lochboisdale. This is a well-known waulking song of the Western Isles and also known on the mainland. The words of the chorus and several of the lines are printed in Alexander MacDonald's *Story and Song from Loch Ness-side*. The tune and chorus are found in the *Gesto Collection*, p. 53, and there is a somewhat similar tune in *Eilean Fraoich*, p. 78. The longest version of the words is in *The MacDonald Collection of Gaelic Poetry*, p. 209, where many of the lines are similar. MacDonald says in his note: 'This is the well-worn theme of unrequited love. The lady to whom the songs were composed was a daughter of MacLean of Boreray, North Uist.' In the Killearnan MS. the song is said to have been taken down from Mrs. J. Macdonald, Moss Cottage, Benbecula. See also K. C. Craig's *Òrain Luaidh*, p. 109; *Songs of the Hebrides*, Vol. II, p. 98, and Vol. III, p. xii.

Mode: Hexatonic, no 6th.

## 87  NIGHEAN DUBH 'S A NIGHEAN DONN

A tune and chorus sung to the same verses as the preceding song 'Gur Tu Mo Nighean Donn Bhòidheach'. From Mrs. John Currie, North Glendale.

Nigh-ean dubh 's a nigh-ean donn, Shiubhl-ainn leat far m'eòl-ais,

Nigh-ean dubh 's a nigh-ean donn Rach-ainn ro' Chinn Tir-e leat, 's dha'n

tir 'san robh mi eòl-ach

*Fonn:* Nighean dubh 's a nighean donn,
Shiubhlainn leat far m'eòlais,
Nighean dubh 's a nighean donn.

### Translation

*Chorus:* Dark-haired maiden, brown-haired maiden, I would follow you to lands unknown.

Mode: Hexatonic, no 2nd.

224

# 88 'M FACA SIBH A' MHAIGHDEAN BHEUSACH?

Ho i ó ho i o hó, Ho i ó ho i a bhó hó, Ió ho i o hó.

'M fac-a sibh a' mhaighd-ean bhéus-ach Ho i ó ho i o hó

*Fonn:* Ho i ó ho i o hó,
Ho i ó ho i a bhó hó,
Ió ho i o hó.

1. 'M faca sibh a' mhaighdean bheusach
Air an dug Niall Òg an éiginn?
'M mullach beinne ri latha gréine,
Gun duin' idir bhith 'nam faisge
5. Ach leanabh òg gun fhalbh gun astar;

'S truagh, a Rìgh! nach bu leis fhéin mi,
'S mi nach ligeadh glaodh na éighe,
Ged a shracadh brollach mo léine;
Ged a shracadh, gum fuaghlainn fhéin i
10. Le snàthad bhig, le snàithean glégheal,
'S nighinn ann an abhainn leum' i,
'S thiormaichinn air bàrr nan geug i.

*Translation*

1. Did you see the modest maiden whom young Neil ravished—on the top of a mountain on a sunny day, without anyone at all near them but a young child not able to walk. 6. Alas, oh King! that I was not his. I would not utter a shout or cry though the bosom of my dress were torn. Though it were torn I would sew it with the little needle and pure white threads. 11. And I would wash it in a leaping river, and dry it on top of the branches.

From Miss Màiri MacRae, North Glendale, who learnt it from Mrs. Ronald Morrison (Bean Raghnaill), South Lochboisdale. For another South Uist version see K. C. Craig's *Òrain Luaidh*, p. 9.

Mode: Irregular, no 2nd or 7th.

## 89 'S MOCH AN DIU GUN D'RINN MI ÉIRIGH

*Fonn:* Hoireann och ù o ho éileadh,
Ho i iù a ho aodh éileadh,
Hoireann och ù o ho éileadh.

1. 'S moch an diu gun d'rinn mi éirigh,
Mas moch an diu 's moch an dé e,
Dhìrich mi suas gual an t-sléibhe,
Fhuair mi gruagach dhonn gun éirigh,
5. Chuir mi 'n lùib mo bhreacain fhéin i;
Thug mi bòid nach éireadh beud dhith,
Nach biodh fios aig neach fo'n ghréin air,
Cha robh fios aig a màthair fhéin air.
Shiubhlainn leat fo choill nan geugan,
10. Shiubhlainn, shiubhlainn, dh'fhalbhainn fhéin leat,
Shiubhlainn fo dhubhar nan geug leat;
Coinnlear òir air bòrd do réitich,
Toil ar càirdean linn le chéile.

# WAULKING SONGS

*Translation*

1. It is early to-day that I arose. If it is early to-day it was earlier yesterday. I ascended the shoulder of the mountain. I found a dark-haired maid lying down. 5. I put her in the fold of my own plaid. I gave a solemn promise that no harm would come to her, that no one under the sun would know of it. Her own mother did not know of it. 9. I would go with you under the branches of the wood. I did go, I would go, I would go away with you. I would go with you under the shadow of the branches. A gold candlestick on your betrothal table. 13. The goodwill of our relations with us both.

From Miss Peigi MacRae, North Glendale. In *Eilean Fraoich*, p. 62, there is a song entitled 'Fhir a' Chinn-duibh, O hi u o' in which five of the lines are similar. The version printed here is incomplete. See K. C. Craig's *Òrain Luaidh*, pp. 46–47, for another South Uist version of the words.

Mode: Ionian: Mixolydian.

## 90 GURA MISE THA FO MHULAD

Ho ro ho ì, hó ro nan, Ho ro chall éil-e, Ho ro ho ì, hó ro nan.

Gur-a mis-e tha fo mhul-ad. Air an tul -aich, 's mór m'éisl-ein

Chunn-a mis-e mo leann-an, Cha do dh'aithn-ich e 'n dé mi.

Mrs. Iain Campbell

## 91 Second tune

Ho ro ho ì, hó ro nan, Ho ro chall éil-e, Ho ro ho ì, hó ro nan.

Gur-a mis-e fo mhul-ad Air an tul -aich, 's mór m'éisl-ein

Cha do dh'fhid-ir, 's cha d'fharr-aid, Cha do ghabh e dhiom sgeul-a.

Luchd nan cal-(a)p-an-an trom-a Chit-e foinn-eamh fo'n éid-eadh.

Miss Mary Smith

228

# WAULKING SONGS

*Fonn:* Ho ro ho ì, hó ro nan,
Ho ro chall éile,
Ho ro ho ì, hó ro nan.

1. Gura mise tha fo mhulad
Air an tulaich, 's mór m'éislein.

Chunna mise mo leannan,
Cha do dh'aithnich e 'n dé mi.

5. Cha do d'fhidir, 's cha d'fharraid,
Cha do ghabh e dhiom sgeula.

Chunna mise dol suas thu
Gu buaile na spréidhe.

'S ann a ghabh e orm seachad
10.     Air each glas nan ceum eutrom.

Air each glas nan ceum lùthmhor
A ghearradh sunndach an fhéithe.

Tha mo leanabh 'nam achlais,
'S mi gun taice fo'n ghréin dha.

15. Cha bu mhise bu choireach,
'S ann bu choireach e fhéin ris.

Mar a théid mi 'nam ònar
Ag iarraidh lòn air gach té dha.

Buaidh a' bhlàir anns an Dòmhnaich,
20.     Le Clann Dòmhnaill nan geurlann.

Luchd nan calpannan troma,
Chìte foinneamh fo'n éideadh.

Luchd nan claidheamhnan geala
Chìte sealladh là gréine.

## Translation

1. It is I that am sorrowful on the little hillock, and great is my grief. I saw my sweetheart and he did not recognize me. 5. He did not perceive, he did not ask, he would not listen to my story. 7. I saw you going up to the cattlefold. He passed me on a grey horse with a light step, on the grey horse of the nimble step, lively at jumping the bog. My babe is in my arms and I without sustenance under the sun for him.

15. I was not to blame, it was himself that was at fault. 17. As I go alone, seeking food of every woman for him.

From Mrs. Iain Campbell, Miss Mary Smith and the two Misses MacRae. See the Kennedy Fraser *Songs of the Hebrides*, Vol. II, Introduction, p. xxii, where it is called 'A Jacobite Song of 1715 from North Uist'. It is also printed in *An t-Òranaiche*, p. 504, where the chorus and first ten lines are similar to this version. This is only a fragment.

See also the Gillies Collection (1786), p. 245; *T.G.S.I.*, Vol. VIII, p. 115, and Vol. XXVI, p. 241; the MacDonald Collection, p. 49 (Killearnan MS., p. 24); K. C. Craig's *Òrain Luaidh*, p. 34; *Gaelic Songs in Nova Scotia*, p. 190. The song was widely known; my husband has recorded versions on Barra and at Loch Carnan in South Uist.

Miss Mary Smith, who was strongly of the opinion that lines 13-18 here belong to another song, added lines 19-24:

Victory on the field on Sunday to Clan Donald of the sharp swords, (21) the men of sturdy legs, which would be seen shapely beneath their garb, (23) the men of bright swords, which would flash in the sunshine.

Miss Mary Smith was right; so far as the words of the song are concerned, two different songs have become confused; one is the complaint of a girl who has been abandoned by her lover, the father of her child, and the other is a song in praise of the valour of the Clan Donald in the Jacobite wars (as printed in the MacDonald Collection).

Mode: Mrs. Iain Campbell—Pentatonic 2:6.
     Miss Mary Smith—Pentatonic 2:(6).

## 92 CHÌ MI BHUAM AIR BRUAICH AN LOCHAIN

Chì mi bhuam air bruaich an loch-ain,
O ho i a ho hi ù ra bho, Ho ro ho ì
's na bhó ì, 's na hao ri ri a ho i ù ra bhó.

*Fonn:* O ho i a ho hi ù ra bho,
Ho ro ho ì 's na bhó ì,
'S na hao ri ri a ho i ù ra bhó.

Chì mi bhuam air bruaich an lochain,
Chì mi na fir a' dol seachad;
Cha doir mi mo raghainn asda,
Fear boineide guirm' is seacaid;
Fear an taighe 'na laigh' gun dùil ris.

### Translation

I see yonder on the banks of the loch,
I see the men passing;
I will not get my choice from among them,
The man of the blue bonnet and jacket;
The man of the house lying without hope for him.

The tune from Miss Màiri MacRae; the words (incomplete) from both Miss MacRae and Mrs. Iain Campbell (Clachair), North Glendale, 1948. For songs with similar lines see: *Eilean Fraoich*, p. 66; *T.G.S.I.*, Vol. XV, p. 143; Tolmie Collection, No. 75; K. N. MacDonald, *Puirt-a-Beul*, No. 47; and K. C. Craig's *Òrain Luaidh*, p. 74. J. L. Campbell has recorded a version in Barra.

Mode: Pentatonic 4:7.

## 93 CHA LABHAIR MI 'N T-ÒRAN

Cha labh-air mi 'n t-òr-an, hì hoir-eann o - ro ho

Hì hoir-eann hì u a, hì hoir-eann o - ro ho.

*Fonn:* Hì hoireann o ro ho,
Hì hoireann hì u a,
Hì hoireann o ro ho.

1. Cha labhair mi 'n t-òran,
   Cha mheòraich mi facal;
   Cha d'fhuair mi raoir cadal,
   'S mi 'm leaba 'nam ònar,
5. 'S mi ri ionndrainn mo leannain,
   Fleasgach fearail ciùin eòlach,
   Thig o Chaisteal nan Ròsan;
   Ach nam faighinn air m'òrdan,
   Bu leat Ceapach na Ströine,
10. Math gu peasair 's gu pònair,
   Math gu corc, is gu eòrna.

   Mìle soiridh, ciad fàilte
   Bhuam gu Màiri 's a faicinn,
   Bean òg a' chùil dualaich,
15. 'S nan gruaidhean dearg daithte;
   'S gura math thig an gùn dhut,
   'S e ùr a's an fhasan;
   'S gura minig a bhà mi
   Muigh air àirigh le d' mhartaibh,
20. Dianamh ìm agus càise,
   Toirt na blàthchàdh gun cheannach,
   Ann am bothag an t-sùgraidh,
   Gun 'ga dùnadh ach barrach.

# WAULKING SONGS

*Translation*

(1) I will not utter the song, (2) I will not remember a word; (3) last night I got no sleep (4) alone in my bed, (5) while I missed my sweetheart (6) a manly quiet wise youth (7) who comes from the Castle of the Roses; (8) but if I were to get my wish (9) Keppoch of the Strone would belong to thee, (10) good for peas and beans, (11) good for oats and barley. (12) A thousand farewells, a hundred welcomes (13) from me to Mary, may I see her, (14) the young woman of curling hair (15) and of red-coloured cheeks; (16) well the gown suits you (17) newly in fashion; (18) often was I (19) out at the sheiling with your cows (20) making butter and cheese, (21) giving butter-milk without recompense (22) in the merry bothy (23) only closed by birch branches.

From Miss Mary Morrison, South Lochboisdale, 1933. A version of the tune is published in the Kennedy Fraser Collection, Vol. IV, Introduction, p. xlv, where it is entitled 'A Harris Salute'. See K. C. Craig's *Òrain Luaidh*, p. 14, and the Tolmie Collection, where there are a few lines similar in the song 'Ho Ro Thugaibh i', No. 73. A version of the air is printed in Seumas Munro's *Am Filidh*, No. 13 of the Appendix. I published this song in the *J.E.F.D.S.S.*, Vol. IV, p. 192.

Mode: Pentatonic 4:7.

## 94 DHIANAINN SÙGRADH RIS AN NIGHINN DUIBH

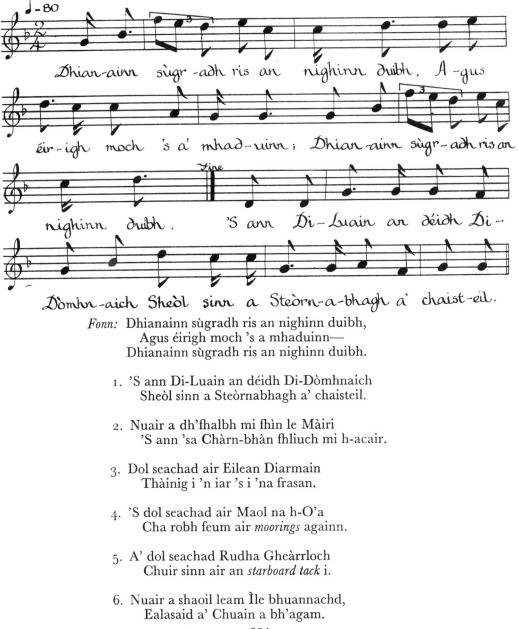

*Fonn:* Dhianainn sùgradh ris an nighinn duibh,
Agus éirigh moch 's a mhaduinn—
Dhianainn sùgradh ris an nighinn duibh.

1. 'S ann Di-Luain an déidh Di-Dòmhnaich
   Sheòl sinn a Steòrnabhagh a' chaisteil.

2. Nuair a dh'fhalbh mi fhìn le Màiri
   'S ann 'sa Chàrn-bhàn fhliuch mi h-acair.

3. Dol seachad air Eilean Diarmain
   Thàinig i 'n iar 's i 'na frasan.

4. 'S dol seachad air Maol na h-O'a
   Cha robh feum air *moorings* againn.

5. A' dol seachad Rudha Gheàrrloch
   Chuir sinn air an *starboard tack* i.

6. Nuair a shaoil leam Ìle bhuannachd,
   Ealasaid a' Chuain a bh'agam.

234

7. *Reef* 'san *topsail*, is dhà 'san *fhòre-sail*,
   Ceann a' *bhoom* an déidh a *laiseadh*.

8. *Reef* 'ga cheangal, 's *reef* 'ga fhuasgladh
   Muir fo cluais is fuaim fo planca.

9. Dhianainn sùgradh ris a' ghruagaich,
   Ri nighinn duinn a' chuailein chleachdaich.

10. 'S bòidheach liom sealladh do chalpa,
    Mar sin t'fhalbh agus t'astar.

11. 'S bòidheach liom nì thu 'n t-éileadh
    A' dol ro'n bheinn ri là frasach.

12. 'S nuair a théid thu null a dh'Éirinn
    Gheibh thu 'm bréid nach fheum am paitseadh.

13. Bidh buill ùr' nach feum an *spliceadh*
    Ris a' mhaighdin-sa tighinn dachaigh.

*Translation*

*Chorus:* I would make sport with the dark-haired maiden, and arise early in the morning. I would make sport with the dark-haired maiden.

1. On a Monday after Sunday we sailed from Stornoway of the castle.

2. When I left with Mary it was at Cairnbaan I wet her anchor.

3. Passing the island of Diarmain, the wind blew from the west with squalls.

4. Passing the Mull of Oa, we had no need of moorings.

5. Passing the point of Gairloch, we put her on the starboard tack.

6. When I thought I had made Islay, it was Ailsa Craig I had.

7. A reef in the topsail and two in the foresail, the end of the boom was lashed.

8. A reef being tied and a reef being loosed, the sea under her sail and a noise under her planks.

9. I would make sport with the lass, with the maiden of the brown curling tresses.

10. Beautiful to me is the sight of your leg, and likewise your carriage and gait.

11. Beautiful to me are you wearing the kilt, crossing the hills on a showery day.

12. When you go over to Ireland you will get a sail that does not need patching.

13. There will be new ropes that do not need splicing on this maiden coming home.

235

# SONGS

From Mrs. John Currie, North Glendale. This song is well known in the Hebrides. A tune nearly similar with the same chorus has been printed in *Eilean Fraoich*, p. 80. In *The MacDonald Collection* there is a poem with the same chorus and three lines similar. The first, tenth and eleventh verses praise a beautiful maiden, but it is the custom to address a sailing ship as though she were a maiden and to attribute to her the charms of her namesake. The singer regarded these lines as most appropriate, but they probably really belong to another song. I printed this in the *J.E.F.D.S.S.*, Vol. IV, p. 151.

Mode: Aeolian.

## 95 CÓ SIOD THALL AIR CEANN MO RÒPA?

*Fonn:* Ill iù ill ò, ill a ro ho,
Ill a ro ho a, ill iù ill ò.

1. Có siod thall air ceann mo ròpa?
   Tha mis', òigear a' chùil bhuidh' ann!

2. 'S muladach mi an tìm a' gheamhraidh,
   Oidhche Shamhna, 's mi gun uighean.

### Translation

1. Who is that yonder at the end of the rope? It is me, the youth of the yellow hair!

2. Sad am I at this time of winter on Hallowe'en night and I without eggs.

From Miss Peigi MacRae, North Glendale, 1943. This is a waulking song about the tricks of Hallowe'en night. It was the custom for the girl to throw a rope over the kiln (surrag na h-àth) where the straw and grain are placed to dry, and to call, 'Who is at the end of my rope?' Her sweetheart would then answer. Another Hallowe'en custom was to 'put a wee bit of the white (of an egg) in a glass of water and if it comes up in wee trees you may look for your sweetheart, but if it stays at the bottom it is a bad lookout.'

Mode: Pentatonic 4:7.

## 96 RÌGH! GUR MULADACH THÀ MI

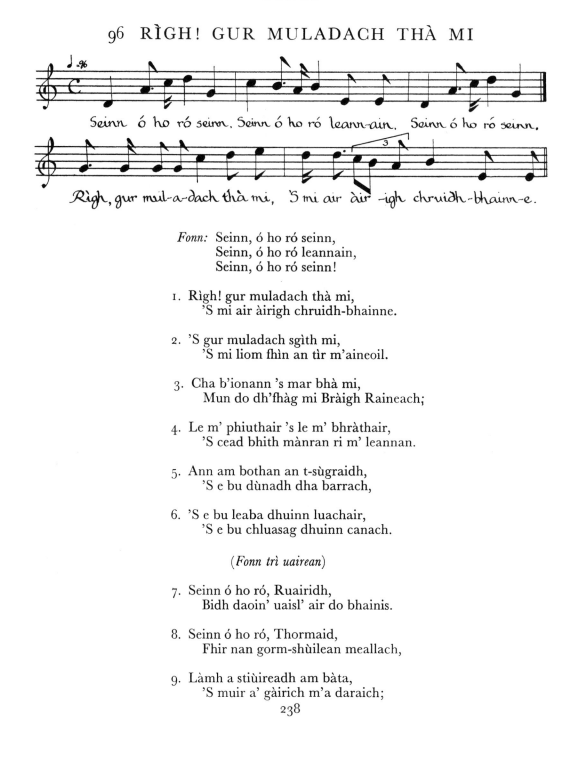

*Fonn:* Seinn, ó ho ró seinn,
    Seinn, ó ho ró leannain,
    Seinn, ó ho ró seinn!

1. Rìgh! gur muladach thà mi,
    'S mi air àirigh chruidh-bhainne.

2. 'S gur muladach sgìth mi,
    'S mi liom fhìn an tìr m'aineoil.

3. Cha b'ionann 's mar bhà mi,
    Mun do dh'fhàg mi Bràigh Raineach;

4. Le m' phiuthair 's le m' bhràthair,
    'S cead bhith mànran ri m' leannan.

5. Ann am bothan an t-sùgraidh,
    'S e bu dùnadh dha barrach,

6. 'S e bu leaba dhuinn luachair,
    'S e bu chluasag dhuinn canach.

(*Fonn trì uairean*)

7. Seinn ó ho ró, Ruairidh,
    Bidh daoin' uaisl' air do bhainis.

8. Seinn ó ho ró, Thormaid,
    Fhir nan gorm-shùilean meallach,

9. Làmh a stiùireadh am bàta,
    'S muir a' gàirich m'a daraich;

10. 'S tu gun stiùireadh i dìreach,
Ro' Chaol Ìle 'na deannaibh;

11. 'S tu gun stiùireadh i tioram,
'S muir a' mire r'a crannaibh.

12. 'S ged nach bi mi 'ga innse,
'S ann an Ìle tha mo leannan.

13. 'S ged nach bi mi 'ga ràitinn,
Thug mi gràdh dhut 's mi 'm leanabh.

*Translation*

*Chorus:* Sing, ó ho ró sing, sing, ó ho ró sweetheart, sing, ó ho ró, sing!

1. O God, I am sorrowful in the sheiling of milch cattle. I am sorrowful and tired, alone in a strange land. Not so was I before I left the brae of Rannoch, with my sister and my brother, and with liberty to dally with my sweetheart. 5. In the bothy of merriment, which was closed by birch-branches, our bed was the rushes, and our pillow was the bog-cotton. 7. Sing ó ho ró, Rory, gentry will attend thy wedding. Sing ó ho ró, Norman, of beguiling blue eyes, (your) hand would steer the boat, while the sea raged around her oak planks. You would steer her straight through the Sound of Islay at full speed. 11. You would steer her dry while the sea was playing around her masts. 12. And although I shall not tell it, my sweetheart is in Islay, and although I shall not say it, I fell in love with you as a child.

From Iain Campbell (Iain Clachair), South Lochboisdale, July 1933. I printed this in the *J.E.F.D.S.S.*, Vol. IV, p. 193. It is a well-known waulking song, and versions of the air and words have appeared in the following collections: *An t-Òranaiche*, p. 13; *Binneas nam Bàrd*, p. 95; the *Celtic Magazine*, Vol. IV, p. 476, where it is described by William MacKenzie as 'a good old pastoral song well known in the Central Highlands'; the *Gesto Collection*, p. 32; Alexander MacDonald, *Story and Song from Loch Ness-side*, p. 251; Miss Lucy Broadwood, *Journal of the Folk-Song Society*, No. 35, p. 292 (noted in Arisaig in 1906); Otto Andersson, 'On Gaelic Folk Music from the Isle of Lewis', *Budkavlen*, 1952, p. 50; Mrs. Kennedy Fraser, *From the Hebrides*, pp. xiii and xiv; recorded in Cape Breton in 1937 by J. L. Campbell from the singing of Mrs. Neil MacInnis, whose forebears came from the Isle of Barra.

Mode: Hexatonic, no 7th.

# 97 MO RÙN AILEIN, HÓ HÒ

*Fonn:* Mo rùn Ailein, hó hò.

1. Dh'éirich mi moch, hó hò,   mo rùn Ailein, hó hò,
   [Maduinn earraich, hó hò,   mo rùn Ailein, hó hò,]
2. Dhìrich mi suas, hó hò,   mo rùn Ailein, hó hò,
   Gual' a' bhearraidh, hó hò,   mo rùn Ailein, hó hò,
3. Lig mi m'uileann, hó hò, *etc.*,   air a' ghàradh, hó hò, *etc.*,
   Dh'amhairc mi bhuam   fad mo sheallaidh,
5. Chunna mi long   steach 'sa bhàghan,
   Có bh'air an stiùir   ach mo leannan?
   Òganach ciùin   foinnidh fearail.

*Atharrachadh fuinn*

Ha la ò éile, hó hò,   ha la ò éile, hó hò

Mìle marbhaisg, hó hò,   ha la ò éile, hó hò,

Luchd nam breugan, hó hò,   ha la ò éile, hó hò,

10. Thog iad ormsa, hó hò, *etc.*,   mo chuid fhéin dhiu, hó hò, *etc.*

Gu robh mo chrios-sa   àrd ag éirigh,

Ma bha, cha b'ann   o'n bhéist ud,

Ach o Sgoilear   Donn na Beurla

Thig an acfhuinn  . . . . . . .[1]

15. Le each crùidheach   nì 'n ceum eutrom.

### Translation

*Chorus:* My love Allan, hó hò, (1) I arose early on a spring morning, I mounted up the shoulder of the ridge, I leant my elbow on the dyke, I looked out as far as I could see.

(5) I saw a ship in the bay. Who was at the helm but my sweetheart, a young man, calm, handsome, brave?

### Change of Chorus

*Chorus:* Ha la ò éile, hó hò, ha la ò éile, hó hò. (9) A thousand curses on the pack of liars. They said it about me, my own share of them, that my girdle was rising.

If so it was not from yonder beast but from the brown-haired Scholar of English, who comes accoutred . . . with a well-shod horse making the light step!

From Mrs. Angus Currie (Anna Ruadh), South Lochboisdale, recorded on wire, 8th November 1950. The speed is increased in the second part, when the soloist first sings the meaningless line 'Ha la ò éile, hó hò' and the other women repeat it as the chorus then and after all the remaining lines of the song. Compare K. C. Craig, *Òrain Luaidh*, p. 39.

Mode: Six note compass.

[1] The reciter missed a half-line here.

## 98 'S MULADACH MI, HO Ì A BHÓ

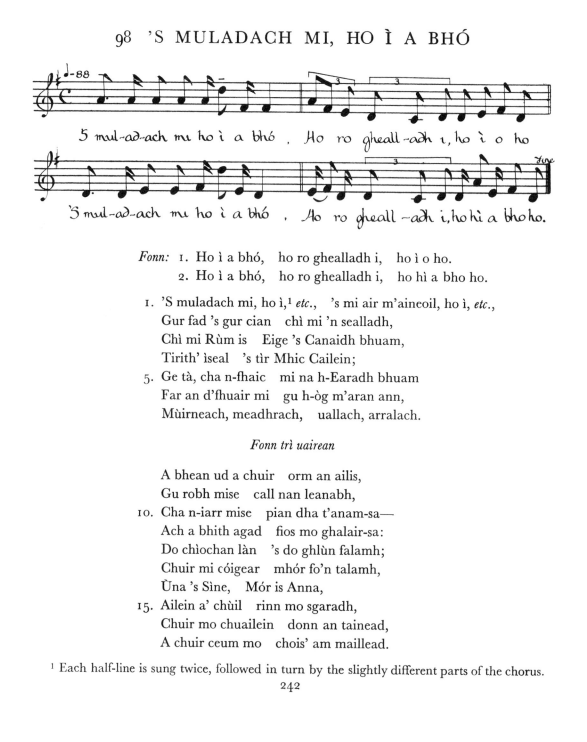

*Fonn:*   1. Ho ì a bhó,   ho ro ghealladh i,   ho ì o ho.
         2. Ho ì a bhó,   ho ro ghealladh i,   ho hì a bho ho.

  1. 'S muladach mi, ho ì,[1] *etc.,*   's mi air m'aineoil, ho ì, *etc.,*
     Gur fad 's gur cian   chì mi 'n sealladh,
     Chì mi Rùm is   Eige 's Canaidh bhuam,
     Tirith' ìseal   's tìr Mhic Cailein;
  5. Ge tà, cha n-fhaic   mi na h-Earadh bhuam
     Far an d'fhuair mi   gu h-òg m'aran ann,
     Mùirneach, meadhrach,   uallach, arralach.

*Fonn trì uairean*

     A bhean ud a chuir   orm an ailis,
     Gu robh mise   call nan leanabh,
 10. Cha n-iarr mise   pian dha t'anam-sa—
     Ach a bhith agad   fios mo ghalair-sa:
     Do chìochan làn   's do ghlùn falamh;
     Chuir mi cóigear   mhór fo'n talamh,
     Ùna 's Sìne,   Mór is Anna,
 15. Ailein a' chùil   rinn mo sgaradh,
     Chuir mo chuailein   donn an tainead,
     A chuir ceum mo   chois' am maillead.

[1] Each half-line is sung twice, followed in turn by the slightly different parts of the chorus.

242

*Translation*

I am sad in an unfamiliar place; far and wide is the sight I see. 3. I see Rum and Eigg and Canna, low-lying Tiree, and the land of Mac Cailein[1]; but I do not see Harris, where I was nourished in my youth, happy and merry, haughty and proud. Yon woman who cast the reproach on me, that I was losing my children, 10. I shall not ask for pain on thy soul, but that thou mayest know my affliction: that thy breasts be full and thy knee empty; I have buried five, Una and Jean, Morag and Anna, 15. long-haired Allan, which bereft me, which thinned my brown hair, and made slow my footstep.

From Mrs. Iain Campbell, South Lochboisdale, 1948. There is a version in *The MacDonald Collection*, p. 254, of which twenty lines are similar, and another in K. C. Craig's *Òrain Luaidh*, p. 81; also manuscript versions exist.

Mode: Irregular; no 4th or 6th.

[1] Chief of the Campbells.

## 99 DH'ÉIRICH MI MOCH MADUINN ÀLAINN

*Fonn:* Fire fàire hò ro hó    o hì o hó

1. Dh'éirich mi moch, o hì o hó,
   Fire fàire hò ro hó,
   Maduinn àlainn o hì o hó,
   Fire fàire, hò ro hó,
   Maduinn àluinn, o hì o hó,
   Fire fàire, hò ro hó,

2. Dhìrich mi suas, o hì *etc.,*    guala ghàraidh, o hì, *etc.,*
   Thiaruinn mi steach    bràighe 'n fhàsaich,
   Lig mi m'uileann    air a' chàrnan,

5. Dh'amhairc mi bhuam    fad' air fàire,
   Chunna mi long    mhór 'sa bhàghan;
   Dé ma chunnaic!    bu neo-cheàrr i,
   Bu lìonmhor oirre    gunna 's cànan,
   Mìle fear fionn    air a h-eàrrlainn;

244

10. Mo leannan fhéin    'n t-aon a b'fheàrr dhiu,
    Fear chòta ghuirm    's léine bàine;
    Gura h-esan    gaol nam bràithrean
    Sheòl a sheachdainn    gus a màireach,
    Ge bè cala    nochd an tàmh iad,
15. Gum bi mire,    cluichd is gàire,
    Iomairt gu tric    air an tàileasg,
    Air na cairtean    breaca bàna,
    Air na dìsnean    geala cnàmha.

*Translation*

1. I arose early on a beautiful morning. 2. I climbed up the shoulder of the ridge, 3. I descended the slope of the moor, I leant my elbow on the cairn, I gazed as far as the horizon. 6. I saw the great ship in the bay. What if I saw her! She was a right ship! 8. Numerous were her guns and cannon. A thousand fair men on board her. My own sweetheart, the best of them, in his blue coat and white shirt. He is the beloved one of the brothers who sailed a week ago to-morrow. Whatever harbour they shelter in to-night there will be mirth in it, 13. games and laughter, frequent playing at backgammon, at the white speckled cards, with the white bone dice.

From Mrs. Mary Steele, Kildonan, South Uist. J. L. Campbell has recorded a version of this song in Cape Breton from Mrs. David Patterson, beginning 'Fliuch a bha mi 'n Coire Bhreacain'. See K. C. Craig's *Òrain Luaidh*, p. 38. The tune as set out here is transcribed from an Ediphone recording. The singer has only sung each half-line once, but for waulking each, except the first, is sung twice, to the different musical phrases.

See *Songs of the Hebrides*, Vol. II, p. 199.

Mode: Irregular, no 4th, 6th or 7th.

## 100 GURA MULADACH A THÀ MI

Gur-a mul-ad-ach a thà mi, Dir-eadh na beinn-e 's ga teàrn-adh.

Hill inn ó hó Huill eo ro bha hó,

Hill ir inn ì hó a ó ro Huill eo a ro ho.

*Fonn:* Hill inn ó hó
Huill eo ro bha hó,
Hill ir inn ì hó a ó ro
Huill eo a ro ho.

1. Gura muladach a thà mi
Dìreadh na beinne 's 'ga teàrnadh,
Hill inn ó hó, *etc.*,

2. Dìreadh na beinne 's 'ga teàrnadh;
Thuit mo chridhe, 's fhad' o'n là sin,
Hill inn ó hó, *etc.*,
Thuit mo chridhe, 's fad' o'n là sin,
Cha tog fiodhull e, no clàrsach,

5. No pìob mhór nam feadan àrda.
'S ann agam fhìn a bha na bràithrean
Dh'iomradh, dh'éibheadh, dh'òladh, phàigheadh,
Chuireadh an cluichd air an tàileasg,
'S air na cairtean breaca, bàna,

10. 'S air na dìsnean geala cnàmha.
'S cha b'e 'n Aoine rinn ur n-àireamh,
Ach a' bhean a bha gun nàire,
Di-Dòmhnaich is Là na Sàbaid,
'S a' chiad Di-Luain an ceann na ràithe.

246

15. 'S truagh, a Rìgh, nach tigeadh ise,
    A làmh leòinte, 's a cas briste,
    'S i 'g iarraidh léigh am beul gach litreach,
    'S gun aon léigh 'san tìr ach mise;
    'S air mo làimh gun dearbhainn misneachd,
20. Lùbainn cnàimh 's gun tàirninn silteach,
    Gus an càirinn i air eislig,
    'S chàirinn ùir air bhruaich a lice.


    'S mise a' bhean dhubhach, dheurach,
    Cha n-ann a lughad mo spréidhe,
25. Ach mu Iain Mùideartach na féile;
    Chunnaic mi latha bha feum ort,
    Latha Cnoc nan Dos bha gleus ort,
    Latha Cill Saighde bha feum ort,
    Dhòirt thu fuil is gheàrr thu féithean,
30. Dh'fhàg thu nàmhaid air dhroch-reubadh;
    'S iomadh fear a bha gu deurach,
    Agus bean air bheagan céille,
    Mnathan òga call an céile,
    'S ionann mise 's mar tha té dhiu,
35. Gun chomas falt mo chinn a reubadh.


    Cha chadal dhomh ach 'nam dhùsgadh—
    Chunna mi do thaigh 'ga rùsgadh,
    'S marcraich' an eich dhuibh air thùs' ann,
    'S marcraich' na fàlaire dùbhghlais,
40. Marcraich' an eich chrùidhich chlisnich,
    Le spuir òir 's le spòig nach bristeadh.


*Translation*

1. Sorrowful am I, climbing and descending the mountain. My heart has fallen—'tis long since that day. Neither fiddle nor harp can lift it, nor bag-pipe of high-pitched chanters.

6. 'Tis I who had the brothers who could play, call (for drinks), drink and pay, who could play at draughts and white-spotted cards, who could play with the white bone dice.

11. It was not the 'Aoine' that counted you, but the woman without shame, on Sunday and the day of the Sabbath and the first Monday at the end of the quarter-year. 15. 'Tis a pity, my God! that she would not come, with her arm wounded and her leg broken, seeking a physician at the beginning of every letter, and no doctor in the country but myself. 19. By my hand I would show courage. I would bend her bones and draw her blood, until I put her on a bier, and put earth on the edge of her tombstone.

SONGS

23. I am a mournful, tearful woman and not because of the scarcity of my cattle, But for generous John of Moidart; I saw the day when there was need of you. 27. On the day (of the battle) of Cnoc nan Dos you were in fine form; on the day of Kilsyth there was need of you. You spilt blood and you cut veins, you left the enemy badly torn. 31. There was many a man who was in tears, many a woman bereft of sense, young women that had lost their husbands. And I am like one of them, not even able to tear my hair.

36. I cannot sleep but am always waking. I saw your house unroofed, and the rider of the black horse in front, and the rider of the dark grey palfrey, the rider of the well-shod spirited horse with his spurs of gold and unbreakable hoof.

*Notes*

*Line 11.* The meaning of this is 'You were not drowned'. The late Father Allan McDonald records the expression 'Àireamh na h-Aoine ort' as equivalent to 'may you be drowned'. It was considered unlucky to bathe on a Friday, and there was a certain 'rann' or verse which if recited in sight of persons bathing, would bring about their drowning. Very few people knew it. There is a long article about this in Father Allan McDonald's South Uist Vocabulary.

*Line 17.* This also refers to Gaelic folklore. It was a custom of persons dispensing charms to cure illnesses to give a letter to sick people. This letter was not to be opened, but was to be put away in a secret place. If it were found and opened, the sick person was liable to get worse. J. L. Campbell obtained this information from Miss Annie Campbell, Iochdar, South Uist.

*Line 25.* Other versions of this song have here 'A Mhic Iain Mhuideartaich na Féile' 'O son of generous John of Moydart'. This would be Domhnall Dubh, who was born around 1615, succeeded his father as chief of Clanranald in 1670, and died on Canna in 1686. He is more likely to be the person referred to as he was active in the Montrose wars. His father, who welcomed the Irish Franciscan missionaries to the Hebrides in 1625, was a very well-known person. He was a staunch royalist, was excommunicated by the Synod of Argyll, and never submitted to the Government.

*Line 27.* Cnoc nan Dos was a battle fought in County Cork, Ireland, in 1647, at which the famous Alasdair mac Colla was killed.

*Line 28.* The battle of Kilsyth was fought on 15th August 1645. The royalist army under Montrose, which included the Clanranald MacDonalds, routed the Covenanters.

*Lines 34-35.* This implies that the extemporizer of the song was his lover, not his legitimate wife, and so could not show her grief openly.

From Miss Mary Smith, South Boisdale. This tune is unlike any I have heard in the Hebrides. Miss Smith, then nearing her eighty-third birthday, sang it with martial spirit and in perfect time. Sometimes omitting the chorus, she would pause after *hill inn ó hó* for four sharp beats to commence the line again.

Two-line verses, repeating the second line of each verse as the first line of the verse following. For another South Uist version of the words see K. C. Craig's *Òrain Luaidh*, p. 102, and *Carmina Gadelica*, V, p. 32. A fragment is in *T.G.S.I.*, XXVII, p. 396.

Mode: Irregular, no 6th or 7th.

## 101 SHAOIL LIOM NACH ROBH POLL NO EABAR

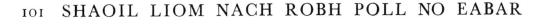

*Fonn:* Fal ill eile ro ho gù,
Ù ra bhó nam b'àill leat mi,
Fal ill eile ro ho gù.

1. Shaoil liom nach robh poll no eabar
   An Eige, gun d'ràinig mi.

2. Shaoil liom gum b'e clachan siùcair
   Bha dlùthadh do ghàraidhean.

3. Shaoil liom gum b'e cruachan mòna
   Bha 'n taigh-còmhnaidh Àrasaig.

### Translation

1. I thought there was neither bog nor muddy stretch in Eigg, until I reached it.

2. I thought that stones of sugar cemented your walls.

3. I thought that the dwelling-house of Arisaig was peat stacks.

Tune, chorus and first two verses from Miss Peigi MacRae; the third verse from Miss Mary Smith, Boisdale. A fragment; compare K. C. Craig, *Òrain Luaidh*, p. 69.

Mode: Pentatonic 2:5.

249

## 102 RINN MI MOCHEIRIGH GU ÉIRIGH

Rinn mi moch-eir-igh gu éir-igh, Hó ró ho laill ó,

Ho ì o ho nàil-ibh i. Hó ró ho laill ó.

*Fonn:* Hó ró ho laill ó,
Ho ì o ho nàilibh i,
Hó ró ho laill ó.

1. Rinn mi mocheirigh gu éirigh,
Cha n-ann a dh'uallach na spréidhe,
No ghleidheadh an fhochainn Chéitein,
Ach a chumail coinneamh ri m'eudail;
5. Mhic 'ic Ailein na bi 'n eud rium,
Tha mi 'n troma ghaol orra cheudghaol,
Tha mi siod mas toil leat fhéin e.
Shiubhlainn, shiubhlainn, dh'fhalbhainn fhéin leat,
Rachainn leat ro' chuan na h-Éireann,
10. Far am bi muir àrd ag éirigh,
Mucan is tuircean is béistean,
Luingeis a' cogadh r'a chéile,
Toirt an iarainn fhuair o chéile,
Mnathan a' caoi, crodh a' geumraich,
15. Crodh is eich an lùib a chéile,
Cha n-aithnich mi mo chuid fhéin dhiubh.

*Fonn trì uairean*

Chuirinn-sa mo gheall, 's mo theanngheall
Dh'fhaodainn siod, ge bè mo cheann e,
Gu leagadh tu a' chreach 'na deannruith,
20. Tighinn le leathad Cothrom Chainnleam[1]
O mhullach beinne gu bial fainge.

[1] 'Gainntir' and 'coimhlidh' in other versions.

250

# WAULKING SONGS

*Fonn trì uairean*

Rachainn leat gu cùl Taigh 'n Dùnain
Far am faighinn modh is mùirn leat,
Daoin' uaisle mu bhòrdaibh dùmhail,
25. Ruidhleadh mu seach air an ùrlar
Le pìob bheag nam feadan siubhlach,
Le pìob mhór nam feadan dùmhail.

*Fonn trì uairean*

Nam bithinn-sa làidir fearail,
Neart Cù Chulainn bhith 'nam bhallaibh,
30. B' aithne dhomh có chùirt a leanainn;
Cha n-e cùirt 'ic 'ille Chaluim,
Cùirt nan gruagach, cùirt nam balach,[1]
Cùirt an Dòmhnaill Duinn[2] nach maireann.

*Fonn trì uairean*

Nam bithinn-sa làidir eòlach,
35. Neart Cù Chulainn bhith 'nam dhòrnaibh,
Chuirinn am blàr le Clann Dòmhnaill,
Le sìol Ailein mhóir na feòladh.

*Fonn trì uairean*

Och is och, mar a tha mise!
An dùthaich a bhith gun cheann-cinnidh,
40. Freasdal làn an dùirn do ghiullan;
Tìm dhuinn, a ghaoil, a bhith tilleadh;
Nan éireadh gach ian le fhine,
Dh'éireadh na Dòmhnallaich linne,
Leathanaich nach leubhadh giorag,
45. Camshronaich bho'n Gharbhbheinn bhiorach—
Bhiodh na Caimbeulaich 'san linnidh!

*Translation*

I arose early, not to herd the cattle or to guard the May braird, but to keep a tryst with my darling. Clanranald, do not be jealous of me. I am deep in love with your first-love; I am so, if you like. I would go, I would go, I would go with you across the Irish sea, where high billows rise, with whales, and porpoises and monsters and ships warring against each other, taking cold iron from each other, with women wailing, and cattle bellowing; cattle and horses mixed up with each other; I do not recognize my own among them.

[1] 'Cùirt a' Ghruamaich', 'cùirt a' Ghallaich' in other versions.
[2] 'Ghuirm' in other versions.

# SONGS

*Chorus three times*

17. I would lay my wager, my firm wager, I could safely do so even if it were my own head, that you would set the lifted cattle running at full speed, coming from the incline of Cothrom Cainnleam [?] from the top of a hill to the entrance of a cattlefold. I would follow you to the back of Taigh an Dùnain, where I would find courtesy and merriment, with gentry closely-packed around the tables, with reels turn about on the floor, with the little pipe of fluent chanters, and the big pipe of thick ones.

*Chorus three times*

27. If I were strong and manly, with the strength of Cù Chulainn in my limbs, I know to what court I would attach myself; not the court of MacLeod of Raasay, (but) the court of maidens and youths, the court of the late Donald Donn.

*Chorus three times*

34. If I were strong and wise, with the strength of Cù Chulainn in my fists, I would fight the battle on the side of Clan Donald, on the side of the race of great Allan of slaughter.

38. Alas, woe is me that the country is without a chieftain, depending on a handful of a boy. It is time for us, my love, to be returning. If every bird (*i.e.* chief) would rise with his clan, the MacDonalds would rise with us, and the MacLeans who know no fear, and the Camerons from pointed Garbh-bheinn, and the Campbells would be in the sea!

From Mrs. Mary Steele (Màiri Bhàn Gillies) from South Lochboisdale and now residing at Kildonan, South Uist. There are perhaps two songs here, if not more, and some of the lines are found in other waulking songs. See *The MacDonald Collection*, p. 242, where sixteen lines are similar and where the foe is the Camerons. In the note concerning the song MacDonald says: 'From internal evidence it appears that this song was composed about 1650.' See another South Uist version of this song in K. C. Craig's *Òrain Luaidh*, p. 94. See *Songs of the Hebrides*, Vol. III, p. xvi, and Vol. IV, pp. xii and xiii.

Mode: Irregular, no 2nd, 3rd or 5th.

# 103 AILEIN, AILEIN, 'S FHAD' DO CHADAL

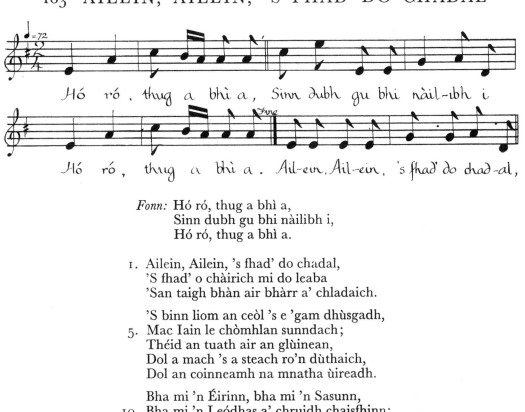

*Fonn:* Hó ró, thug a bhì a,
Sinn dubh gu bhi nàilibh i,
Hó ró, thug a bhì a.

1. Ailein, Ailein, 's fhad' do chadal,
   'S fhad' o chàirich mi do leaba
   'San taigh bhàn air bhàrr a' chladaich.

   'S binn liom an ceòl 's e 'gam dhùsgadh,
5. Mac Iain le chòmhlan sunndach;
   Théid an tuath air an glùinean,
   Dol a mach 's a steach ro'n dùthaich,
   Dol an coinneamh na mnatha ùireadh.

   Bha mi 'n Éirinn, bha mi 'n Sasunn,
10. Bha mi 'n Leódhas a' chruidh chaisfhinn;
    Cha n-fhaca mi sguab no dais ann,
    Na pill chriathraidh na pill fhasgnaidh.

### Translation

Allan, Allan, long is thy slumber, long it is since I made your bed in the white house at the top of the beach. Sweet to me is the music that wakens me, the son of Iain with his happy band; the people will go on their knees, going in and out through the country, going to meet the new wife.

I was in Ireland, I was in England, I was in Lewis of the white-footed cattle. I did not see a sheaf of corn or a hay mow, a sieve for riddling or a winnowing fan.

From Miss Annie MacDonald, Lochboisdale. The tune and chorus are related to No. 64 in the Tolmie Collection. The words to the latter are superior. See also K. C. Craig's *Òrain Luaidh*, p. 7.

Mode: Hexatonic, no 6th.

## 104 A' BHEAN IADACH

O 's e an t-àilgh-eas. Hùg ò, Chuir dha'n tràigh mi,
Hùg ò. A bhuain duil-isg, hu ri a bhò,
No bhuain bhàir-neach, Hùg ò.

1. O, 's e 'n t-àilgheas, hùg ò    chuir dha'n tràigh mi, hùg ò
   A bhuain duilisg, hu ri a bhò,    no bhuain bhàirneach, hùg ò
   A bhuain duilisg, hùg ò    no bhuain bhàirneach, hùg ò
   'Nighean ud thall, hu ri a bhò    'n cois na tràghad, hùg ò
   Nighean ud thall, *etc.,*    'n cois na tràghad, *etc.,*
   An truagh leat bean òg    's i 'ga bàthadh?'
5. 'Cha truagh, cha truagh,    's beag mo chàs dhith!'
   ''S ann a bhios tu    staigh 'nam àite;
   Sìn do chas dhomh,    sìn do làmh dhomh!
   Cirb do d' bhreacan    mas e 's fheàrr leat!
   Nach truagh a nochd    mo thriùir phàisdean!
10. Fear dhiu bliadhna,    fear a dhà dhiu,
   Fear beag eile    'm feum a thàlaidh!
   Ach Iain bhig,    laoigh do mhàthar,
   Cha n-fhaigh thu nochd    cìoch do mhàthar;
   Ged a gheobhadh    's beag as fheàirrde,
15. 'S ann a bhios i    lomlan sàile!
   Fuar mo leaba,    fliuch le sàile;
   'S buidhe bhean òg    théid 'nam àite,
   Gheobh i ciall is    gheobh i nàire,
   Gheobh i caoirich    mhaola, bhàna,
20. Gheobh i crodh-laoigh    's aighean dàire!
   Thig an coite    'n seo a màireach,
   Bidh m'athair oirre    's mo thriùir bhràithrean,
   'S deagh-Mhac an t-Saoir    air ràmh-bràghad,
   'S gheobh iad mise    'n déidh mo bhàthadh,

254

25. Mo chòta gorm    an uachdar sàile,
    'S mo bhroids airgid    air cloich làimh rium,
    'S mo phaidirean    'n lag mo bhràghad;
    Ceil e, ceil e    air mo mhàthair,
    Gus an éirich    ghrian a màireach!'

Bha dà nighinn ann, agus bha fear a' suirghe orra, agus bha iad ri taobh a chéile; agus cha robh fios aige gu dé 'n rud a dheanadh e, cha b'urrainn e na dhà a phòsadh.

Agus dh'fhalbh e, is phòs e aointé, 's bha an té eile ann 's i iadach. Bha ise riamh iadach, agus bha i staigh a' deanamh phlànaichean riamh, fiach am faigheadh i cur as dha'n té eile; cha robh fios aice-se dé na plànaichean a gheobhadh i riamh air son cur as dha'n té eile, bha i cho iadach.

Co dhiù, bha triùir phàisdean beag aig an té eile, agus bha an leanabh a bha 'n seo aice. Smaointich i gun dànaig là briagh, briagh, briagh, teth—bha an tràigh goirid dhaibh, agus smaointich i gun doireadh i leatha 'n seo dha'n tràigh i. Agus 's e seo an rud a rinn i, thànaig i agus thug i leatha am boireannach a bha an seo dha'n tràigh, agus dh'fhàg i staigh na pàisdean aice 's i gun a bhith ach mionaid shìos a's an tràigh a' buain dhuileasg agus bhàirneach shìos dha'n tràigh.

Bha clachan caol air choireigin ann, 's chaidh iad a null    agus bha iad air an tràigh co dhiù, agus bhuain iad bàirnich 's a chuile sian a's an tràigh. Shuidh iad ann a shineachd, agus thuit an té aig an robh a' chlann, thuit i 'na cadal.

Bha ise (an té iadach) air an *lookout* air a son fhéin, ach co dhiu, dh'fhalbh ise agus liagair ise air falbh cho socair 's a ghabhadh deanamh, liagair i air falbh, agus chunnaic i an lìonadh a' tighinn; agus dìreach nuair a gheobhadh i a nall air an t-sruthan a bha an seo, thànaig i nall air, agus shuidh i air an taobh a bhos.

Agus bha an té eile, cha do dhùisg i riamh gus na dhùisg an làn i, 's i gus a bhith bàite. Agus an uair sin thòisich i air deanamh an òrain air an sgeir; agus bha ise (an té iadach) bhos air an taobh a bhos dha'n linnidh a bha an sin, agus bha am boireannach eile thall.

Lig i leis a' bhoireannach a bàthadh ann an sin, agus thànaig i fhéin dhachaigh chon an duine aig a' bhoireannach, gus i fhéin a dhol 'na h-àite, a dh'fhuireach còmhla ris. Thànaig i dhachaigh, agus an leanabh a bha an seothach, bha e caoineadh, 's a' rànaich, 's a' lasagaich; 's thug i uice am pàisde a bha an seo. 'S gu dé 'n rud a thug i leatha ach a chuile facal riamh dha'n òran a rinn am boireannach eile, màthair na cloinne, thug i leatha a chuile facal riamh dha'n òran. Agus bha i 'ga ghabhail, agus an duin' aice, 's e tuathanach a bh'ann, agus bha e muigh mu'n chrodh agus mu'n chuile sian; agus thànaig an duine chon an doruis, agus chual' e ise gabhail an òrain, agus sheas e 'san dorus; agus dh'éisd e ris a chuile guth riamh dha'n òran, is chuir e mach as an taigh i.

*Translation*

## THE JEALOUS WOMAN

The Wife:

1. O! it was desire[1] that sent me to the strand
   To pick dulse and gather limpets.
   'Girl over yonder beside the shore
   Have you no pity for a young wife who is drowning?'

[1] Most other versions of the song have 'Cha b'e 'n t-àilgheas' 'It was *not* desire', which seems to make better sense, in view of the story.

# SONGS

The Jealous Woman:

      5. 'I have no pity, little do I care about her!'

The Wife:

        'You will be established in my place;
        Stretch out your foot to me, stretch your hand to me.
        The corner of your plaid if you prefer it!
        Wretched to-night are my three children!
    10. One of them a year old, one two years,
        Another little one in need of being lulled to sleep!
        Little Iain, your mother's dearest,
        To-night you will not get your mother's breast;
        Though you got it, it would be of little good,
    15. Full it will be of salt water.
        Cold is my bed, wet with brine,
        Fortunate is the young woman who will go in my place,
        She will get wisdom, she will get modesty[1],
        She will get white hornless sheep,
    20. She will get cows in calf and heifers for bulling!
        The boat will come here to-morrow,
        My father and my three brothers will be on her,
        With good MacIntyre at the bow oar.
        They will find me after my drowning,
    25. My blue coat floating on the sea,
        My silver brooch on a stone beside me,
        And my beads around my neck;
        Hide it, hide it from my mother
        Until the sun rises to-morrow.'

Once there were two young women, and a man was courting both of them; they lived beside each other. He didn't know what to do, as he couldn't marry them both.

He went and married one of them, and the other one was jealous. She was always jealous, and always at home making plans to do away with the first one; she didn't know what plans she might find to do away with the first one, she was so jealous.

The first one had three children, and she had this baby. She (the jealous one) thought that a very fine, warm day had come—the shore was near at hand, she thought that she would take the first one with her to the shore. This is what she did, she came and took the first one with her to the shore, and she (the first one) left her children at home thinking she would only be a minute down on the shore getting dulse and limpets.

There were some kind of narrow stepping stones there, and they went across, and were on the shore, and they picked the limpets and so on on the shore. They sat down there, and the mother of the children fell asleep.

She (the jealous one) was on the lookout for herself, but she went and sneaked away as quietly as she could, she sneaked away, and she saw the flood tide coming; and just when she could get across the stream there, she came over, and she sat down on the landward side.

---

[1] *I.e.* she will get wisdom and modesty in the husband whose wife she is superseding.

The other one never woke until the high tide woke her, when she was about to be drowned. And then she began to make the song, on the rock; and the jealous one was on the other side of the water there, and the mother over (on the rock).

The jealous one let the other one drown there, and came home herself to the drowned one's husband, to take her place, to go to stay with him. She came home, and this baby, it was crying, and bawling, and sobbing; and she took the child to her. And what had she brought with her but the song that the other woman, the mother of the children, had made, she brought with her every single word of the song. And she was singing it while the husband, who was a farmer, was outside around the cattle and everything; and the husband came to the door, and he heard her singing the song, and he stood in the doorway; and he listened to every single word of the song, and put her out of the house.

The tune and words of the song were taken down from Iain Campbell (Iain Clachair) in April 1932. The story behind the song was recorded on wire by Anna Ruadh Currie on 9th November 1950. I have replaced two English words, 'jealous' and 'baby' she used by their Gaelic equivalents, otherwise the story is given exactly as she told it.

The tale of the jealous woman who entices her sister to the rocks at low tide so that she be caught by the sea and drowned and the woman marry the husband is the same theme as 'Binnorie', a folk tale found in Europe. This song is known from Lewis to the south of Ireland, and versions of the words have been published in several collections; and I have seen three tunes in print. One, in *An Gàidheal*, Vol. II, p. 165, was found in Sollas, North Uist, and the title is given as 'Tuireadh Bean Mhic an t-Saoir'. Miss Tolmie collected the same air in North Uist, and it is used by Mrs. Kennedy Fraser as the air for 'Land of Heart's Desire', see her Vol. II, p. 34, while in the same volume is the song 'Sea Tangle', p. 56, which is made up of two of the *Bean Iadach* tunes, of which the second is similar to Mr. Campbell's. A verson of this air is also in the Tolmie Collection, No. 50, under the title 'Bean Mhic A' Mhaoir'. There is another tune to the same words in the same collection, No. 51, which was used by Mrs. Kennedy Fraser as the air for her 'Barra Love Lilt', Vol. III, p. 98. I have also noted a similar tune to Mr. Campbell's with an interesting version of the words from Mrs. Mary Steele, Kildonan, South Uist.

Compare also K. N. MacDonald's *Gesto Collection*, p. 119, and his *Puirt-a-Beul*, p. 44, where Skye and Eigg versions are given; the Patrick MacDonald Collection, No. 11; the *Inverness Collection of Highland Music*, p. 35; K. C. Craig, *Òrain Luaidh*, p. 1, contains a version of the words; another appeared in the *Sydney Post Record* in Nova Scotia in 1937. Professor Otto Andersson published a Lewis version of the air with a few lines of the song in *The Budkavlen*, 1952, p. 47. Mr. Angus Matheson has drawn my attention to versions in the MacLagan MS, No. 119, and in Ó Muirgheasa, *Dhá Chéad de Cheóltaibh Uladh*, pp. 380, 451, 452; and in *Ossian*, contributed by Mr. Alexander Nicolson. Each line, as set out here, is sung twice with slightly differing chorus.

Recently my attention has been drawn to the fact that a good version of the words of this song, and the story accompanying it, are to be found in *Twixt Ben Nevis and Glencoe*, by the Revd. Alexander Stewart (1885: pp. 205-211), who says that the song is claimed by the people of Uist, Skye, Mull, Morvern, and other places in the Highlands.

Mode: Hexatonic, no 2nd.

## 105  AILEIN DUINN

*Fonn:* Ailein Duinn, ó hì, shiubhlainn leat,
Hó ri rì ri u ho, e o hùg hoireann ó,
Ailein Duinn, ó hì, shiubhlainn leat.

1. 'S gura mise th'air mo sgaradh,
Cha n-eil sùgradh nochd air m'aire,
Ailein Duinn, ó hì, *etc.*,

Cha n-eil sùgradh nochd air m'aire
Ach fuaim nan siantan 's miad na gaillinn,
Ailein Duinn, ó hì, *etc.*

258

Ach fuaim nan siantan 's miad na gaillinn
Dh'fhuadaicheadh na fir bho'n chaladh.
5. Ailein Duinn, a luaidh nan leannan,
Chuala mi gun deach thu fairis
Air a' bhàta chaol dhubh dharaich,
'S gun deach thu air tìr am Manainn—.
Cha b'e siod mo ragha caladh
10. Ach Caolas Stiadair anns na h-Earadh,
No Loch Miabhaig anns na beannaibh.
M'iarratas air Rìgh na Cathrach
Gun mi dhol an ùir no 'n anart,
An talamh toll, no 'n àite falaich,
15. Ach 'sa bhall 'san deach thu, Ailein!
Ailein Duinn, a luaidh mo chéille!
Gura h-òg a thug mi spéis dhut;
'S ann a nochd as truagh mo sgeula,
'S cha n-e bàs a' chruidh 'san fhéithe,
20. Ach cho fliuch 's a tha do léine,
Muca mara bhith 'gad reubadh;
Ged bu liomsa buaile spréidhe
'S ann a nochd bu bheag mo spéis dhith.

Ailein duinn, a chiall 's a nàire!
25. Chuala mi gun deach do bhàthadh—
'S truagh, a Rìgh! nach mi bha làimh riut
Ge bè sgeir no bodha 'n tràigh thu,
Ge bè tiùrr an d'fhàg an làn thu;
Dh'òlainn deoch, ge b'oil le càch e,
30. A dh'fhuil do chuim, 's tu 'n déidh do bhàthadh.

*Translation*

Chorus: Brown-haired Allan, ó hì, I would go with thee; hó ri rì ri u ho, e o hùg
hoireann ó,
Brown-haired Allan, ó hì, I would go with thee.

1. I am tormented, I have no thought for merriment to-night but (only) for the sound of the elements and the strength of the gales which would drive the men from the harbour. 5. And brown-haired Allan, my darling sweetheart, I heard you had gone across (the sea) on the slender black boat of oak, and that you had gone ashore in the Isle of Man. That was not the harbour I would have chosen but Caolas Stiadair in Harris or Loch Miabhaig amongst the hills. 12. My prayer to God in heaven, let me not be put in earth or in shroud, in a hole in the earth or a secret place, but in the spot where you have gone, Allan! 16. Brown-haired Allan, my heart's darling, I was young when I fell in love with you. To-night my tale is wretched. It is not (a tale of) the death of cattle in the bog but of the wetness of your shirt and (of how) you are being torn by whales. 22. Although I had a fold of cattle, little to-night would

I esteem it. Brown-haired Allan, my dear beloved! 25. I heard you had been drowned, alas, o God, that I was not beside you on whatever skerry or rock you were cast, on whatever wrack the high-tide had left you. 29. I would drink a drink, in spite of everyone, of your heart's blood, after you had been drowned.

From Iain Campbell, South Lochboisdale, December, 1933. Two-line verses, the second line of each verse being the first line of the following verse. I published this song in the *J.E.F.D.S.S.*, Vol IV, p. 149, with notes. Lines 21, 22 and 23 were given me by his daughter Mary. A fuller version of this song is printed by Rev. A. MacLean Sinclair in *Gaelic Bards 1715–1765*, p. 251. He gives the following account of the circumstances of the composition:

'Allan Morrison, son of Roderick Morrison of Stornoway, was a sea-captain. He generally traded with his vessel between Stornoway and the Isle of Man. In the spring of 1786 he left Stornoway in his vessel to go to Scalpay, Harris, for the purpose of going through the ceremony of marriage contract, *an réiteach*, with Annie Campbell, daughter of Campbell of Scalpay. A furious storm having sprung up, the vessel was swamped; and Captain Morrison and all on board sank with it. The broken-hearted Annie wasted away through grief and died a few months afterwards. Whilst her relatives and friends were crossing over in boats from Scalpay to Rodel, where she was to be buried, they were overtaken by such a violent storm that the coffin had to be thrown overboard. Shortly after her death Captain Morrison's body was found at the Shiant Isles. A few days later her own body was found at the same place. Whether they were buried side by side or not, they should have been.'

It was Donald Campbell of Scalpay, an ancestor of Annie, who refused to betray Prince Charles to Rev. Aulay MacAulay, great-grandfather of Lord MacAulay, in 1746.

There are twenty-six lines from Rev. Kenneth MacLeod printed in the Kennedy Fraser *Songs of the Hebrides*, Vol. I, p. 129, with the tune from Miss Frances Tolmie's Collection. There is a very good version in *An t-Òranaiche*, p. 124. A very incomplete version is printed in the appendix to the *Gesto Collection*, p. 61. The following five lines may be noted:

> Mas e cluasag dhut a' ghaineamh,
> Mas leaba dhut an fheamain,
> Mas e an t-iasg do choinnlean geala,
> Mas e na ròin do luchd faire,
> M'achanaich gu Rìgh na Cathrach, *etc.*

'If the sand is your pillow, if the seaweed is your bed, if the fish are your white candles, if the seals are your (death-bed) watchers, I pray God in Heaven, etc.'

The Editor adds the note:

'A Lament by a lady in Harris for her lover who was drowned off the coast, and a prayer that she might be buried nowhere but in the place where he was lying. She died of grief, and when her body was being conveyed to Pabbay for burial, a fearful storm arose, and the coffin was cast overboard. At the same moment a form was seen, supposed to be that of Allan, who stretched out his arms and bore it away to the depths of the sea.' See also an account by the late John N. MacLeod in Gaelic in the *Stornoway Gazette*.

An incomplete version of this song was recorded from Mrs. MacLean, Beaver Cove, Cape Breton, by J. L. Campbell and myself in 1937. Mrs. MacLean's ancestors came from the Isle of Barra.

It must be pointed out, however, that there has been some confusion between this song and others of the same metre on the same kind of subject. In particular, the four lines quoted from the *Gesto Collection* and the last five lines of the song printed here are found elsewhere. Compare the Tolmie Collection (*J.F.S.S.*, No. 16, pp. 204, 212 and 225). There is a song apparently addressed to another Ailein Donn (recorded by us from Roderick MacKinnon in Barra and Mrs. MacLean in Cape Breton).

With regard to line 29, it is interesting to compare the fourth verse of the lament for Gregor MacGregor as printed in *Bàrdachd Ghàidhlig*, and Professor W. J. Watson's note on it drawing attention to a similar passage in the story of Deirdre and Naoise, pp. 244, 328.

Compare also the pibroch *Cumh na Peahair* in Donald MacDonald's *Collection of the Ancient Martial Music of Caledonia*, p. 53, where it is stated that when Alasdair MacDonell of Keppoch and his brother were murdered, 'their natural Sister, frantic with Grief, Expired at their side, Swallowing their Blood.' This took place in 1663. See also *Cumha ni mhic Raonuill* in D. C. MacPherson's Duanaire, p. 22: '*Thainig ur fuil thar mo bhrògan | 'S teann nach d'òl mi fhin mo leòr dhi.*'

Compare also: *Òrain a' Mhòid*, XI; *Father Allan's Island* (Amy Murray), p. 151; *T.G.S.I.*, Vol. XXVII, p. 394; K. C. Craig's *Òrain Luaidh*, p. 105; *Scottish Home Industries* (1895), p. 25 (music only); *Hebridean Folksongs*, Vol. I, pp. 44 and 161.

Mode: Hexatonic, no 2nd.

## 106 'S ANN DI-LUAIN RO' LÀ FHÉILL MÌCHEIL

*Fonn:* Ò ro na hùg ò,
Seinn o ho ro nàilibh,
Ò ro na hùg ò.

1. 'S ann Di-Luain ro' Là Fhéill Mìcheil
   A fhuair mi 'n dìnneir a chràidh mi,

2. Agus suipeir gun aoibhneas,
   Ged nach roinn mi ri càch i.

3. Och, a Dhia, mar tha mise!
   Bean gun mhisneach gu bràch mi.

4. Bean gun mhàthair, gun athair,
   Gun fhear-taighe, gun bhràthair.

5. Mac Aonghuis a Barraidh,
   'S e a sgar mi 's a chràidh mi.

6. M' eudail mhór do chùl dualach,
   Chì mi bhuam air bhàrr sàile.

7. 'S tu 'nad shìneadh 'san tiùrra,
   Far 'n do bhrùchd a' mhuir-làn thu.

8. Iad 'gad tharruing eadar fearaibh,
   Null gu Baile na Tràghad,

9. Ann an ciste chaoil, chumhaig
   Air a dubhadh[1] 's a tàirneadh.

1 'Dubhadh'; coffins used to be blackened with blacklead.

10. Tha na taighean 'gan rùsgadh
    'S fear 'gan cùmhdach 's 'gan càradh.

11. Null gu Baile na Trianaid,
    Far 'm bu lìonmhor mo chàirdean.

12. 'S mi ri coimhead nan mara
    A' cur fairis a' bhàta.

13. Mo thriùir bhràithrean innte 's m'athair,
    Is fear mo thaighe, 's e chràidh mi.

*Translation*

1. It was on Monday before St. Michael's Day that I got the dinner that hurt me and the joyless supper, although I cannot share it with the rest. O God! how sad is my plight! I am a woman bereft of courage for ever. A woman without mother, without father, without husband, without brother. 5. Son of Angus from Barra, it is he that has bereft me and grieved me. I see your dearly beloved curly locks on the top of the salt wave, and you stretched in the seaweed where the high tide has left you. They are carrying you between men across to Baile na Tràghad, in a narrow, slender coffin, blackened and nailed. 10. The houses are stripped (of thatch) and a man is covering and mending them. 11. Over to Baile na Trianaid where many of my friends are (buried). 12. And I watching the sea capsizing the boat. 13. My three brothers in her, and my father, and my husband, it is this that pained me.

The tune, chorus and thirteen verses were given me by Miss Peigi and Miss Màiri MacRae, Mrs. John Currie and Mrs. Flora MacIntyre during 1935. Versions of this poem, all with some lines similar to this, have been printed in the following collections: *The MacDonald Collection*, p. 351; *An Duanaire*, p. 25, where it is entitled 'A' Bhantrach'; K. C. Craig's *Òrain Luaidh*, p. 53 (another South Uist version). In the Kennedy Fraser Collection, Vol. I, p. 115, is a tune entitled 'Sea Sorrow' which is related to this one, and on p. 17 of the same volume is a poem containing six of the lines printed here. Verse 10 is difficult to understand in this song, though it appears in both the *Duanaire* and *MacDonald Collection* versions in somewhat similar form:

Tha mo thaighean 'gan rùsgadh,
'S cha tionndaidh mo ghràdh rium.

and

Tha do thaighean 'gan rùsgadh,
Feur 'gan cùmhdach 'sa Chàrnaich.

'Baile na Trianaid' is in North Uist close by the North Ford.

Mode: Six note compass, no 7th.

## 107 HÓ RO, GUR TOIL LINN ANNA!

Hó ro gur toil linn Anna,
Hé ho gur toil linn Anna,
Hó ro gur toil linn Anna.

1. Cha dian mise clò gu sìorruidh,
   Cha chroch mi m'iarna ri tallan.

2. 'S ged tha mise seo 'nam shìneadh,
   'S iomadh nì tha air m'aire.

3. Mi 'nam shìneadh air na bòrdan,
   Dh'fhalbh an fheòil a bha mu m' chnamhan.

4. Sin nuair a thuirt Peigi Anndra
   'Tha an t-am a bhith aig a' bhainfh'each.'

5. Sin nuair a thuirt Màiri Dhòmhnaill
   ''S fheàrr dhut tòiseachadh air ceaille.'

6. 'Na faigheamaid air a dheilbh e
   Dh'fhalbhamaid leis ris a' ghealaich.'

7. Thuirt Màiri riuth' an uair sin—
   'Cha n-fhaigh sibh luadhadh ri'r maireann!'

264

*Translation*

Hó ro, we love Anna. 1. I will never more make tweed, I will not hang a hank of wool on the wall. 2. Though I am lying here, many a thing is on my mind. 3. I am stretched here on the boards (hard bed), gone is the flesh that was on my bones.

4. It was then that Peigi Anndra said, 'It is time it was at the weaver.' 5. Then Donald's Mary said, 'It would be better to start making a ball of wool. If we could get it warped we would go on with it by moonlight.' 7. Màiri Anndra then said, 'You will never get it waulked in your life-time' (*i.e.* at your slow rate).

Composed by Mrs. Catriona Campbell MacDonald, South Lochboisdale. Given by Miss Peigi MacRae, North Glendale.

Mrs. MacDonald was a sister of Iain and Seonaidh Campbell, and like them was gifted in composing Gaelic verse and with the same remarkable memory for poetry and songs. Mrs. MacDonald, as her words describe, was an invalid when she composed these lines and died not long afterwards. Two of the names she mentions in her song are contributors to this book, Miss Peigi and Miss Màiri MacRae. Màiri Dhòmhnaill is Miss Mary Currie. The weaver was Peigi Iain Bharraich. The waulking they prepared for was duly held at her house, where she, lying on her bed in the kitchen, sang this song.

Mode: Hexatonic, no 4th.

# ÒRAIN BASAIDH—CLAPPING SONGS

## 108  COISICH AGUS FAIGH DHOMH CÉILE

Fàil ill éileadh ho a ó éileadh,
1. 'Coisich agus faigh dhomh céile,'
Fàil ill éileadh ó ho ro i.
`'S math is aithne dhomh do chéile,
Iain 'Ill Easbuig bheir mi fhéin dhut,
Tuathanach math 's deagh-làmh fheuma,
5, Coinnleir òir air bòrd an réitich,
Freagair siod, ma 's toil leat fhéin e!'

# CLAPPING SONGS

*Translation*

Fàil ill éileadh ho a ó éileadh,
1. 'Step out and get me a sweetheart,'
Fàil ill éileadh ó ho ro i.
'Well I know your sweetheart,
John son of Archibald I'll give you,
5. A good farmer and useful hand,
A golden candlestick on the betrothal table,
Answer that, if you yourself want to !'

From Miss Peigi MacRae.

Mode: Aeolian, weak 2nd.

## 109  Ó, CÓ BHEIR MI LIOM?

Ó, có bheir mi liom air an luing Éireannaich?
'S e mo ghràdh bheir mi liom air an luing Éireannaich.

Ó, có bheir mi liom air an luing Éireannaich?
'S gur e Iain bheir mi liom air an luing Éireannaich.

*Translation*

O, whom shall I take with me on the Irish ship?
It is my love I shall take with me on the Irish ship.

O, whom shall I take with me on the Irish ship?
It is John I shall take with me on the Irish ship.

From Miss Màiri MacRae, Glendale, 1930. An 'Òran Basaidh' or 'Clapping Song'. When the tweed is shrunk sufficiently it is rolled up tightly and two women, facing each other, clap it hard in quick time. In this song, sung for that occasion, they will pair off for fun the young folk that are attending the waulking. One may call, 'Whom shall John take on the Irish ship?' and her partner replies, 'It is Peggy he will take.' In Glendale the term they used was *òran coilich* and to call out a name was 'A Mhàiri, bheir thusa dhaibh an coileach'. There is a version of this song wherever there are waulkings, and the fullest and best version for words I have seen is *An Duanaire*, p. 121. See also for words and tune Kennedy Fraser, Vol. I, p. 161; the Tolmie Collection, No. 20; and for words *MacTalla*, Vol. X, p. 51.

Mode: Pentatonic 4:7.

17    The ruin of the Inn on the shore of Loch Eynort, the chief harbour of South Uist in the old days. Beinn Mhór is on the right

18 Roderick MacCormick's house at Loch Eynort. Saithe drying in the sun

19  Driving Highland cattle to the Fair at Gerinish

20  Selling horses at Gerinish

21   Mrs Iain Campbell (Bean Iain Chlachair) with her Hebridean sheep

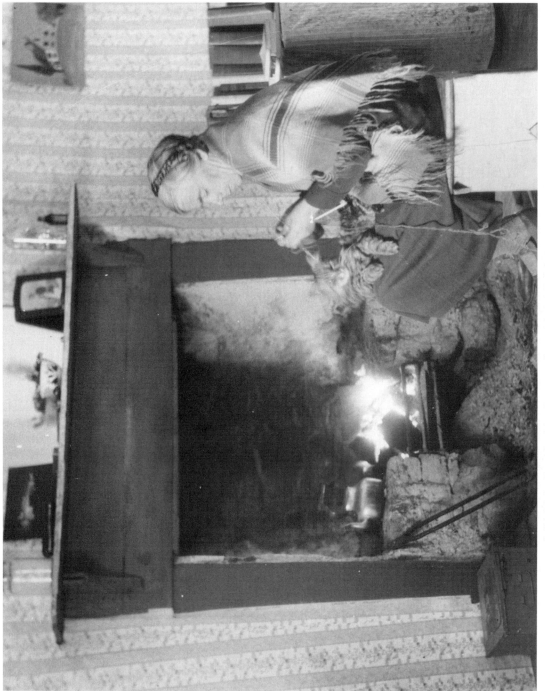

22 Màiri MacRae beside the peat fire with 'Uilleam Dona' (Wicked Willy)

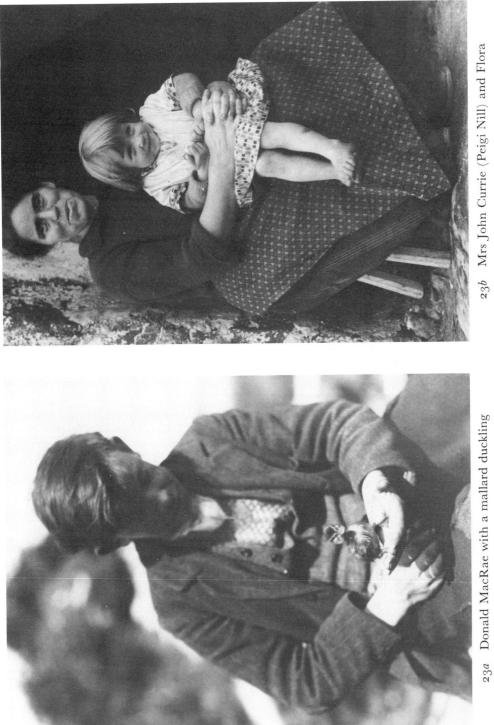

23b   Mrs John Currie (Peigi Nill) and Flora

23a   Donald MacRae with a mallard duckling

24*b* Mrs Alasdair Currie twists her wool on a spindle or *fearsaid*. She wears a hand-knitted shawl and *drocaid* skirt

24*a* Miss Mary Smith

25   Peigi MacRae milking Dora, who wears a *buarach* or fetter

26a  Seonaidh and Peigi Campbell with neighbours take the mackerel from the nets.

26b  Angus John and James Campbell in the *St Bride*

27   Mrs Roderick MacLeod (Bean Ruairi a' Chùbair) carding wool

28 Spinning with a distaff or *cuigeal*

29   Bean Ruairi at her spinning-wheel. The *crois-iarna* for measuring wool
hangs on the wall

30   A roll of hand-made tweed and balls of blanket wool

31   The children in their Hallowe'en guise

32   Calum and Catherine Paterson with flail (*sùiste*) and sieve (*criathair*)

# RECITERS

★

IAIN CAMPBELL (Iain Clachair: Iain Mac Dhòmhnaill 'ic Iain Bhàin), crofter and mason, South Lochboisdale; born about 1858, died 1932. Like his brother he was a poet, and some of his poems were taken down by Fr. Allan McDonald and Dr. George Henderson at various times between 1889 and 1893. He gave songs 96, 104 and 105, and cures. (Plates 7*b*, 21.)

MRS. IAIN CAMPBELL (Màiri nighean Iain Ruaidh 'ic Aonghuis 'ic Ruairi), his wife, gave songs 26, 35, 36, 44, 47, 51, 77, 86, 90, 92 and 98, and proverbs. (Plate 21.)

RODERICK CAMPBELL (Ròidseag), merchant seaman, son of Iain Campbell, was a bard like his father and uncle, and composed song 6.

SEONAIDH CAIMBEUL (Seonaidh mac Dhòmhnaill 'ic Iain Bhàin), crofter fisherman, South Lochboisdale, brother of Iain Campbell; born 1859, died 1945. He was also a poet, and about a hundred of his songs have been taken down by Mr. John MacInnes, of which forty-five were published in 1936 in a book called *Òrain Ghaidhlig le Seonaidh Caimbeul*. He was also a story-teller. He gave the words of 'Duan na Càisg' and song 23, some cures and the six stories given here in translation. Some of his poems were previously taken down by Fr. Allan McDonald, who says that his family belonged to the branch of the Campbells known in South Uist as 'Caimbeulaich an Urrais'. (Plates 5*b*, 15.)

ANGUS JOHN CAMPBELL (Aonghus Iain), son of Iain Campbell, crofter fisherman, South Lochboisdale, gave songs 5, 8, 10, 11, 12, 13, 15, 22 and 25, a Hogmanay ballad and various cures and proverbs. (Plates 5*b*, 16, 26*b*.)

MRS. MARY CAMPBELL MACLEOD, South Lochboisdale, daughter of Iain Campbell, gave songs 86 and 105.

MRS. ALASDAIR CAMPBELL (Seònaid nighean Aonghuis 'ic Ailein Mhóir, Bean Alasdair 'ic Dhubhghaill), North Glendale, gave song 9.

269

# RECITERS

MRS. ANGUS CAMPBELL (Màiri nighean Iain 'ic Ruairi 'ic Iain 'ic Fhionnlaidh, Bean Aonghuis Ruaidh 'ic Dhubhghaill), South Lochboisdale, gave songs and proverbs. (Plates 3*b*, 8.)

MRS. ANGUS CAMPBELL (Bean Aonghuis Bhig), gave some proverbs.

MRS. ALASDAIR CURRIE (Mary Ann nighean Coinnich Bhig 'ic Thormoid 'ic Coinnich) (a MacKinnon from Dalibrog) gave song 49, dyes and recipes. (Plates 4*b*, 24*b*.)

DONALD CURRIE, son of Alasdair Currie, gave ballad no. 2. (Plate 6*b*.)

MRS. ANGUS CURRIE (Anna Ruadh nighean Dhòmhnaill 'ic Ailein 'ic Iain 'ic Fhionnlaidh), South Lochboisdale, gave songs 45, 97 and 104.

MRS. DONALD CURRIE (Agnes nighean Sheonaidh Gallacher), born at Lochboisdale, gave songs 16, 19, 22, 29, 34, 37, 39, 41, 46, 48, 61, 62, 73 and 83, and various proverbs. She is particularly good at lullabies and *puirt-a-bial*.

MRS. JOHN CURRIE (Peigi Nill 'ic Steafain, Bean Iagain Dhòmhnaill Mhóir), North Glendale, gave songs 3, 4, 7, 16, 21, 23, 33, 38, 52, 64, 66, 87, 94 and 106, and dyes. (Plate 23*b*.)

MISS PEIGI CURRIE (Peigi Dhòmhnaill 'ic Eóghainn), South Lochboisdale, gave various cures.

MRS. ANGUS MACDONALD (nighean Dhòmhnaill 'ic Ealaig, Bean Aonghuis 'ic Iain 'ic Aonghuis Mhóir), South Lochboisdale, gave various proverbs and dyes.

MISS ANNIE MACDONALD (Anna nighean Raghnaill 'ic Iain 'ic Lachlainn), born at Lochboisdale, now living on Canna. She gave songs 28, 56, 69, 78, 83, 85 and 103.

JOHN MACDONALD (Iagain Theàrlaich 'ic Aonghuis Mhóir), South Lochboisdale, gave the 'Ballad of the Smithy'.

MRS. JOHN MACDONALD (nighean Eachainn Bhig, Bean Iagain Theàrlaich 'ic Aonghuis Mhóir), South Lochboisdale, gave various cures.

MISS MARY MACDONALD (Màiri nighean Ruairidh 'ic Dhòmhnaill 'ic Dhòmhnaill 'ic Aonghuis), South Lochboisdale, gave various cures and dyes.

RODERICK MACDONALD (Ruairi am Posta: mac Raghnaill 'ic Ruairi 'ic Raghnaill), formerly postman, North Lochboisdale, gave song 24.

MRS. FLORA MACINTYRE (Floraidh nighean Ailein 'ic Caluim, Bean Chaluim Dhòmhnaill 'ic Iain Chaluim), Glendale, gave song 106.

NEIL MACLENNAN (Niall mac 'Illeasbuig Fhearchair 'ic Iain Ruaidh 'ic Mhicheil), postmaster at Lochboisdale and formerly R.S.M. of the Camerons, gave song 8. His aunt, Marion MacLennan, had a wonderful knowledge of folklore, some of which she gave to Alexander Carmichael, the Revd. A. MacDonald, Killearnan, and Fr. Allan McDonald. The family came originally from Harris.

# RECITERS

MRS. INA MACLENNAN FRASER, formerly at Lochboisdale, now living at Staffin, Isle of Skye, sister of Neil MacLennan, gave various cures.

REV. MURDO MACLEOD, formerly minister of the Church of Scotland at Dalibrog, now at Valparaiso, Chile, gave songs 5, 14 and 75.

MISS PEIGI and MISS MÀIRI MACRAE (Clann Anndra na h-Àirigh Molaich), North Glendale, I have already described in the general introduction. Their parents came originally from Harris. They gave songs 1, 2, 8, 10, 11, 17, 20, 23, 24, 30, 31, 32, 36, 37, 40, 41, 42, 50, 53, 54, 55, 57, 58, 59, 60, 65, 67, 68, 70, 71, 72, 74, 76, 77, 78, 80, 81, 82, 84, 85, 88, 89, 90, 91, 92, 95, 97, 101, 106, 107, 108, and 109; also many proverbs, recipes, cures and dyes. (Plates 3a, 7a, 10, 16, 22, 25.)

FINLAY MARTIN (Fionnladh Dhòmhnaill Mhartainn), Dalibrog, gave various cures.

RONALD MORRISON (Raghnall mac Eóghainn), South Lochboisdale, gave various cures. (Plate 6a.)

MRS. RONALD MORRISON (Bean Raghnaill 'ic Eóghainn), South Lochboisdale, gave song 88. (Plate 6a.)

MISS MARY MORRISON, her daughter, gave song 93.

MISS MARY SMITH (Màiri Smios nighean Iain 'ic Phàdruig), South Boisdale, aged 89 in 1954, gave songs 27, 77, 84, 85, 91 and 102. Her grandfather, Patrick, was a very famous *seanchaidh* who gave much material to Alexander Carmichael, and her father Iain gave Ossianic ballads to Dr. George Henderson. (Plate 24a.)

MRS. MARY STEELE (Màiri Bhàn nighean Dhòmhnaill 'ic Ailein), Kildonan, sister of Mrs. Angus Currie, gave songs 79, 82, 99, 100, 102 and 103.

DUNCAN MACDONALD (Dunnchadh mac Dhòmhnaill 'ic Dhunnchaidh 'ic Iain 'ic Dhòmhnaill 'ic Thormoid), Peninerine, the famous Gaelic storyteller, gave me the words of song 13 while on a visit to Canna in the summer of 1951.

(I am much obliged to Mr. John MacInnes, Gerinish, originally from South Lochboisdale, for information concerning the Gaelic patronymics of many of the reciters.)

# FIRST LINES OF SONGS
# AND BALLADS

★

# FIRST LINES OF SONGS

# FIRST LINES OF SONGS

# APPENDIX

THE following seventeen songs were included in an article on 'Gaelic Folksongs from South Uist' which I was invited to contribute to *Studia Memoriae Belae Bartók Sacra*, published in Budapest in 1956. As this volume cannot have been seen by many readers in Scotland or America, I think it is worth reprinting them here. The songs were chosen on purpose to illustrate the different types of song extant in the Gaelic oral tradition of South Uist. Only one, number 7, had appeared earlier in the original edition of *Folksongs and Folklore of South Uist*.

M.F.S.

### 1. Latha mór a ghàbhaidh

*Òran Mór*                    Sung by Peigi MacRae, Glendale.

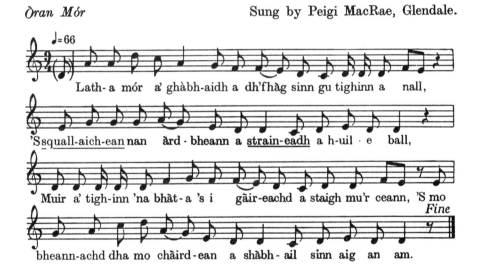

*Translation*

The great day of danger, we left to sail across, with squalls of the high hills straining every rope, the sea coming aboard and laughing around our heads; my blessing on my friends who saved us at the time.

# APPENDIX

Song composed to a traditional tune by *Calum Ruadh MacKinnon*, Barra, who died around 1933.

## 2. A' dol seachad Port Grianaig

*Sailing Song*                     Sung by Peigi MacRae, Glendale

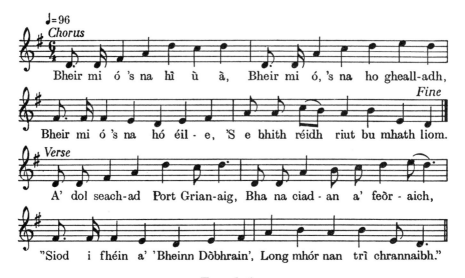

Bheir mi ó 's na hì ù à, Bheir mi ó, 's na ho gheall-adh,

Bheir mi ó 's na hó éil - e, 'S e bhith réidh riut bu mhath liom.

A' dol seach-ad Port Grian-aig, Bha na ciad - an a' feòr - aich,

"Siod i fhéin a' 'Bheinn Dòbhrain', Long mhór nan trì chrannaibh."

### Translation

Chorus : Bheir mi ó, *etc.*, I would prefer to be friends with thee.
Verse : Going past Greenock, hundreds were asking, „That's her, the *Ben Dorain*, the great ship of three masts."

## 3. 'S truagh, a Rìgh, nach b'e 'm màireach

*Love Song*                     Sung by Agnes Currie, Lochboisdale.

Ó fail i rinn, ill e rinn O ho ró i o é

Fail i rinn ill e rinn Ó ho rinn ó.

'S truagh, a Rìgh, nach b'e 'm màireach An latha dh'fhal(a)bhadh mo bràthair,.

Gheobh-ainn leisg-eul no dhà air, A ghràidh, bhith 'gad thùirs'.

Ó fail i rinn ill e rinn, ó ho rinn ó.

*Translation*

Sad, o Lord, 'twas not tomorrow, the day my brother would depart. I would get an excuse or two, my love, to lament you.

Cp. *Òranaiche*, 176, 178.

## 4. An cluinn thu mi, mo chailin donn?

*Love Song*                                Sung by Mrs. John Currie, Glendale.

An cluinn thu mi, mo chail-in donn? Teann nall is

thoir an air-e dhomh! Tha mór-an ann am

bar-ail dhiù Gur òg an leann-an dhòmhs' thu.

*Translation*

Will you hear me, my brown-haired girl? Come over and pay attention to me! Many of them are of the opinion that you are (too) young a sweetheart for me.

279

# APPENDIX

Cp. *Eilean Fraoich*, p. 13. Mrs. Currie first learned this song in Eriskay.

## 5. 'S i nighean mo ghaoil

*Love Song*                                    Sung by Peigi MacRae, Glendale.

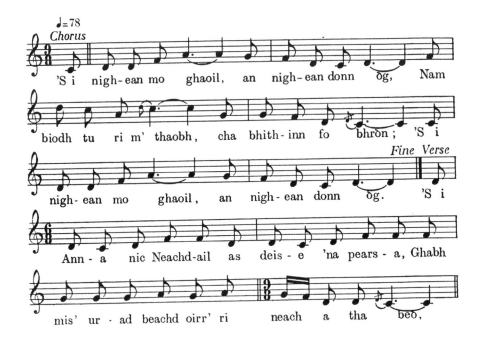

*Translation*

Chorus : The lass that I love is the young brown-haired girl ; if you were beside me I would not be sad ; the lass that I love is the young brown-haired girl.

Verse : 'Tis Annie MacNicol who is neatest of person, I took as great a notion to her as to anyone alive.

Cp. *Orain a' Mhoid*, II, p. 9 ; Angus MacLeod, *The Songs of Duncan Ban MacIntyre*, p. 102. The words of the chorus and opening verse are practically the same as in Duncan Ban's song, but the other verses Peigi MacRae sang, though on a similar subject, were different.

# APPENDIX

## 6. Éirich 's na dean tionndadh rium

Sung by Peigi MacRae, Glendale.

Éir-ich 's na dean tionnd-adh rium, Gur h-e mo dhiùmb a choisinn thu! Dean
cad-al soc-air air mo chùl-aibh, Sùgr-adh cha bhi nochd ag-ainn!
'S olc an ob-air dhu'sa daonn-an Bhith tighinn dhachaigh air an daoraich;
Chosg-adh tu do chuid dha'n t-saoghal, 'S dh'aognaich fear do choltais mi.

*Translation*

Get up and don't you turn to me, 'tis my anger you have earned.
Turn your back and go to sleep, tonight there'll be no love-making.
Ill the ploy you're always at, coming home drunk again ; you would
spend your worldly goods — such a husband vexes me.

## 7. Cha bhi mi 'gad thàladh

*Lullaby*

Sung by Peigi MacRae, Glendale.

O bà, o bà, o bà, o ì, O bà, o
bà, o bà, o ì, O bà, o bà, o bà, o ì, Cha
bhi mi 'gad thàl-adh Bho'n shàr-aich thu mi. O

# APPENDIX

*Translation*

O bà, o bà, o bà, o ì, I will not rock you to sleep, since you have worn me out.

## 8. A Bhólagan, a bhó chiùin

*Milking Song*　　　　　　　　Sung by Agnes Currie, Lochboisdale.

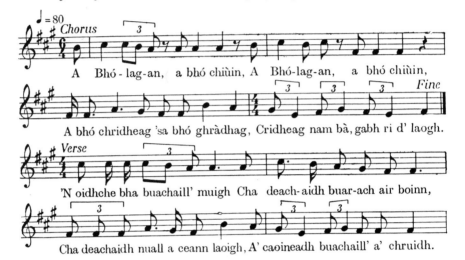

A Bhó-lag-an, a bhó chiùin, A Bhó-lag-an, a bhó chiùin,

A bhó chridheag 'sa bhó ghràdhag, Cridheag nam bà, gabh ri d' laogh.

'N oidhche bha buachaill' muigh Cha deach-aidh buar-ach air boinn,

Cha deachaidh nuall a ceann laoigh, A' caoineadh buachaill' a' chruidh.

*Translation*

Chorus : Bólagan, gentle cow, Bólagan, gentle cow, dear little cow, beloved little cow, dearest of cows, take to your calf.

Verse : The night (the) herdsman was outside no fetter was put on a cow, no calf uttered a low, lamenting the herdsman of the cattle.

## 9. Hó Mhàiri, hó bheag

*Children's Song*　　　　　　　Sung by Agnes Currie, Lochboisdale.

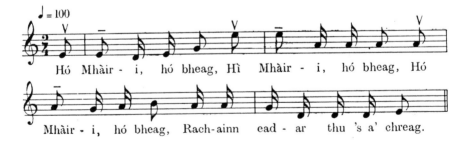

Hó Mhàir - i, hó bheag, Hì Mhàir - i, hó bheag, Hó

Mhàir - i, hó bheag, Rach-ainn ead - ar thu 's a' chreag.

# APPENDIX

Hó Mary, hó bheag, I would go between you and the crag.
Children's Song of a type often heard — "I would go between you and the wind, I would go between you and death, where the raven would make a cry."

Cp. Tolmie Collection, No. 23.

## 10. 'S ann tha 'n còmhradh grinn aig an fhitheach

*Children's Song*        Sung by Peigi MacRae, Glendale.

'S ann tha 'n còmh-radh grinn aig an fhith - each,

Sin nuair thuirt an fhaoil-eag, 'na laigh' air a maod-ail.

"Cha n'eil an fheòil cho daor nach fhaod sinn aic - e suidh - e";

'S ann tha 'n còmh-radh grinn aig an fhith - each.

Sin nuair thuirt an cal- (a)m-an 'na suidh' air a h-carr-(a)b-all "Tha'n

t-am ag - ainn bhith fal - (a)bh 's na seal-(a)g-air - ean air tighinn!"

*Fine*

'S ann tha 'n còmh-radh grinn aig an fhith - each.

# APPENDIX

The raven has pleasant talk : then the seagull, lying on her belly, said, »Meat is not so dear that we can't sit down at it.« The raven has pleasant talk.

Then the dove, sitting on her tail, said, »It is time for us to be going, the hunters are coming!« The raven has pleasant talk.

## 11. A rì a ró a, cailleach a' bhreabadair

*Dance Song*                                    Sung by Peigi MacRae, Glendale.

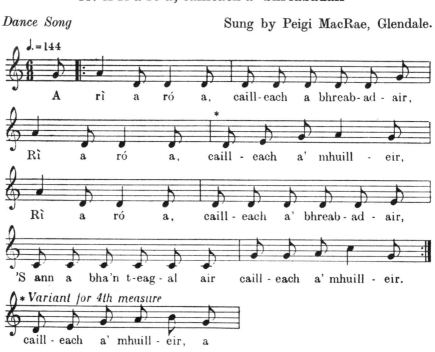

A rì a ró a, caill-each a bhreab-ad-air,

Rì a ró a, caill-each a' mhuill-eir,

Rì a ró a, caill-each a' bhreab-ad-air,

'S ann a bha'n t-eag-al air caill-each a' mhuill-eir.

*Variant for 4th measure*

caill-each a' mhuill-eir, a

*Translation*

A rì a ró a, the weaver's old wife, rì a ró a, the miller's old wife, rì a ró a, the weaver's old wife, the miller's old wife had the fright of her life.

284

# APPENDIX

## 12. Beil, a chailleach, a' bhrà

**Quern Song**
Sung by Annie MacDonald, Lochboisdale.

Beil, a chaill-each,'a' bhrà, Beil, a chaill-each,a' bhrà, Beil, a chaill-each, a' bhrà, 'S fear a' tigh-inn 'gad iarr - aidh! Gu dé 'n t-aod-ach a th'air? Tha lùir - each air, tha bàirl - ig air, Tha seann-chraic-eann brath-ann air; Beil, a chaill-each,a' bhrà, Beil, a chaill-each,a' bhrà, Beil, a chaill-each, a' bhra, 'S fear a' tigh-inn 'gad iarr - aidh!

*Translation*

Grind the quern, old wife, grind the quern, old wife, grind the quern, old wife, a man is coming to ask for you! What clothing does he wear? He wears a tattered cloak, he wears rags, he has an old quern-skin on! Grind the quern, old wife, grind the quern, old wife, grind the quern, old wife, a man is coming to ask for you!

Cp. *MacDonald Collection*, p. 334, lines 24—26.

A quern is a hand mill of two circular flat stones for grinding meal. The top stone rotates by being pushed round by a wooden pin, in a jerking, irregular manner.

# APPENDIX

## 13. 'S gura mise tà làn airteil

*Waulking Song*　　　　　　Sung by Annie MacDonald, Lochboisdale.

Fail iù ill ò ho ro éil - e, Fail
iù ill à ro hù a hó Fail iù ill ò ho ro éil - e.

'S gur-a mis - e tà làn airt-eil Dìr-eadh 's a' teàrnadh na leac-aich.

*Variant: Chorus.*

Fail iù ill ò ho ro éil - e, Fail iù ill ò ro hù a ho a

*Variants for second line of verse*

1.

'S math tha fios a'm dé chum bhuam thu,

2.

Bha té eil' aig bail - e 'gad bhuann-achd.

3.

Gun mhart dubh ann, gun mhart ruadh ann.

## Translation

I am full of sorrow, climbing and descending the hillside.

Cp. K. C. Craig, p. 59.

## 14. Hó a, hù a, nighean dubh

*Love Song*                                    Sung by Agnes Currie, Lochboisdale.

*Translation*

Chorus : Hó a, hù a, black-haired lass, brown-haired lass, hó ri ri a, pretty black-haired lass, hó a hù a, black-haired lass, brown-haired lass.

Verse : Brown-haired lass of bright bosom, I would meet you on the moorland.

# APPENDIX

## 15. Thug mi gaol do dh'Iain

*Waulking Song*                        Sung by Peigi MacRae, Glendale.

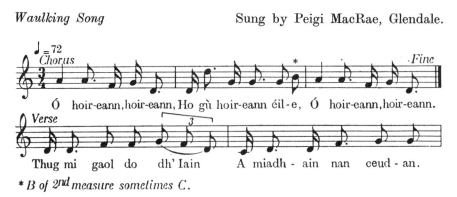

Ó hoir-eann, hoir-eann, Ho gù hoir-eann éil-e, Ó hoir-eann, hoir-eann.

Thug mi gaol do dh'Iain     A miadh-ain nan ceud-an.

*\* B of 2nd measure sometimes C.*

### Translation

Verse : I gave love to Iain, from amongst hundreds.

This may not be the usual first line. The singer only remembered a fragment.

## 16. Ill iù, ó, cha d'fhuair mi 'n cadal

*Waulking Song*                        Sung by Peigi MacRae, Glendale.

Ill iù, ill eó, ill-ean is ó, Ill iù, ó, cha

d'fhuair mi 'n cad-al, Ill iù, ill eó, ill-ean is ó.

Dh'fhiadh-aich an sgiob-air air bòrd mi,

'S rinn an ròg-air e mo ghlac-adh.

288

# APPENDIX

Chorus : Ill iù, *etc.*, I did not get sleep.
Verse : The skipper invited me on board, and the rascal seized me.

Fragment of waulking song. Cp. K. C. Craig, p. 86.

## 17. Chì mi 'm báta seach an rubha

*Waulking Song*                    Sung by Peigi MacRae, Glendale.

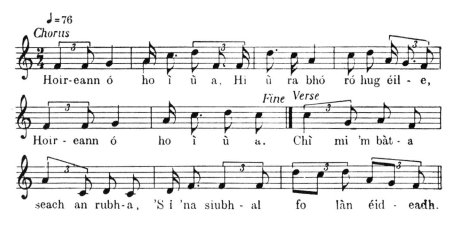

Hoir-eann ó   ho   î   ù   a,   Hi   ù   ra bhó   ró hug éil - e,

Hoir - eann ó   ho   î   ù   a.   Chì   mi 'm bàt - a

seach an rubh-a,   'S i 'na siubh - al   fo   làn éid - eadh.

*Translation*

I see the boat go past the point, moving under full sail.

Cp. K. C. Craig, p. 114.

289

# NOTES

1. Seven of Calum Ruadh MacKinnon's other songs were published by Colm Ó Loch-lainn in his *Deoch Slàinte nan Gillean*, Dublin 1948.

6. This is the refrain and the sixth verse of a song by Ailean Dall MacDougall (1750–1828), the subject being a wife's scolding of her husband for taking too many drams of whisky. See the 1829 edition of his poems, pp. 77, 78.

7. See p. 137 of this book.

8. There is a version of the words in *Carmina Gadelica*, I 266.

10. A version of this song was taken down by Fr Allan McDonald from John MacKinnon ('Iain Mac an Tàilleir'), Daliburgh, South Uist, on 4th December 1894. This has refrain and three verses, the second with one line missing. Another version, five verses and refrain, recorded by the late Dr Calum MacLean from Mrs Annie Arnott, Kilmuir, Skye, and two other verses recorded by Ian Patterson from Mrs Kate Dix, Bernera-Harris, with a musical transcription of the first, was printed in the first number of *Tocher*, published by the School of Scottish Studies, in 1971.

    From these and from Peigi MacRae's version, the story behind the song becomes clear. The farmer's mare has died, and the birds of prey, the eagle, raven, crow, and seagull, have come to feast on the dead body. The dove is sitting on the tail, keeping watch to warn the others of the hunters' approach. The farmer's dog is thinking about his chance at the feast. Each of the animals utters a verse of the song. In Fr Allan McDonald's version, the refrain is:

    > 'S ann tha 'n còmhradh binn
    >     aig an fhitheach,
    > Air an làiridh dhuinn,
    >     thug i dhuinn an t-sitheann.

    'The raven has sweet conversation about the brown mare, she
    has given us meat.'

    From this it is clear that the 'her' of Peigi MacRae's version refers to the mare, not mentioned there.

12. See *Carmina Gadelica* V 246, for a version of the text, and I 252 for a description of the process of making meal with the quern. The 'quern skin' was an old skeep-skin on which the quern was placed.

# NOTES

13. There is a version of this song in Campbell and Collinson, Hebridean Folksongs Vol. I p. 80 (No. XIII), musical transcriptions pp. 272–278.

16. There will be a version of this in *Hebridean Folksongs* Vol. III, no. CXIV, recorded from Mrs Neil Campbell, Frobost, South Uist.

17. See Hebridean Folksongs Vol. I no XXI, p. 108, musical transcriptions pp. 296–298.

# BIBLIOGRAPHY

★

(The original spelling and accentation of titles is reproduced)

## MUSIC

A' CHOISIR-CHIÙIL. The *St. Columba Collection of Gaelic Songs*. Bayley & Ferguson, Glasgow, London.

AN COMUNN GÀIDHEALACH. Publications. *Òrain a' Mhòid*, 1924-1938. *Coisir a' Mhòid*, the Mod Collection of Gaelic Part Songs, 1896–1925, 2 vols. *Coisir na Cloinne*, Forty Gaelic Songs for Rural and Juvenile Gaelic Choirs. Alexander MacLaren & Sons, Glasgow.

ANDERSSON, Professor Otto. 'On Gaelic Folk Music from the Isle of Lewis'. *The Budkavlen*, 1952. Åbo, Finland.

BROADWOOD, Lucy E. 'Twenty Gaelic Songs', with Notes, *Journal of the Folk Song Society*, *No. 35*, December 1931. 'Ten Gaelic Folk Songs', with texts and tunes, *Journal of the English Folk Dance and Song Society*, Vol. I, No. 1, 1932; 'Eleven Gaelic Songs', *ibid.*, Vol. I, No. 2; 'Eleven Gaelic Folk Songs', *ibid.*, Vol. I, No. 3. Cecil Sharp House, 2 Regent's Park Road, London, N.W.

CAMPBELL, Alexander. *Albyn's Anthology* or a Select Collection of the Melodies and Vocal Poetry peculiar to Scotland and the Isles hitherto unpublished. Collected and arranged by Alexander Campbell. Author of *The History of Poetry in Scotland; A Journey through the Different Parts of Scotland, etc., etc.; The Modern Scottish and English Verses adapted to the Highland, Hebridean, and Lowland Melodies written by Walter Scott, Esq., and other Living Poets of the First Eminence*, two volumes, 1816.

CAMPBELL, Donald, Esq. *A Treatise of the Language, Poetry, and Music of the Highland Clans. With Illustrative Traditions and Anecdotes and Numerous Ancient Highland Airs*. D. R. Collie & Son, 19 St. David Street, Edinburgh, 1862.

CAMPBELL, John Lorne. *Highland Songs of the Forty-five*. John Grant, Edinburgh, 1933.

CELTIC MELODIES: *Being a Collection of Original Slow Highland Airs, Pipe Reels, and Cainn-tearachd never before published*. Selected and arranged by a Highlander (MS. with notes). Published by R. Purdie, Edinburgh, 1823.

293

# BIBLIOGRAPHY

CLÀRSACH A' GHLINNE. *The Harp of the Glen*. Twenty-five Gaelic Songs arranged with simple accompaniments by Jennie Given, A.R.C.M. Paterson's Publications Ltd., Glasgow and London.

DOW, Daniel. *A Collection of Ancient Scots Music for the Violin, Harpsichord or German-Flute*. Never before printed. Consisting of Ports, Salutations, Marches or Pibrochs &c. Edinburgh. *Circa* 1780.

DUN, Finlay. *Orain na'h-Albain*, a collection of Gaelic Songs with English and Gaelic Words and an Appendix containing traditional Notes to many of the Songs. The Pianoforte accompaniment arranged and revised by Finlay Dun. Edinburgh. No date.
    (Published about 1860. The Preface contains what may be the earliest discussion of the modality of Gaelic folktunes.)

EILEAN FRAOICH: Lewis Gaelic Songs and Melodies. An Comunn Gàidhealach Leódhais, Stornoway, 1938.

FRASER, Captain Simon of Knockie. *The Airs and Melodies Peculiar to the Highlands of Scotland and the Isles, communicated in an original, pleasing and familiar style; Having the lively airs introduced as medleys to form a sequence to each slower movement; With an admired plain harmony for the Piano forte, Harp, Organ or Violincello, intended rather to preserve Simplicity than load with Embellishment.* Edited by Captain Simon Fraser and chiefly acquired during the interesting period from 1715 to 1745, through the Authentic Source narrated in the Accompanying Prospectus. Mr. John Gow, Hanover Street, Edinburgh and London, 1816.

—— New edition revised by Wm. MacKay, Secretary to the Gaelic Society of Inverness, and containing the corrections and additions by the Compiler's son, the late Angus Fraser. Hugh MacKenzie, Bank Lane, Inverness, 1874.

GESTO COLLECTION: see K. N. MacDonald.

GLEN, John. *Early Scottish Melodies*. Edinburgh, 1900.

GUNN, Rev. Adam, M.A., and MACFARLANE, Malcolm. *Orain agus Dain le Rob Donn Mac-Aoidh*. New Edition. Containing several original and hitherto unpublished melodies collected in the Reay Country; sketch of the bard and his times; dissertation on the Reay Country dialect; a full glossary of uncommon words; and a supplementary chapter on the bard's surname. Glasgow, 1899.
    (Contains forty-five airs in staff and sol-fa notation.)

INVERNESS COLLECTION OF HIGHLAND PIBROCHS, LAMENTS, QUICKSTEPS, AND MARCHES, THE, carefully and effectively arranged for the Pianoforte, and containing some of the most popular and favourite airs of the Highlands of Scotland. Inverness, no date.

KENNEDY FRASER, Marjory, and MACLEOD, Kenneth. *Songs of the Hebrides*, Vol. I (1909), Vol. II (1917), Vol. III (1921). Boosey & Co. Ltd., London; *From the Hebrides* (1925), Paterson, Glasgow.

MACDONALD, Keith Norman. *The Gesto Collection of Highland Music, including the second part or appendix of 67 pages.* Printed by Oscar Brandstetter, Leipzig, 1895.

—— *Puirt-a-Beul or Mouth Tunes suitable for Dances, Games, etc.* Alexander MacLaren & Sons, Glasgow, 1901 and 1931.

MACDONALD, Patrick. *A Collection of Highland Vocal Airs never hitherto published. To which are added a few of the more lively Country Dances or Reels of the North Highlands & Isles. And Some Specimens of Bagpipe Music.* By Patrick MacDonald, Minister of Kilmore in Argyllshire. (The Collection made by Patrick and his brother, Joseph MacDonald.) Edinburgh. No date (about 1780).

# BIBLIOGRAPHY

MacMillan, Rev. John, of Barra. *Gaelic Songs of the Isles of the West*. Translations and Stories by Patrick MacGlynn, M.A., D.Lit. Music arranged by F. W. Lewis, F.R.C.O., L.R.A.M. Boosey & Co. Ltd., London, 1929, 1930, 2 vols.

Matheson, William. *The Songs of John MacCodrum*. Scottish Gaelic Texts Society, 1938. (Contains twenty-three genuine traditional airs to which some of these songs are sung in Uist.)

Morison, Duncan. *Ceòl Mara. Songs of the Isle of Lewis*. J. & W. Chester, London, 1935.

Murray, Amy. *Child Songs in the Island of Youth*. (Article printed in the *Celtic Review*, Vol. II, p. 314. Contains six songs taken down on Eriskay in 1905, which are reprinted in the following book.)

—— *Father Allan's Island*. New York, 1920. (Contains twenty-six authentic transcriptions of traditional Gaelic folksongs noted on Eriskay, which is the island referred to in the title, in 1905.)

O Lochlainn, Colm. *Deoch-Slàinte nan Gillean. Dornan òran a Barraidh*. Under the Sign of the Three Candles, Dublin, 1948.

Òrain Dà Ghuthach. *Gaelic Duets*, Book I, Alexander MacLaren, Glasgow, 1928.

Shaw, Margaret Fay. 'Six Hebridean Folk Songs', *Journal of the English Folk Dance and Song Society*, 1943: 'Seven Hebridean Folk Songs', *ibid.*, 1944 (Vol. IV, Nos. 4 and 5).

Stewart, Charles. *The Killin Collection of Gaelic Songs*. With music and translations. Edinburgh, 1884.

Tolmie, Frances. '105 Songs of Occupation from the Western Isles of Scotland with Notes and Reminiscences.' 'Notes on the Modal System of Gaelic Tunes', by Miss A. G. Gilchrist and Miss Lucy E. Broadwood. *Journal of the Folk Song Society*, No. 16, being the 3rd part of Vol. IV. 19 Berners Street, London, W.1, 1911.

Whyte, Henry (Fionn). *The Celtic Lyre*, a collection of Gaelic songs, with English translations. Music in both notations. Edinburgh, 1898.

## TEXTS

Cameron, Rev. Hector. *Na Bàird Thirisdeach*, The Tiree Bards. Stirling, 1932.

Campbell, Lord Archibald. *Records of Argyll*: Legends, Traditions and Recollections of Argyllshire Highlanders. William Blackwood & Sons, Edinburgh & London, 1885.

Campbell, J. F. *Leabhar na Féinne*: Heroic Gaelic Ballads collected in Scotland chiefly from 1512 to 1871. London, 1872.

Campbell, J. L. *Fr. Allan McDonald of Eriskay: Priest, Poet and Folklorist*. Oliver & Boyd, 1954.

—— *Sia Sgialachdan*: Six Gaelic Stories from Uist and Barra. Edinburgh, 1938.

Campbell or Caimbeul, Seonaidh. *Orain Ghàidhlig le Seonaidh Caimbeul* (Seonaidh mac Dhòmhnaill 'ic Iain Bhàin), air an toirt sìos le Iain Mac Aonghuis: air an deasachadh le Iain Latharna Caimbeul. Printed in Dunfermline for the author in 1936; second edition in 1937.

Carmichael, Alexander. *Carmina Gadelica*, Vols. I–VI. Oliver & Boyd, Edinburgh.

Christiansen, Dr. Reidar Th. *The Vikings and the Viking Ward in Irish and Gaelic Tradition*. Oslo, 1931.

Craig, K. C. *Òrain Luaidh Màiri Nighean Alasdair*, air an cruinneachadh le K. C. Craig. Glasgow, 1949. (Contains texts of 155 waulking songs taken down from a reciter, aged 80, at Snaoiseabhal in South Uist.)

# BIBLIOGRAPHY

GILLIES, John. *Sean Dain agus Orain Ghaidhealach*, air an tabhairt o Dhaoin Uaisle, araid an Gaeltachd Alba, don fhear fhoillsicheadh Eoin Gillies. Clo-bhuailt' am Peairt, 1786. Collection of Ancient and Modern Gaelic Poems and Songs, transmitted from Gentlemen in the Highlands of Scotland to the Editor. Printed in Perth.

GOODRICH FREER, A. *The Outer Isles*. London, 1902. (Contains a good deal of folklore material collected by Fr. Allan McDonald in South Uist and Eriskay.)

MacDONALD, Rev. A., Kiltarlity, and MacDONALD, Rev. A., Killearnan. *The MacDonald Collection of Gaelic Poetry*. Inverness, 1911. (A good deal of the material printed here was collected in South Uist and Benbecula.)

MacDONALD, Alexander, Inverness. *Story and Song from Loch Ness-side*. Being principally Sketches of Olden-Time Life in the Valley of the Great Glen of Scotland, with particular reference to Glenmoriston and vicinity. Inverness, 1911.

McDONALD, Rev. Allan. *Comh-Chruinneachadh de Laoidhean Spioradail*. Oban, 1893. See also J. L. Campbell, A. Goodrich Freer, Amy Murray, and note on manuscript sources.

MacDONALD, Rev. Archibald, *Uist Bards*. Glasgow, 1894.

MacDONALD, Keith Norman. *MacDonald Bards from Mediæval Times*. Edinburgh, 1900.

MacDONALD, Màiri. 'Joseph MacDonald.' *Scots Magazine*, October 1953.

MacDONALD, Ranald. *Comh-Chruinneachadh Orannaigh Gaidhealach*. Edinburgh, 1776. (The first printed Scottish Gaelic anthology, usually called the Eigg Collection.)

MacFARLANE, Malcolm. *Binneas nam Bàrd*. Bardic Melody, a book in which the poems, songs and ditties of the Scottish Gaels are exhibited along with their airs. Stirling, 1908.

MacKENZIE, John. *Sàr-Obair nam Bàrd Gaelach*, or the Beauties of Gaelic Poetry. Edinburgh, 1865.

MacKINNON, Lachlan, M.A. *Cascheum nam Bàrd*. Inverness, 1939.

MacLEAN SINCLAIR, Rev. A. *Clàrsach na Coille*. Glasgow, 1928 (second edition).

—— *The Gaelic Bards*, from 1411 to 1715; from 1715 to 1765; from 1775 to 1825. Published at Charlottetown, P.E.I., and Sydney, Nova Scotia.

—— *Comhchruinneachadh Ghlinn-a'-Bhaird*. The Glenbard Collection of Gaelic Poetry. Charlottetown, P.E.I., 1888.

MacLEOD, Angus, M.A., B.Sc., F.E.I.S. *The Songs of Duncan Ban MacIntyre*. Scottish Gaelic Texts Society, 1952.

MacLEOD, Malcolm. *Modern Gaelic Bards*. Stirling, 1908.

MAC LEÒID, Iain N. *Bàrdachd Leódhais*. Alexander MacLaren & Sons, Glasgow, 1916.

MAC-NA-CEARDADH, Gilleasbuig. *The Gaelic Songster. An t-Òranaiche*: no Co-Thional Taghte do Òrain Ùr agus Shean, a' chuid mhòr dhiubh nach robh riamh roimhe ann an clò. Glasgow, 1879.

MacPHERSON, Donald. *An Duanaire*: A new collection of Gaelic Songs and Poems (never before printed). Edinburgh, 1868.

PATTISON, Thomas. *The Gaelic Bards, and Original Poems*. Glasgow, second edition, 1868.

SHAW, Margaret Fay. 'Hunting Folksongs in the Hebrides.' *National Geographic Magazine*, February, 1947.

SINTON, Rev. Thomas, Minister of Dores. *The Poetry of Badenoch*. Collected and edited, with translations, introductions, and notes. Inverness, 1906.

STEWART, Alexander and Donald, A.M. *Cochruinneacha Taoghta de Shaothair nam Bard Gaeleach*. A choice Collection of the Works of the Highland Bards, collected in the Highlands and Isles. Edinburgh, 1804.

# BIBLIOGRAPHY

TURNER, Patrick. *Comhchruinneacha do dh'Orain taghta, Ghaidhealach,* nach robh riamh roimhe clo-bhuailte gus a nis, air an tional o mheodhair, air feadh Gaidhealtachd a's Eileine na h-Alba. Edinburgh, 1813.

WATSON, Professor James Carmichael. *Gaelic Songs of Mary MacLeod.* Edited with translations. Glasgow, 1934.

WATSON, Professor William J. *Bàrdachd Ghàidhlig.* Specimens of Gaelic Poetry, 1550-1900. (Second edition.) Stirling, 1932.

WHYTE, Henry. *The Celtic Garland of Gaelic Songs and Readings.* Glasgow, 1920.

## JOURNALS AND PERIODICALS

*An Gàidheal* (formerly *An Deo-Gréine*), monthly magazine of An Comunn Gàidhealach.

*The Celtic Magazine.* A monthly periodical, Inverness, 1876–1888.

*The Celtic Monthly.* 1893–1917, Glasgow. Edited by John Mackay.

*The Celtic Review.* Published quarterly, 1904–1916, Edinburgh, London and Dublin.

*Éigse: A Journal of Irish Studies.* Published by Colm O Lochlainn for the National University of Ireland. Dublin, 1939–

*Gairm.* Quarterly Gaelic Magazine. Glasgow, 1952–

*Mac Talla.* Printed and published at Sydney, Nova Scotia, by the late J. G. MacKinnon. Weekly 1892–1901, fortnightly 1901–1904.

*Northern Chronicle,* Inverness. (Weekly Gaelic column.)

*Ossian.* A magazine published from time to time by Glasgow University Ossianic Society.

*Scottish Gaelic Studies.* Issued by the Celtic Department of the University of Aberdeen. Printed by the Oxford University Press, Humphrey Milford, from 1926.

*Stornoway Gazette,* Stornoway. (Weekly Gaelic column by John N. MacLeod.)

*Sydney Post Record.* Sydney, Nova Scotia. (Gaelic column.)

*Transactions of the Gaelic Society of Inverness.* Published from 1871 on.

## RECORDINGS

Gaelic Folksongs from the Isle of Barra: five double-sided twelve-inch discs, together with book of words and translations, published by the Linguaphone Institute, 207 Regent Street, London W.1., for the Folklore Institute of Scotland, originally recorded by J. L. Campbell on Barra in 1938. One of them, No. IX, is a version of a song in this book ('S muladach mi, ho i a bhó, p. 242). The book of words contains an excellent description of a waulking, written by Miss Annie Johnston.

## MANUSCRIPT SOURCES

Important collections of the words of South Uist songs, particularly of waulking songs, made by the late Fr. Allan McDonald (who also compiled an invaluable vocabulary of South Uist words and phrases); the late Donald MacCormick; Mr. Donald MacIntyre; the Rev. A. MacDonald, Killearnan; and the Very Rev. Canon Duncan MacLean, exist in manuscript. I have been fortunate enough to have had access to this material, some of which it is to be hoped will be published, which has been helpful for clearing up obscurities in the text, but I have not incorporated readings from these sources in the versions I print here.

# ADDENDA

SINCE the preceding words were written, Fr. Allan McDonald's Collection has been published by the Dublin Institute for Advanced Studies under the title of *Gaelic Words and Expressions from South Uist and Eriskay* in 1958, and Donald MacCormick's Collection of waulking songs has been edited by my husband and published as the first volume of *Hebridean Folksongs* by the Oxford University Press, with musical transcriptions by Francis Collinson; two further volumes, containing more waulking songs from South Uist and Barra, are being prepared for publication.

Donald MacCormick's Collection contains versions of the following songs in this book: numbers 77, 82, 89, 93, 98, 99, 100, 102, and 105. The second and third volumes of *Hebridean Folksongs* will contain versions of numbers 79, 90, 92, and 97.

In 1956 I contributed the tunes and opening verses of seventeen traditional Gaelic songs from South Uist to *Studia Memoriae Belae Bartók Sacra* (pp. 427–43), of which fifteen are additional to those printed in this book.

In 1960 the School of Scottish Studies at Edinburgh University published a long-playing disc of Gaelic and Scots folksongs, which included twelve traditional Gaelic songs, and in 1972 another long-playing disc (No. 3 in the Scottish Tradition series) of six waulking songs, a clapping song, and a port-a-bial, under the title of 'Waulking Songs from Barra'. One of these is a version of No. 97 here. Various traditional Gaelic songs have been printed from time to time in the School of Scottish Studies' periodical *Tocher*.

Amongst other publications of interest are Francis Collinson's *Traditional and National Music of Scotland* (1966), and Helen Creighton and Calum MacLeod's *Gaelic Songs in Nova Scotia* (1964); while an important paper was read to the Gaelic Society of Inverness on 28 March 1958 by Miss Ethel Bassin on 'The Debt of Marjory Kennedy-Fraser to Frances Tolmie' (*T.G.S.I.*, Vols. XXXIX–XL, pp. 334–49). At the time of her decease Miss Bassin left a nearly completed book on the life and work of Frances Tolmie, which it is greatly to be hoped will be published.

# INDEX

(references are to the English translation)

# INDEX

# INDEX

Corpse, salt and nails placed on, 13
Cothrom Cainnleam [ ? ], 252
Cotton, 126
*Craobh* (a cloud) foretelling wind direction, 5
Cravat (*crabhàta*), 217
Crofter-fishermen, 1, 3
Crofters Act of 1886, 12
Crofts, 2, 3, 5, 7, 12
*Cronan* (a croon), *see* 136, 156
*Crotal*, used for making dyes, 53, 177, 181; superstition regarding it, 13
Cruisie-lamp (*cruisgein*), 6
Cù Chulainn (hero of the Ulster Cycle), 252
*Cunntais an t-Sleamhnain* (charm to heal styes), 49
Cures: asthma, 47; bealing, 48; burns, 48; chilblains, 48; cold blisters, 47; constipation, 48; corns, 48; dropsy, 50; earache, 47; *groimmaothain*, 48; headache, 47; heartburn, 48; indigestion, 48; jaundice, 50; lumbago, 49; 'Morning After', 50; nose bleed, 49; rheumatism, 49; scalds, 48; scrofula, 49; skin irritations, 49; sore feet, 49; sore throat, 47; splinters, to remove, 47; sprains, 47; stiff neck, 47; stomachache, 48; strains, 47; styes, 49; tonic, 50; toothache, 49; warts, 49; whooping-cough, 50; worms, 50
Cures for animals: cataract, 51; colds, 51; constipation, 51; cough, 51; dry disease, 50; lump on horse, 51; lump in throat of sheep, 51; staggers, 51; tonic for a cold, 51

Dalibrog, 11, 12, 15
Dances, Highland, 16, 71, 83, 252
Daorghlas, 29, 30
Days and Dates of special significance: Sunday, 13; Monday, 34; Tuesday, 15; Friday, 13; Saturday, 34; February 1st, 14, 21; May 3rd, 13; June 9th, 21; June 29th, 22; September 29th, 14, 22
Dearg mac Dreighinn, 29
Death, warning or omen, 9, 13, 23
Diarmaid, 30
Dice (*disnean*), 245, 247
'Diùram mac Iain 'ic Lachlainn 'ic Ruairi', 139
Divination, 8, 14, 237
'Dòmhnall Mac Sheumais', 216
'Donald' (? MacDonald of Sleat), 83
Dornie MS., 153
Drowning, death by, 81, 101, 105, 255, 259, 263
Drums, 95
Dun-a-Berty (Dunaverty), Castle of, 131
Dunvegan, 60

'Eàrrlainn' (part of a ship), 244

Easival, 5
Easter, Lay of, 26–8; — -morning tradition, 14
Education Act of 1872, 74, *see also under* English
Eggs (used in Hallowe'en divination), 237
Eigg, Isle of, 243, 249
Eilein Diarmain, 235
Eilein Ruadh, 87
Eisteddfod, 75
Emigrant Songs, 71, 79
England, 93, 221, 253
—, Union of Scotland with, 74
English language (*Beurla*), 87, 125, 127; its corrupting influence on Gaelic through schools and broadcasting, 17, 74; knowledge of it a mark of learning, 217, 241
Eoligarry, 7
Eriskay, Isle of, 15, 28, 75, 81, 90, 91, 147, 155
—, Sound of, 7, 8
Estate, proverbs about the, 41–2
— Officer, 11; in proverb, 42
Europe, 104
Evictions, 11, 12, 75
Evil Eye, 7
Exciseman, the, 89, 90, 178

Factor, the (*am Bàillidh Mór*), 126, 127; in proverb, 42
Factors, 11
Fair, the (*féill*), 123, 126
Fairies, the, 169
Fank, 251
Ferguson, Donald, of Boisdale House, 2
—, John, Tacksman of Bornish, 127
—, Rob, Tacksman of Drimore, 127
Fever epidemic, 12
Fiann, the, 31
Fiddle, the, 83, 247
Fingalian ballads, *see* Ossianic ballads
Fionn Mac Cumhail, 29
*Fir-chlisne* (Northern Lights), 5
Fire, the, 5; proverbs about, 39; prayer for smooring, 19, *see also* Peat
First footing, 14
Fish:
　　Bream (*carbhanach*), 199
　　Cuddies, used in cure, 48
　　Haddock, bone used in cure, 48
　　Herring, 3, 9; salt herring, 3, 4, (in cure) 50
　　Lythe (*liùghag*), 199
　　Saithe, dried in the sun, Pl. 18
　　— -oil, for lamp, 6; in cures, 48, 50
Fishing, as livelihood, 3; proverbs about, 36

# INDEX

# INDEX

# INDEX

# INDEX

# INDEX

Thatch, on grain stacks, 4; on houses, 4, 5, 17, *see also* Houses

Thimble (*miaran*), 15

Thomas the Rhymer, 63–5

Thompson, S., and A. Aarne (classification of folk-tales), 59, 61, 63

Three Questions, story of, 62

Tide, spring, 3, 21, 57

Tongs, as protection against evil, 8, 9; in cures, 47, 49

'Tormod', 238

Traveller, commercial, 127

Triads, 33–4

Trousers (*briogaisean*), 177

Tweed (*clò*), 3, 6, 72, 207, 265, Pl. 30, *see* Waulking

'Uamh an Oir' (the Cave of Gold), 132, 133

Uist, South, mentioned in proverbs, 45; in story, 60; in songs, 79, 81, 101, 223

'Una', 242

Vaccination, 127

Victoria, Queen, 81

Water-horse (*each uisge*), 11, 171, 172

Waulking (*luadhadh*), description of, 6, 7, 72–4; in song, 265

— songs, *see* Contents, *also* 15, 136, 155, 204

Waulking songs, structure of, 73

Weaveress (*bainfh'each*), 6, 127

Weaving terms:
    *deilbh* (warping frame), 265
    *iarna* (hank of wool), 265
    *lianradh*, Pl. 29

Weaving, lucky day for setting the loom, 21

Wedding, 15, 16; hens for wedding feast, 15

Wednesday (*Di-Ciadain*), 87

Whelks, white (*Gille-fionndrainn*), used in cures, 50, 51

Whisky, 14, 57, 89, 90, 123, *see* 'Politician', Spey Royal

'Whisky Galore', 90

Wind, proverbs about the, 34, 35, *see craobh, snàithlin*

Wine, given to horse, 153

Witches, 7

Wood, the (*coille*) (songs mentioning woods must have been made on the mainland), 227

Wool, 3; carding and making into *rolagan*, 6, Pl. 27; ball of (*ceaille*), 265; in proverb, 44; used in cure, 49; dye recipes for, 53–5; from Soay sheep, 177, *see* Spinning

—, blanket, 3, 72, Pl. 30

Worldly wealth, proverbs about, 42–3, *see also under* Animals: Cattle

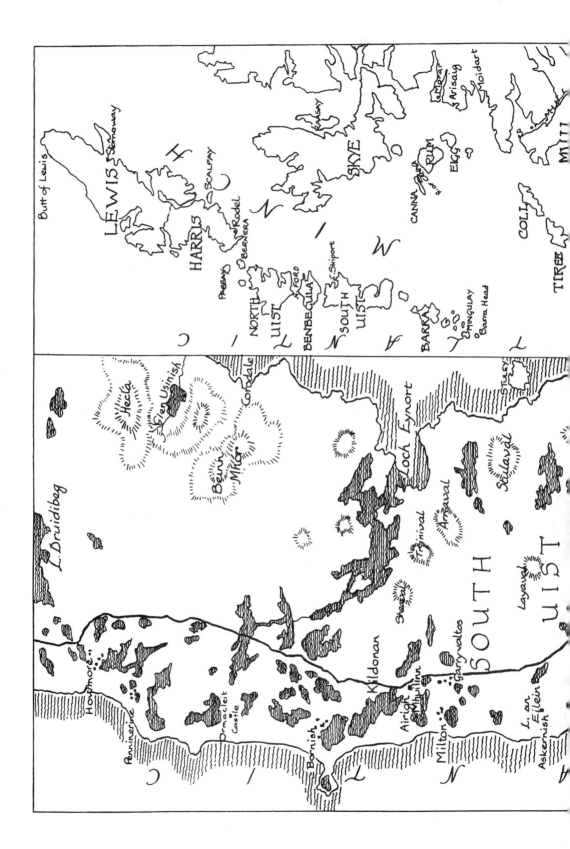

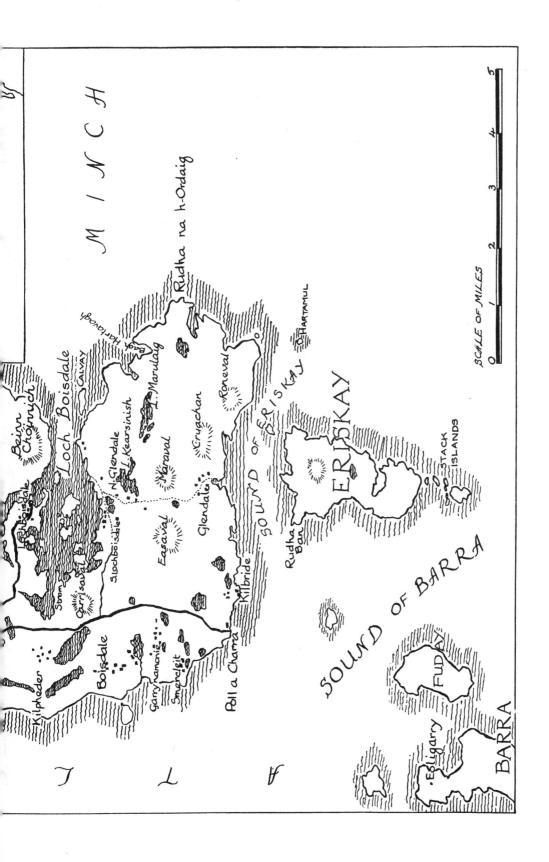

MINCH

Beinn Chaunych

Loch Boisdale

CALVAY

Bagh Hartavagh

Marulaig

L. Kearsinish

N. Glendale

Maraval

Grygachan

Reneval

Rudha na h-Odaig

O HARTAMUL

SOUND OF ERISKAY

ERISKAY

Rudha Ban

STACK ISLANDS

Easaval

Glendale

Sloc bo-isdales

Garrisaval

Strom

Kilbride

Poll a Charra

SOUND OF BARRA

Boisdale

Garrynamonie

Smerclyt

Kilpheder

FUDAY

Eoligarry

BARRA

SCALE OF MILES

0    1    2    3    4    5

UIST